Texas Food Companies

A Tasty Guide

Rhonda Cloos

Republic of Texas Press

Library of Congress Cataloging-in-Publication Data

Cloos, Rhonda.
  Texas food companies: a tasty guide / Rhonda Cloos.
     p. cm.
  Includes bibliographical references (p.).
  ISBN 1-55622-877-5
  1. Groceries—Texas—Catalogs. 2. Food industry and trade—
Texas—Guidebooks. I. Title.

TX354.5 .C56   2001   2001041934
664'.0025764—dc21   CIP

Printed in the United States of America

ISBN 1-55622-877-5
10 9 8 7 6 5 4 3 2 1
0109

All inquiries for volume purchases of this book should be addressed to Wordware
Publishing, Inc., at 2320 Los Rios Boulevard, Plano, Texas 75074. Telephone
inquiries may be made by calling:

(972) 423-0090

Contents

Contents

Chapter 3

Chapter 4

Chapter 5

Contents

Chapter 8

Chapter 9

To Mark, Michael, and Marlee

Many people helped shape this book. Heartfelt thanks to:
- ★ Dianne Stultz, editor, Ginnie Bivona for her encouragement and wit, and Tamra Andrews for the connection to Ginnie;
- ★ My mother, who is with me in memory, for inspiring a love of food; my father who gave me the writing gene; and my sister Barbara, who is a walking thesaurus;
- ★ Preston Gee, for his creativity;
- ★ My friends, who enthusiastically shared their favorite Texas foods;
- ★ And the helpful Texas food association folks who took time to talk with me.

A Texas-sized thank you goes to the people behind the food companies mentioned on these pages. Your stories are inspiring and fascinating, and your kindness is most appreciated. Keep making those palate-pleasing products!

This book was written in memory of my dear friend and fellow author, Chuck Meyer.

Introduction: Lone Appetit!

Texas is home to over twenty million people and almost one thousand food manufacturers. That boils down to one food company for every 20,000 Texans, which translates to a lot of good eating in the Lone Star State. Lots of lips are being licked with a taste of Texas pride.

Foods made in the Lone Star State range from peach jam to spicy sausage to whiskey-filled chocolates, and all flavors in between. A pickle maker puts out over four million pounds of the cucumber delights a year (that's five pounds of pickles per Texan). A baker near Houston adds spirit to chocolate cake by adding whiskey like they did in the days before Prohibition. A dairy near San Antonio pours fresh milk the old-fashioned way, into glass bottles. From the Red River to the Gulf and the Piney Woods to the desert, Texans are churning out foods with a spirit of pride and a sense of good taste.

Up north in the Panhandle, a popcorn company came up with a way to make the snack more tender. Ready for some heat? Go down south to Beaumont where Ant Hill Production grinds pepper seasonings so hot that the July air may feel cooler than your mouth! Head west to Abilene where Billy Beans "I Scream" salsa will make you shout with joy. If your taste buds want more of the hot stuff, head further west to El Paso. There, the Kerr family is busy brewing sauces so spicy they boast names like Snake Bite Salsa and Chipotle Cha Cha Cha. Speaking of chipotle peppers, the talented Sanderson family puts them into a steak sauce worthy of any Texas prime cut.

Ready for a real firehouse bowl of red? Corpus Christi is home to Texas Firehouse Chili. The owners still fight fires, but on their days off they bring some heat into the kitchen with salsas, sauces, and chili mixes. Top off the fiery fare with a slice of New York, Texas, Cheesecake. It is smooth, rich, and creamy, and best of all it is handmade near Texas's own "Big Apple."

If you think you'll have to saddle up your car to sample fine Texan cuisine, relax, kick back, and head to the nearest grocer. You can even pick up your phone or click your mouse for mail order delights. Whether you live in or out of the Lone Star State, you can dip, rub, splash, and savor to your Texan heart's content.

Unlike high tech, food making in Texas is not a new trend. Smack in the middle of the state, Austin may be known for megabytes, but Texans throughout the state have been taking mega-bites of original Lone Star foods for years. The little creamery in Brenham (aw come on, even if you're a new Texan you know the name) has been making ice cream for over ninety years.

Texas is a melting pot where pioneers from around the world settled the land and built their lives. Our native foods reflect their rich culture and tastes. Warm climates are known for spicy foods and—this should not be a surprise—Texas is no exception. We probably have as many types of salsa as there are ears of corn in Iowa. While the fiery condiment may come out only on taco night in other states, salsa goes on everything in Texas. Some eat it plain, scraping the bottle with a spoon in passionate pursuit of every last hot drop.

While Texas-made foods are eaten everywhere in the Lone Star State, they also leave the homeland, tantalizing taste buds from coast to coast. The Texas food phenomenon has spawned numerous restaurants, fast food eateries, and cravings for a bit of Texas heat. In winter, there may be as many Texas chili mixes heading north as there are birds flying south.

Blending tastefully with the spice and heat is the well-known truth that Texans are a creative bunch. The fact that the Lone Star State is home to acres of lush gardens in August says something about the ability of its people to think outside the box. The creativity and pioneer spirit native to Texans adds up to food combinations that simply wouldn't be considered anywhere but here. Where else would you find sirloin tamales?

Texas Food Companies: A Tasty Guide takes you on a dining chair tour of the unusual edibles created by Texans. It is virtually impossible to cover all foods made in the state without ending up with a volume too big for even a Texas-sized bookshelf. The result is a behind-the-scenes look at just over one hundred manufacturers. It is important to note that new companies are being blended each day, stirring up original concoctions sure to delight the Texas tongue.

Chapters are divided by category such as "Cakes, Cookies, and Baking Mixes." Reflecting true Texas pioneer spirit, the companies featured make food items that are among the most unusual around. You will relish in the stories of the founding fathers and mothers of these companies and how their unique products came to be. Tales will warm your heart and tease your taste buds.

One word of caution: Mouths tend to water and lips get licked as the scrumptious sauces, delightful desserts, and other fabulous foods come to life on these pages. You may want to keep some chips and salsa within reach.

Chapter 1
Cakes, Cookies, and Baking Mixes

Things are hot in Texas! Ovens are fired up all over the state, filling the Lone Star air with the sweet aroma of cookies, cakes, and other mouth-watering desserts. In Texas tradition, bakery items are packed with ingredients we adore like native pecans, rich chocolate, and fresh creamery butter. More and more Texans are cranking their pride up a notch, enjoying desserts baked in the shape of the state.

Fruitcakes are another state favorite, and once again pecans take center stage. From October through December, thousands of fruitcakes are taking form (some in the shape of Texas!) around the state.

In addition to fruitcakes, many desserts featured in this chapter are available whether you live in or out of state, or even out of the country. Like Texans on their way to a chili festival, baked goods travel well, making them ideal mail order items. So sit back, relax, and enjoy reading about these heavenly ovenly creations baked with pure and simple TLC (Texas Love and Care).

Aunt Doe Doe's Gourmet Foods

1421 N. 77 Sunshine Strip
Harlingen, Texas 78550
Phone: (956) 428-0199
Fax: (956) 428-0300
Toll-Free: (877) 428-0199

Dorothy Hinojosa spent twenty years perfecting her rum cake recipe before finally being convinced that people would love to buy it! At first she sold the flavorful rum cakes through her sister's business until

1

demand was so high her sister suggested she start her own company.
Armed with her secret rum cake recipe,
Dorothy moved to a commercial kitchen
and baking became a full-time
enterprise.

Images Photography

Next she needed a company name.
Dorothy's nephew, who was six-and-a-
half at the time, lovingly called her Aunt
Doe Doe. With his permission, Aunt Doe
Doe's Gourmet Foods was in business. Now her nephew is on hand to
help his aunt at gourmet shows and with other aspects of marketing.

Customers are extremely fond of Aunt Doe Doe's creations, and
some comments catch her off guard. More than once she has been
asked if she is happily married (after all, the way to a man's heart is
through his stomach). Others, after sinking their teeth into her buttery
cakes with that fabulous rum flavor, have said the cake is "to die for," or
that they have "died and gone to heaven." In other words, these are not
your ordinary rum cakes. One bite is all it takes to realize that Aunt
Doe Doe could rule the world with her rum cakes. The texture is moist
and the cake bursts with flavor. And then, of course, there is the rum,
which adds just the perfect amount of zip. Aunt Doe Doe tops off her
cakes with fresh pecans, which seem to soak up even more of that succulent rum flavor.

What makes Aunt Doe Doe's cakes stand out? Dorothy says it is all
in the way the ingredients are mixed and that she uses "the best rum
out there." (No, she is not telling what brand that is!) Dorothy makes
the award-winning rum cakes herself and obviously loves what she
does.

Aunt Doe Doe's rum cakes come in four flavors: Original, Chocolate, Orange, and Lemon. The buttery Original remains the most
popular. Each cake is packaged in a platinum tin before being boxed and
shipped. The cake's shelf life, in its original wrapping, is about
forty-five days at room temperature or about ninety days in the refrigerator. The cake will keep a year if frozen. (Who could wait that long?)

Where to Buy. Aunt Doe Doe's has a permanent booth at the
gourmet market in Dallas. She also takes orders by phone, mail, and
fax, and she is working on a website (check www.auntdoedoes.com).

Gift boxes arrive in perfect condition, sure to impress anyone lucky enough to receive an Aunt Doe Doe's cake.

⭐ Austin Cheesecake Company

15824 Chatham Wood Drive
Austin, Texas 78717
Internet: www.austincheesecakes.com

Austin Cheesecake Company, founded by Lori and Craig Mayer, is a newcomer to the Texas food scene. But while the company has a short history, Lori is no stranger to the food business. A former caterer and food major in college, she knows what it takes to create a culinary success. Lori's novel idea of selling pre-made cheesecake mixes has been a Texas hit.

Lori had two goals when concocting her product. The first was to formulate a pre-made mix, allowing people to create a luscious home-made cheesecake in just a few minutes. The second was to develop a cheesecake large enough for a family but not so gigantic that it could feed the entire neighborhood. After all, these are rich desserts! The result of Lori's creativity is a mix containing all of the nonperishables needed for a six-inch cheesecake that easily serves six people. The kit includes crust ingredients, dry cake mix, and topping. Simply add the perishables, combine in a mixer or food processor, and in a few minutes your home will be filled with the aroma of a homemade cheesecake baking in the oven.

Austin Cheesecake Company caters to our taste buds with a variety of flavors including Hazelnut Cappuccino, Lemon Tart, Margarita, Strawberry Margarita, Milk Chocolate, Chocolate Cappuccino, Chocolate Irish Cream, Bluebonnet (with an edible Texas Bluebonnet decoration), Blueberry Lemon, Piña Colada, Brownie, Caramel Apple, and Gingerbread. Crusts complement the flavor of each cake, as do the toppings, which include hot fudge and caramel sauce to name two. Gingerbread cheesecake, complete with an edible gingerbread man topping, is a Christmas favorite.

Need an elegant way to serve your cheesecake? Austin Cheese-cake Company sells pottery platters handcrafted in Conroe, Texas, and perfectly sized for the company's six-inch cheesecakes. Designs range from a bright "Fiesta" to a colorful "Tulip." Festive Thanksgiving and Christmas plates are also sold.

Where to Buy. Austin Cheesecake Company mixes are available in gift stores, gourmet shops, and directly from the Internet. Customers have the option of purchasing only the mix or a full set, which includes the mix, baking pan, and pottery platter. The "Texas-Style Cheesecake Mix and Gift Pack" includes the six-inch springform pan, recipe, one cheesecake mix (you choose the flavor), and a gift card.

C.H. Guenther & Son, Inc. (Pioneer Brand)

P.O. Box 118
San Antonio, Texas 78291
Phone: (210) 227-1401
Toll-Free: (800) 531-7912
Fax: (210) 227-1409
Internet: www.chguenther.com

The oldest continuously family-owned food company in Texas began with a fascinating tale of a young man who left his European homeland for adventure in America. It is a story dusted with family pride, ambition, and a pioneer spirit.

On May 5, 1848, Carl Hilmar Guenther left his homeland of Germany bound for America. Against his parents' wishes, Hilmar (he was called by his middle name because his father's name was Carl Gottfried Guenther) took a giant step toward a new life. He could have stayed in Germany and enjoyed the comforts of home and family, but Hilmar was in search of something new.

Knowing his mother and father would object, Hilmar, who was twenty-two years old at the time, did not tell them he was America bound. They would find out later.

Hilmar had heard that Wisconsin was brimming with German immigrants, so he headed there and stayed for a few years. In the meantime, although his father was disappointed that his son left home, he implied that he would help him financially.

Having enjoyed his stay in Wisconsin, Hilmar had a desire to travel south. He left the northern state in October 1850 and arrived a few months later in Texas. A location near Fredericksburg was attractive to Hilmar because of its strong German influence. When his father sent money, he used it to begin construction on a flour mill. This was a lengthy process, but after a series of ups and downs, the mill opened its doors for business in 1851.

Once the mill was underway, it was time for Hilmar to find a wife. He enjoyed the company of a German girl named Dorothea Wilhelmine Pape, and he married her in 1855 when she was sixteen and he was twenty-nine.

Over the next few years it was clear that the small Fredericksburg economy limited the mill's growth. A drought threatened production (the mill was powered by water) and Hilmar wanted to expand. He felt that it would be wiser to expand in a larger city and decided on nearby San Antonio. In 1859 he bought land to build a flour mill in the Alamo city, which at that time boasted a population of more than 8,000 people.

Hilmar's parents continued to send financial support as he built the new mill. On the mill's property, he also had a home constructed, which would house the entire Guenther family that eventually grew to seven children.

When the railroad expanded to San Antonio, it opened up new opportunity for supplying customers from further distances. In addition, San Antonio was growing rapidly and had more than 30,000 residents by the 1880s. The German population made up about 25 percent of the city, and Hilmar's mill was right in the middle of a neighborhood of German immigrants. Life was good when in 1878 Hilmar employed two of his sons and changed the name of his company from Guenther's Mills to C.H. Guenther & Sons.

San Antonio's growth continued, and the family business prospered. But soon an event would occur that damaged the family ties. One of Hilmar's sons, Arthur, left his father's company and with a brother-in-law opened his own mill. Again the name of Hilmar's mill was changed; this time C.H. Guenther & Sons was changed to C.H.

Guenther & Son. You can only imagine the hurt a father would feel if his own son opened a competing business.

The competition was short-lived, however, and just a few years later, Arthur returned to his father's business. More tragedy was to follow when Hilmar's other son, Fritz, died after a lengthy illness and Hilmar's wife, Dorothea, died of cancer at age fifty-eight.

Then Arthur Guenther left his father's business for a second time and again formed his own company, this time with a different relative. A dispute regarding use of the "Guenther" name landed the two companies in court. At that time businesses used their company names rather than brand names. By the time the dispute was settled, the idea of using brand names had taken hold, and C.H. Guenther & Son came up with "Pioneer" as its top brand. Hilmar's picture was placed on every Pioneer product so that customers would know that it was made by C.H. Guenther.

Although Hilmar's son Arthur was now a competitor, there were other Guenther family members to help with the business. The youngest son, Erhard, was vice president and general manager, and Hilmar's son-in-law Adolf Wagner was secretary. When Hilmar died on October 2, 1902, at age seventy-six, he knew that these family members could carry on the successful flour milling operation.

Erhard led the business into the twentieth century, and another family member was already moving up the ranks. Hilmar's grandson Adolph G. Beckmann worked at the mill beginning in 1907. Erhard and his family continued to live in the original Guenther house located at the mill, although they had it extensively updated and renovated in 1915.

In 1909 C.H. Guenther & Son started a tradition that would last for many years. They commissioned calendar plates made in Dresden, Germany. These china gift plates initially featured a monthly calendar around the rim and an attractive design in the center.

In the meantime, the company prospered under Erhard's leadership. The government presence in the area was a plus for business, and C.H. Guenther & Son had a contract to supply the military with thousands of pounds of flour.

In the early 1920s they opened a twenty-story-tall grain elevator with the brand name "Pioneer" lighting up the top. The company's success continued despite the Depression, and further expansion occurred throughout the 1930s. Also during that time, Pioneer flour was sacked in printed cloths attractive enough to be made into dresses or draperies. It was an innovative idea during a time when many people could not afford to buy new clothes or window coverings.

When the Depression ended, World War II began. The collector plates, first made in 1909, could no longer be made in Germany because of the war so a company in Indiana took over production. Because of government contracts, the Guenther mill operated at full force during the war years. Hilmar's son Erhard Guenther remained president until 1945 when he passed the gavel to Adolph Guenther Beckmann. The mill had grown considerably under Erhard's tenure, and this trend continued while Adolph was in charge.

A test kitchen opened, and in 1948 a biscuit mix was developed. A pancake mix followed. The Texas Food Fair of 1952, held in Houston, featured an eight-layer 1,500-pound cake made from Pioneer mixes. When completed, the cake stood nearly as tall as an adult.

Growth continued, and in 1985 the company introduced a Country Gravy mix to consumers. Today the gravy line consists of twelve varieties, including three nonfat mixes. In 1987 the company expanded its product line to frozen yeast rolls with the purchase of Texas Custom Bakery near Dallas.

More innovation was to follow. In the early 1990s Pioneer biscuit and baking mixes became available in resealable containers, offering the ultimate in convenience. The company was the first in-plant manufacturer of these canisters. And in 1995 the company purchased the White Lily Foods Company, makers of White Lily Flour.

Today the brands include Pioneer, White Wings, White Lily, and Country Gravy. White Lily products include flour, cornmeal, and mixes such as Blueberry Pancake, Apple Cinnamon Muffin, and Chewy Fudge Brownie. White Wings products include flour, tortillas, and tortilla mixes. And of course, the Pioneer Brand—the company's oldest—is a popular line of flour and pancake and baking mixes. There are about one hundred products in all!

Products are sold throughout the South and Midwest and are sought after by others around the country. My friend Susan Whitman says that when her mother visits from Pennsylvania, she leaves room in her suitcase for transporting the delicious Pioneer Non-Fat Buttermilk Pancake Mix back home.

C.H. Guenther & Son remains in the family. Robert Schupbach, brand manager for Pioneer/White Wings, is a fifth-generation family member. The president is Richard DeGregorio, and more than ninety of the company's shareholders are descendants of Carl Hilmar Guenther.

C.H. Guenther & Son is believed to be the oldest family-owned business in Texas and the oldest continuously operated family-owned milling company in the country. If you are interested in learning more fascinating details about the Guenther family and the mill, I highly recommend reading *C.H. Guenther & Son at 150 Years: The Legacy of a Texas Milling Pioneer* by Lewis. F. Fisher (Maverick Publishing Company, 2001). The author does an outstanding job of tracing the family's history and explaining the details of what it was like to construct a mill during the nineteenth century. Family and mill photos, old advertisements, and early package designs add to the delight of this informative book.

Where to Buy. C.H. Guenther & Son brands are sold at grocery stores throughout the South and Midwest.

A Tasty Visit

The Guenther House®
205 E. Guenther Street
San Antonio, Texas 78204
Phone: (210) 227-1061
Toll-Free: (210) 235-8186
Internet: www.guentherhouse.com

Built in 1859 as the residence of Carl Hilmar Guenther and family and renovated in 1915 for son Erhard and his family, The Guenther House is a popular San Antonio tourist destination and a journey back in time. The home, listed on the National Register of Historic Places, houses a museum, restaurant, and store.

Gingerbread

Gingerbread houses and villages are a European old-world tradition. When settlers from the region moved to Texas, they carried along this centuries-old custom.

★ Chocolate Chix

1829 E. Levee Street
Dallas, Texas 75207
Phone: (214) 744-2442
Fax: (214) 744-2449
Toll-Free: (877) 246-2449
Internet: www.chocolatechix.com

When Cheryl Surano first made her mother's mushroom-shaped meringue cookies with their sinfully rich chocolate layer, she had no idea that they would become a gourmet sensation.

Cheryl's story began in the mid-1990s when she served the cookies at a party. Her guests were instantly hooked on the combination of light meringue and European chocolate. (And at only twenty-five calories a piece, they are a dream come true!) Realizing that pastry tube talent is a necessary ingredient, Cheryl's friends shied away from making their own mushroom-shaped wonders, and demand grew. Cheryl spent the entire 1995 Christmas season baking cookies.

Ultimately a friend introduced the scrumptious chocolate meringue cookies to a Neiman Marcus buyer, and the store began selling them. Rave reviews kept the orders coming, and Cheryl needed more space. She moved into a 5,400-square-foot commercial kitchen, where she now has seven full-time employees. Today's cookies are as delightful as her first batch.

Every company needs a name, and Cheryl came up with Chocolate Chix because of the egg white meringue (from chickens!) and, of course, the chocolate.

Each unique mushroom-shaped cookie boasts a generous layer of dark European chocolate separating the top of the mushroom from its stem. The smooth chocolate shares the spotlight with the crunchy meringue. All ingredients are natural, and the taste is fresh and pure. And of course, the appearance will add elegance to any fine dessert tray.

The cookies are available in three flavors: Original, Mint, and Pecan. Each variety is packaged in its own elegant hexagonal box: white for Original, silver for Mint, and gold for Pecan. The lid has a large cellophane mushroom design cut into it, allowing a peek inside, and the sides of the box feature whimsical mushroom cutouts.

Because this is a very delicate product, packaging is an important issue. Cheryl experimented until she came up with the idea of individually wrapping each cookie for maximum freshness and a longer shelf life. She now has specialized equipment to seal the individual cookies (like a fortune cookie wrapper) so that they stay crunchy over time.

Where to Buy. Chocolate Chix cookies are available at Neiman Marcus stores, the Norm Thompson catalog, the Dean and DeLuca store in New York, and gourmet or high-end gift shops. The cookies are not sold on the Internet, but the Chocolate Chix website contains a lot of interesting information and photos. Look closely at the photo and you will see a dark area between the mushroom top and stem. This is the luscious layer of European chocolate.

⭐

Collin Street Bakery

401 W. Seventh Avenue
Corsicana, Texas 75110
Phone: (903) 872-8111
Toll-Free: (800) 248-3366
Fax: (903) 872-6869
Internet: www.collinstreetbakery.com

In 1896 master baker Gus Weidmann journeyed from Wiesbaden, Germany, to Corsicana, Texas. Among the cherished items he carried over from his homeland was his recipe for "Christmas Cake." When he met up with entrepreneur Tom McElwee, the two put a bakery on the lower floor of a hotel. Celebrity guests, such as Will Rogers, took a liking to the Deluxe Fruitcake, and word spread. When John Ringling, of circus fame,  ordered cakes for his friends all over the world, the mail order business was born. More than one hundred years later, these signature fruit-cakes are shipped from the Corsicana bakery to every state in the nation and nearly two hundred countries.

One and a half million pounds of pecans are placed into the Collin Street Deluxe™ Fruitcakes every year, accounting for 27 percent of each cake. The pecans are cracked and processed at the company's plant (Navarro Pecan Company) located near the bakery. The fruit-cakes are baked and packaged by a staff of eighty, which grows to eight hundred during the holiday season. During this busy time, four large ovens churn out 80,000 pounds of fruitcakes a day for fifty days, yield-ing a whopping four million pounds of fruitcake. That's about one and a half million cakes in three sizes: Regular, Medium, and Large. Each one is beautifully decorated with carefully placed pecans and colorful cherries.

Many Corsicana area residents are dedicated to their bakery jobs; some tasty careers have spanned more than four decades. The only recipe change occurred over fifty years ago when the company switched from pure butter to vegetable shortening to lengthen the shelf life (an important factor in cakes being shipped around the world).

In addition to employee dedication, customer loyalty has also played a significant role in Collin Street's success. The bakery is proud that 80 percent of its customers reorder every year, and that many new ones are attracted through word of mouth. Some customers have been coming back for half a century, while others call each year to see if they are on anyone's fruitcake gift list. If not, they order their own. The cus-tomer list reads like a Hollywood gala event, featuring such celebrities as the late Steve Allen and his wife Jayne Meadows, Vanna White, the Dom DeLouise family, Lyle Lovett, Zubin Mehta, Robert Stack, and many more.

In addition to the fruitcake, gift recipients are impressed with the company's traditional tin. It is estimated that millions of these collect-ibles are floating around homes, holding sewing supplies, kitchen utensils, cookies, and other items. The attractive tin features the Alamo and other familiar Lone Star sights.

Collin Street Bakery is busy baking year round, with different vari-eties depending on the season. At Easter you might enjoy their cheesecake, carrot cake, or a host of other cakes including, of course, the fruitcake.

Where to Buy. Collin Street Bakery accepts orders via fax, phone, mail, and the Internet. The products are not sold in stores, but the company's brochures and catalogs note that delivery is "guaranteed anywhere in the world." They send reminder notices to existing customers, making gift giving even easier. The website is well done, with beautiful photography, as well as questions and answers regarding the cakes and bakery.

Over 300,000 visitors are welcomed to this unique bakeshop every year. Guests enjoy an old-fashioned ten-cent cup of coffee, free samples, and assorted cookies, pies, cakes, breads, candies, and pastries. A handicapped accessible lounge is available for a relaxing break.

A Tasty Visit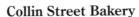

Collin Street Bakery
Corsicana, Texas
Toll-Free: (800) 292-7400

The Collin Street Bakery is open to visitors seven days a week and is located fifty miles west of Dallas on I-45.

Country Fruitcakes, Etc.

Rt. 2, Box 412
Normangee, Texas 77871
Phone: (936) 396-6636
Internet: www.alpha1.net/~ashannon

Andrea Shannon calls her cake "A fruitcake that non-fruitcake lovers love." It contains no citron, no raisins, no peel, no spices, and no preservatives, but what it does contain is sure to please. Great flavor and the shape of Texas give these creations a treat for the eye as well as the palate.

Andrea purchased the business in 1993 and stands proud of her colorful creations. Starting with an "old southern family recipe," Country Fruitcakes are made primarily of native pecans and walnuts blended with fruits and just enough batter to hold the tasty concoction together.

The fruitcakes are mixed the old-fashioned way, and the homemade taste leaves no doubt that a great deal of TLC is poured into each one. Premium nuts and fruit are blended with the batter by hand and baked to perfection on a real Texas ranch. (Yes, they are *authentic* country fruitcakes!) Each one is carefully hand decorated, adding color and drama to a buffet table or festive holiday meal.

During the holiday season, Andrea bakes almost nonstop, sometimes handling over one hundred pounds of batter in a batch. Although the Texas-shaped fruitcake is the company's signature product, Country Fruitcakes are available in three other sizes: Ring, Loaf, and Mini-Loaf (a popular stocking stuffer). Custom orders are also taken.

Country Fruitcakes is known for its personal service, which continues from the time the order is taken until it is packaged and shipped. If she is not baking, Andrea can likely be found at the country post office, shipping as many as fifty packages at a time. The fruitcakes leave rural Normangee (pronounced "Norman G."), heading all over the country, and to Canada and European destinations such as France and Germany. Andrea promises that gifts arrive perfectly "anywhere in the world."

Where to Buy. Country Fruitcakes' products are available locally in the Normangee area and through phone and mail orders. The website offers company information, photos of how the cakes are set into the unique packaging, and a printable order form. Gift givers will rejoice in the ease of simply sending their list to Country Fruitcakes, who will ship out the items along with a greeting.

✪ Gladder's Gourmet Cookies, Inc.

P.O. Box 539
Lockhart, Texas 78644
Toll-Free: (888) 398-GLAD (4523)
Fax: (512) 398-6323
Internet: www.gladders.com

If you want homemade cookie taste without homemade cookie effort, Gladder's Gourmet has some treats for you. This company has earned its

"Gourmet" name because quality is at the forefront.

In the early 1980s John Glader owned an ice cream shop in Austin, and in 1984 he created a recipe for delicious homemade oatmeal cookies. John, inspired by a grade school teacher who called him *Gladder* instead of *Glader*, then founded the cookie business. A team player, John is happy—or rather, glad—that the company name is different from his own. He believes that the success is a reflection of the dedicated team of twenty-five who work with him.

In 1994 Gladder's moved into its 20,000-square-foot production facility located outside of Austin in Lockhart, Texas. There, Gladder's Gourmet has a wholesale bakery, a retail bakeshop, and a mail order and Internet business that serves the rest of the world. You have probably sunk your teeth into a Gladder's cookie without knowing it because they are distributed to companies who "proudly put their label on our cookies" as well as sandwich shops and pizza parlors. If you have had a cookie with a homemade taste and texture and no commercial aftertaste, it may have been a Gladder's.

There are a host of other flavors and products in addition to the original Old Fashion Oatmeal Cookie. The Classic Cookie line includes Chocolate Chip, Chocolate Chunk, Chocolate Chunk Pecan, Cinnamon Pecan, White Chocolate (plain or with pecans or macadamias), Cranberry Crunch, Old Fashion Sugar, Peanut Butter, Triple Chocolate Chip, and—believe it or not—that is just a partial list! In all, there are about twenty varieties of cookies and bar cookies, such as blondies, brownies, and lemon bars. The cookies are generously sized and full of fresh ingredients such as high-quality chocolate chips and chunks, chewy raisins, and fresh nuts. Bar cookies have a moist, cake-like texture and are amply sized. The brownies, for example, have a rich chocolate flavor and chocolate chunks to add a pleasant surprise. The products are certified kosher.

Chocolate Chip stands out as the company's most popular Classic Cookie, and one bite will tell you why. Each cookie contains just the right amount of high-quality chocolate. John's original treat, Oatmeal Raisin, boasts a soft and chewy texture and fresh flavor reminiscent of the ones Mom made.

The company's Internet orders arrive packed in a brown bag inside a box so that customers do not have to spend a lot on packaging costs. Gifts can be ordered in tins or baskets. In the past, limited edition tins have been issued, and they are a possibility for the future. These tins are becoming collector's items so be sure to save yours if you get one. One tin, depicting an airplane scene, showed up in an antique store. (The flying theme was used because when he is not working, John enjoys flying airplanes and teaching formation flying.)

Where to Buy. If you are driving through Lockhart, stop by Gladder's Gourmet retail bakery for some fresh-baked cookies. The bakery is a popular spot for local ranchers, who take time out to enjoy a few fresh baked cookies. If you are not in the area, order by phone, fax, mail, or online. You can order cookies by the dozen—a fun gift for someone special, including yourself!

A Tasty Visit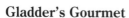

Gladder's Gourmet
Lockhart, Texas 78644
Toll-Free: (888) 398-GLAD (4523)

Visit the Gladder's Gourmet bakery in Lockhart and load up on fresh-baked cookies. You'll be *glad* you did!

Lady Walton's Gourmet Cookies

151 Regal Row, Suite 118
Dallas, Texas 75247
Phone: (214) 630-9101
Toll-Free: (800) 552-8006
Fax: (214) 630-7360
Internet: www.ladywalton.com

Next time you are strolling through a gourmet shop or upscale grocery store, step into the imported cookie aisle and look for a product made in the Lone Star State. That's right, mixed in with items from abroad is a delicate cookie made in Dallas.

Lady Walton's Gourmet Cookies was named for Lady Walton in England, whose descendent, Susan Walton, founded the company in 1988. Susan now serves as chairman, while Mary Elizon Walton is the president.

The cookies, based on a Dutch recipe for stroup waffles (also known as stroopwafels), contain a rich, creamy filling sandwiched between two thin and crispy old-fashioned European waffle wafers. Fillings include Creamy Dark Chocolate, White Chocolate Amaretto, Dark Chocolate Mint, Chocolate Cinnamon Cappuccino, White Chocolate Raspberry, White Chocolate Lemon Honey, and White Chocolate Ginger. White Chocolate Raspberry, White Chocolate Amaretto, and Creamy Dark Chocolate are the most popular varieties.

These unique cookies are generously sized (over three inches in diameter), yet elegant. Together, the creamy filling and crispy waffle provide a delectable blend of taste and texture. The cookies maintain their handmade quality thanks to custom European equipment purchased by the company and delivered to its Dallas plant. Open a package and you will be hard pressed to find two cookies that are exactly alike. The waffle edges are just slightly irregular, adding to their elegance.

The cookies add a refined touch to a cookie platter, a complementary texture to a scoop of ice cream, and a sense of indulgence to a cup of coffee or tea. The waffle has just a hint of sweetness, serving as the perfect backdrop for the rich filling. One taste and you will see why Lady Walton's holds its own in the European cookie aisle.

Where to Buy. Lady Walton's Gourmet Cookies are available at grocery stores and gourmet shops and through catalog and phone orders. The website offers ordering information as well as photographs. A variety of package sizes are available to suit your needs, including a gift tin, canister, or holiday gift box. They are also available individually wrapped. Call the toll-free number for availability in your area. Remember that you won't find Lady Walton's in the main cookie aisle, so check the import section.

Stroopwafel

The stroopwafel is a syrup-based waffle cookie first made in Holland during the eighteenth century. Visitors to the land of tulips and windmills continue to enjoy these Dutch delicacies.

Laura's Cheesecakes

109 N. Madison
Mt. Pleasant, Texas 75455
Phone: (903) 577-8177
Fax: (903) 577-8179
Toll-Free: (800) 252-8727
Internet: www.laurascheesecakes.com

A Dangerfield, Texas schoolteacher named Laura had another lesson to teach, but this one was outside the classroom. She developed a recipe for a classic cheesecake and taught customers just how scrumptious a cheesecake could be! In 1995 Monica Walden purchased the company, moved it to Mt. Pleasant, and has been filling the town with pleasant aromas ever since.

Initially, Monica planned only a retail shop, called Main Street Bakery, located in a downtown square antique shop. Her customers had other plans. After savoring the creamy, rich cheesecakes they wanted to ship them to family and friends. In other words, they wanted to spread the tasty "Mt. Pleasantries" around the country.

The mail order business was born, and now Laura's Cheesecakes are shipped throughout the United States. In order to maintain their freshness, they are frozen prior to being sent via two-day air. During the Christmas season, over a hundred cakes are baked each day, and about five thousand are shipped out.

Despite these huge numbers, each cheesecake is baked by hand. One of the original bakers stayed with the company when Monica purchased it, and Laura's special recipe is still used. Quality is important, and the cakes contain only the finest cream cheese, fresh eggs, sugar, and sour cream. When the rich desserts come out of the oven, the handmade attention to detail continues, from slicing all the way through packing and shipping.

Laura's Cheesecakes come in a variety of flavors, offering something for everyone. The bakery's most unique and popular product is called The Sampler. Six different flavors comprise this ten-inch, four-and-a-half-pound cheesecake. There are eighteen slices in all, including three slices of each of six flavors. Those flavors are Classic, Brownie Swirl, Raspberry Swirl, Apple Streusel, Turtle, and Blueberry.

Where to Buy. If a trip to Mt. Pleasant is not in your plans, order Laura's Cheesecakes by mail, phone, fax, or the Internet. A catalog highlights the cheesecakes and contains color photos and detailed descriptions. Monica welcomes custom phone orders.

A Tasty Visit 🍽

Main Street Bakery
(located inside Antiques & Uniques, on the downtown square)
Mt. Pleasant, Texas
Phone: (903) 577-8177

Hours: 10-4 Monday-Saturday (Holiday hours are different, so call first.) Mt. Pleasant is located along Interstate 30, about 62 miles west of Texarkana. Shop for antiques and locally made pottery and jewelry before enjoying a delicious lunch and slice of cheesecake.

⭐ Marotti Biscotti

749 Redwing
Lewisville, Texas 75067
Phone: (972) 221-7295
Fax: (972) 436-4547
Internet: www.mbiscotti.com

Who says you have to go to Italy for *real* biscotti? From its base in Lewisville (near Dallas), Marotti Biscotti bakes authentic biscotti, suitable for dunking. If you want to go to Italy, you will need another reason!

Owners Jo-Ann Marotti and Glenn Mancini grew up in New York, where they began selling their traditional biscotti in 1985. About six years later they moved to the Lone Star State.

Glenn explains that real biscotti are labor intensive. To achieve that classically dry texture so well suited for dipping, the process involves baking and rebaking. First the dough is mixed, shaped into a loaf, and then baked. Then it is cooled and cut at just the right time—and that's the tricky part—before rebaking. You have to know what you are doing because if they are cut too soon, the finished product will be too moist, but if you wait too long, it will be too hard, even by biscotti standards! Marotti Biscotti cookies are rolled and cut by hand just like they were centuries ago. There is no added butter or oil. The biscotti contain only flour, sugar, eggs, chocolate, nuts, seeds, dried fruits, pure flavors, and leavening.

Marotti Biscotti offers both Americano and Italiano biscotti. The Americano flavors reflect this country's tastes: Maple Walnut, Chocolate Cashew (deep chocolate with milk chocolate bits and tropical cashews), Lemon Almond, and Chocolate Macadamia. Italian versions are divided into two types: Southern and Northern Italy. Southern Italian choices are Anise, Lemon Poppy, and Triple Fruit and Nut. Northern Italian varieties include Chocolate Almond Chip, Mocha Nut, Quaresimale, and Raisin Spice, inspired by the region's Germanic folks. Quaresimale, called a classic Lent tradition, is a Tuscan treasure featuring whole almonds and hazelnuts.

Marotti Biscotti goes beyond biscotti, offering other pastries such as brownies and buttery shortbread to name a few. Biscotti are available in a choice of package sizes. Purchase in bulk or gift tins, depending on your needs.

Where to Buy. Phone, fax, or mail orders are taken, and the company's website contains a printable order form. The site is very informative, featuring clear product descriptions and ordering hours.

Mary of Puddin Hill

P.O. Box 241
Greenville, Texas 75403-0241
Phone: (903) 445-2651
Toll-Free: (800) 545-8889
Fax: (903) 455-4522
Internet: www.puddinhill.com

Over fifty years ago something special, other than the Baby Boomer generation, was born. Mary of Puddin Hill started selling fruitcakes for the first time. The family recipe, now one hundred and fifty years old, is still in use. Today two generations of family ownership preside over the company. And there is not just one Mary guaranteeing these fruit-cakes, there are two (one is nicknamed "Pud"). The recipe was handed down from Great-Grandmother Mary Horton, who started the tradition of serving fruitcake at family gatherings.

Greenville, Texas

In 1948 Mary and Sam Lauderdale founded the company when they were students at the University of Texas. Sam is the quality control expert, having earned his real name, which is Sample.

The owners are proud of their fruitcakes, which contain about one-third native Texas pecans, as well as cherries, dates, and pineapple held together with a light batter. If that doesn't get your taste buds fired up, the company makes a host of other products, including chocolates, cakes, cookies, candies, and other treats.

The fruitcakes come in a variety of shapes and sizes and even fla-vors. There is an Apricot Fruit Cake, Pecan Fruit Cake, Walnut Fruit Cake, and that's just for starters. Pecan Little Puds and Thingamajigs (white or milk chocolate covered caramel and pecans) come boxed together, making a lovely gift presentation. Apricot Little Puds and Praline Pecan Pie Minis are other excellent bite-sized selections. Fruit Cake Bars make an ideal stocking stuffer!

The company also sells a line of Carolina Flavors, beverage and cooking syrups. They sweeten hot ciders and nogs, add to the glaze on ham or sweet potatoes, and enhance a number of baked items.

By the way, Puddin Hill got its name from the black dirt land, family owned for generations and resembling chocolate pudding.

Where to Buy. Mary of Puddin Hill takes orders through their mail order catalog, by phone, fax, and online. You can also purchase from their retail shop. A seasonal holiday store is located in North Park Mall, Dallas.

A Tasty Visit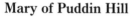

Mary of Puddin Hill
Greenville, Texas 75403-0241
Toll-Free: (800) 545-8889

Hours: Monday - Friday 10 a.m. - 5 p.m. (seasonally on Saturdays). Visit Mary of Puddin Hill, watch candy being made, and enjoy free samples. The on-site retail store sells company-made items.

⭐ Miss Sophia Fine Handicrafts (Old World Gingerbread)

1825 Levee Street
Dallas, Texas 75207
Phone: (214) 741-6800
Internet: www.misssophia.com

A set of Russian storybooks given to little Miss Sophia (the owner's daughter), was the inspiration for this Dallas-based company. The books featured elaborately decorated villages with houses, trees, and a clock tower. For Christmas 1996 the family made their own gingerbread villages to give as gifts for family and  friends. At the time, their company sold handmade pillows and decorative accessories (hence the name Sophia Fine Handicrafts). After the villages were crafted, they were placed in the studio's window before being given as gifts. People began noticing—and even buying—the gingerbread sensations sitting in the window. Soon the Bloodworth family started selling ready-made gingerbread houses. While these items were quite popular, there was a growing demand for kits that allow people to construct their own gingerbread houses.

Today Miss Sophia Fine Handicrafts sells gingerbread kits, making it easy and fun for any family to build creations all their own. Select several kits and put together your own village. (Won't your neighbors be impressed?) The packaging features little Sophia fashioned to look like an elf.

There are a variety of kits available, including an Elf Haus, Clock Tower, Country Dacha, Hanukkah House, Peasant Cottages, and Tannenbaum Trio. For Easter there is a Tisket Tasket Easter Basket to build or Sunny Bunny with Easter Egg Cookies. A Halloween kit is in the works. Each set includes everything you need for the finished product. The gingerbread is baked and pre-cut, and all candy and other decorations are included. Just add water to the icing and put it all together.

The kits have achieved national fame, appearing on such television shows as *Oprah* and *The View*.

Where to Buy. Miss Sophia Old World Gingerbread kits are sold at Rice Epicurean Markets and through the Internet or via mail order. The company's website features a printable order form for those who prefer mail order.

New York, Texas, Cheesecake® Co.

211 N. Palestine
Athens, Texas 75751
Phone: (903) 677-6706
Toll-Free: (877) NYTXCCC (877-698-9222)
Fax: (903) 677-5605
Internet: www.nytxccc.com

New York City is renowned for its rich, creamy cheesecakes. Well I have great news for Texans! There is no need to head up to the Big Apple for a bite of this popular dessert. You can get one from the New York, Texas, Cheesecake Co. and enjoy a scrumptious slice of heaven made in the Lone Star State!

The history of this fabulous East Texas company is drizzled with good taste and a few interesting twists. It all started with a bed and breakfast inn overlooking the hills of New York, Texas. In 1985 the owner—a writer—served the inn's guests a cheesecake made from a century-old family recipe. A local baker named Fayrene Miller prepared the cakes back then and is still baking them to this day. (Fayrene is pictured preparing one of her incredible creations.)

Eventually the owner sold the company to two women. Sadly, someone left a freezer door open during a holiday season, and the owners lost thousands of dollars' worth of products. You can only imagine how many cheesecakes would be in the company's freezer during the Christmas season. After this chilling (or rather, thawing) event, the shop flooded and the owners shut it down until it was purchased by a man named Tony Hartman, who moved the company across the street.

During this time, hundreds of miles away in the West Texas town of Odessa, Bud and Nancy Hicks were loyal cheesecake customers. Bud purchased New York, Texas, Cheesecakes as holiday gifts for his dear Aunt Jo, who lived out in the country south of Weatherford. He would order the cake and call to tell her when to expect it. On the delivery day, Bud would get a call from his aunt, letting him know that she was at home waiting for her cake. Often, while they were on the phone, Aunt Jo would see the delivery truck heading down the road and she'd yell to Bud, "STOP him! STOP him! Oh, there goes my cheesecake!" Then she would run outside and wave down the truck. Aunt Jo was serious about her love for these cheesecakes. One taste and you will understand why.

Have you ever loved a product so much you thought about buying the company? Well that is what happened in the next twist of this cheesecake tale. Bud Hicks was so fond of the cakes that he and his wife bought the company from Tony Hartman in May 2000. Bud had retired from his Odessa construction business, and he was attracted to the idea of owning a company that produced a top quality product. He and Nancy moved east and became the proud new owners of the New York, Texas, Cheesecake Co.

What is the secret behind this delectable dessert? The answer in a nutshell is that each cake is baked from scratch, using the first owner's century-old Pennsylvania Dutch recipe. The original copy of the recipe is worn but is still around, written on old-fashioned paper with one corner missing.

Fayrene makes the cheesecakes in small batches. She carefully cracks each egg, squeezes the juice from fresh lemons, and uses only the finest cream cheese to make the light and fluffy cheesecakes. This creamy mixture is poured into a delicious graham cracker crust and baked to perfection.

Vendors have tried to sell Bud on the idea of using pre-cracked eggs or bottled lemon juice, but he and Fayrene prefer the old-fashioned way. It pays off because the cheesecakes have a fresh home baked taste.

Brace yourself for the outstanding flavor assortment: Original, Turtle Praline, Chocolate Amaretto, Chocolate, Black Forest, White Chocolate, White Chocolate Raspberry, Key Lime, Amaretto, Strawberry, Raspberry, and Blueberry.

Turtle Praline is an Original flavored cake with a swirl of fresh ingredients such as peanuts, Texas pecans, and chocolate. Key Lime is made from fresh lime juice and has a subtle tartness and characteristic lime color. The Chocolate variety contains rich chocolate, giving it a delightful taste. Each flavor reflects the fresh ingredients placed into it, and eating a slice is pure indulgence. Take a bite and you will say, "I see what you mean."

Popular holiday choices include Christmas Cake and Pumpkin to name a few. If you have a special flavor in mind, just give the folks at New York, Texas, Cheesecake Co. about five days' notice, and Fayrene will whip up a custom blend. Her more unusual creations include Grand Marnier and even black-eyed pea cheesecakes (for the Athens Black-Eyed Pea Festival).

An assortment called "Premies" contains cupcake-sized miniature versions of the larger cakes complete with a graham cracker crust. Seventy-two assorted Premies arrive in a charming Texas-shaped box ready for a Texas-sized party!

New York, Texas, Cheesecake Co. offers delicious "guilt-free" cheesecakes for those on special diets or people with diabetes. They are available in Original, Raspberry, Strawberry, Blueberry, and Chocolate and are 98 percent fat-free with less than one gram of fat per piece.

All cheesecakes are available in three sizes. The two-pound cake serves six to ten; three-pound serves ten to twenty; and four-pound serves fifteen to thirty cheesecake lovers. The cakes are frozen and shipped year round by two-day air in a cold pack wrap designed to keep them chilled. When they arrive they can be refrozen for four or five months or refrigerated for four to five days. Run a knife under warm water to cut the cake. If you want to save a few slices for a special treat, take them out, seal in a plastic bag, and freeze.

Many agree that these cheesecakes are out of this world. New York, Texas, Cheesecake Co. has won numerous awards and honors and has been featured in local and national publications and on television and radio shows. The cake has been named the "Best Mail Order food product of the year" by *Bon Appetit* magazine.

By the way, if you are wondering about New York, Texas, it was named around 1860 in good humor because it was the opposite of bustling New York City. The community had not much more than a cemetery and a church.

The folks at New York, Texas, Cheesecake Co. are extremely personable. It seems that the Texas version of New York is a friendly place serving up some great tasting cheesecakes.

Where to Buy. Purchase cheesecakes from New York, Texas, by mail, phone, fax, and the Internet. You can also find them at a variety of food shows around Texas, including Junior League shows and wine and food fairs, and at the retail shop in Athens.

A Tasty Visit

New York, Texas, Cheesecake® Co.
211 N. Palestine
Athens, Texas 75751
Phone: (903) 677-6706
Toll-Free: (877) 698-9222
Hours: Tuesday - Saturday 11 a.m. - 5 p.m.

When in East Texas, stop by for a scrumptious slice of cheesecake and a cup of hot coffee. Friendly staff will give you a hearty East Texas welcome. The bakery is located in a historic building that has been renovated. It is situated on Palestine Street one block north of the courthouse square. While you are there, be sure to buy a cheesecake to go!

The Original Ya-Hoo! Baking Company (Miss King's)

5302 Texoma Parkway
Sherman, Texas 75090-2112
Phone: (903) 893-8151
Toll-Free: (888) 869-2466
Internet: www.yahoocake.com

In 1944 Eunice King returned to Texas and—yahoo—are we glad she did! A missionary in Brazil for six years prior to starting the bakery, she returned home and initially taught home economics for the Texas Agricultural Extension Service. Her specialty was helping people in rural Texas learn proper food canning techniques.

A talented baker, Miss King developed new baking methods and eventually opened a tearoom in her hometown of Sherman. Located in a Victorian home on downtown Mulberry Street, it was called the Pecan House Tea Room. If that didn't keep her busy enough, she also ran a bakery on Texoma Parkway, where loyal customers enjoyed her delicious creations.

Ultimately Miss King's merged with the Ya-Hoo! Cake Company now located on the site of her original bakery.

Today the company offers a wide variety of cakes and other desserts. The Original Ya-Hoo! Cake™ is a delicious combination of pure chocolate, Texas pecans, and rich cherries blended into a moist Texas-shaped cake. The company's catalog features a variety of mouth-watering desserts. Choose from about forty different cakes, including fruitcakes (in a range of sizes, including individual), Yellow Rose™ Lemon Cake, coffee cake, cheesecake, pecan loaf, and much more. For those who have an extra craving for sweets, the company offers brittles, chocolates, truffles, and caramels.

The people at Ya-Hoo! take baking as seriously as Miss King did, using only fresh ingredients to give their products a homemade taste. The cakes and other items arrive in festive tins, boxes, or crates.

Where to Buy. You can purchase the cakes at the Outpost Store in front of their bakery in Sherman, Texas. Occasionally you may find their products in retail stores. The sure-fire way to get your cake and eat it too is to order from the company's toll-free number, by mail, fax, or through the website.

A Tasty Visit 🍴

The Original Ya-Hoo! Baking Company Outpost Store
5302 Texoma Pkwy. (Just north of I-75 and Hwy. 82)
Sherman, Texas (60 miles north of Dallas)

Visit the Original Ya-Hoo! Baking Co. Outpost Store and purchase their delicious cakes and other tempting items!

⭐ Penny's Pastries

P.O. Box 10506
Austin, Texas 78766
Toll-Free: (866) 302-3663

Before moving to Austin in 1992, Penny McConnell's retail bakery was popular in the other Capital City (i.e., Washington, D.C.). While her bakery cases displayed beautiful cookies and pastries, inside Penny's mind a new idea was taking shape. As a bakery owner, she recognized the challenge in finding the time to  create intricately decorated cookies while running a retail operation. And that was the spark for Penny's Pastries ala Austin.

Today Penny McConnell runs a wholesale business, rolling out hundreds of thousands of ornate hand-decorated cookies each year. Instead of running a retail bakery, Penny sells her cookies to them, which allows her to focus her time and energy on baking and decorating these edible masterpieces.

Penny's Pastries' line of roll and cut cookies are all made in Austin and hand decorated with glazes or sparkling sugars. During the busy times, Penny's staff grows to as many as thirteen "cookie designers."

The dough is rolled by machine, hand cut, and then baked to perfection. When cooled, the designers work their magic, transforming the buttery shapes into hand-decorated masterpieces. And while the cookies score high marks in appearance, they excel in flavor as well. Ingredients such as real butter and pure vanilla and almond extracts assure that each cookie tastes as good as it looks.

Shapes of all types roll out of the company's oven, with hearts being the most popular. Penny has placed the shape of Texas in a heart, and a house in a heart as well. She is open to customers' ideas and welcomes custom orders.

One reason Penny's Pastries is so popular is that it is very difficult to bake cookies that look and taste as good. Penny teaches classes at Central Market and shares her recipe with just about anyone who asks.

Where to Buy. Penny's Pastries are sold in gourmet stores, coffeehouses, and bakeries in Austin, Dallas, Houston, and San Antonio. Orders are accepted by phone, and Penny is working on a website (check www.pennyspastries.com).

★ Wunsche Bros. Chocolate Whiskey Cake

PMB 223
20770 Hwy. 281 N, Ste. 108
San Antonio, Texas 78258-7500
Phone: (210) 497-1539
Toll-Free: (888) 333-CAKE (2253)
Fax: (210) 497-2674
Internet: www.whiskeycake.com

In 1988 the Wunsche Bros. Café in Spring, Texas, began selling a rich chocolate whiskey cake. The combination of chocolate, whiskey, and pecans was so popular that requests for mail orders poured in.

Today the company's mail order business is thriving. The cake arrives in the company's original tin, decorated in Texas style, along with "The Legend of the Wunsche Bros. Chocolate Whiskey Cake." You'll have to read the legend yourself to get the whole story, but here is a tidbit to entice you. Back in 1919, just before Prohibition, the old Wunsche Bros. Hotel and Saloon had to do *something* with its leftover whiskey. Can you guess?

The whiskey cake was created at that time, serving as the inspiration for today's version. The cake is dense and rich, containing hardly any flour but a lot of chocolate, and of course, the whiskey! All this goodness packed into one single layer cake makes it weigh about as much as many two-layer cakes.

The cake remains a popular dessert to patrons of the Wunsche Bros. Café and to cyberspace visitors as well. Whiskey is a natural preservative, making it an ideal mail order product. It stays fresh up to two months in the tin or up to six months if frozen. It is best enjoyed with a glass of ice-cold milk.

Select the two-pound Whiskey Cake or a dozen quarter-pound Mini Chocolate Whiskey Cakes for great stocking stuffers. The two-pound cake is a popular corporate gift and a tasty tradition for chocolate lovers everywhere.

The company has expanded its line beyond the Whiskey Cakes. Other treasures include Mama Jean's Rum Cake, Homemade Texas Fudge in a variety of flavors, and Rio Grande Texas Pecan Pralines.

Where to Buy. If you are in the Houston area, you can enjoy a slice of cake or buy a whole one at Wunsche Bros. Café. Otherwise, order by phone, fax, or directly from the company's website.

A Tasty Visit

Wunsche Bros. Café

Spring, Texas (20 miles north of Houston)

(281) 350-2233 (call for specific hours and directions)

Visit the Wunsche Bros. Café, a historic landmark, and enjoy a meal topped off with a slice of the famous Chocolate Whiskey Cake. The café is open for lunch and dinner seven days a week, except for Monday when no dinner is served.

Chapter 2

Candy, Nuts, and Honey

Candy, nuts, and honey add crunch and sweetness to the state fare. From chocolates to pralines, and peanut patties to toffee, Texans are fond of the sweeter things in life.

There is no shortage of chocoholics in this state. Whether chocolate is eaten by itself or layered with other treats, it is a Lone Star favorite. In the 1700s chocolate was among the foods the Europeans brought to the United States. Today Texas confectioners add a touch of creativity to chocolate, sculpting it into the shape of the state or the Alamo, mixing it with nuts and caramel, or slathering it on top of freshly made toffee. The Texas heat can play tricks on chocolate, but advanced packing methods allow state-made candies to be shipped virtually anywhere, any time of year, and still arrive in whole pieces rather than in a puddle.

In addition to chocolate, native peanuts and pecans are at home in Texas-made candies. Confections seem to come alive with crunchy nuts, which also serve to cut the sweetness in such favorites as pralines and peanut patties. When it comes to making sweets in Texas, the common word is "handmade." What could be sweeter than confections made by the hands of a Texan?

Texas beekeeping is an art and science we can all be thankful for with each succulent drop of honey. Getting stung is a daily part of beekeeping (aw, it's nothin', they say). Think about that and send a heaping tablespoon of thanks to local beekeepers for their willingness to persevere and continue to bring us some of the best honey in the world.

When you read this chapter, be prepared for some serious cravings as visions of pralines, peanut patties, and other sweet treats drift before your eyes. Sweet dreams!

All American Snacks, Ltd. (White Trash)

P.O. Box 3
Midland, Texas 79702
Phone: (915) 687-6666
Toll-free: (800) 840-2455
Fax: (915) 687-6969
Internet: www.allamericansnacks.com

The story behind All American Snacks is all-American proof that kitchen secrets can become business realities.

The kitchen where it all began is in Midland, Texas, and the three women in the story are Lexie Kauffman, Sheri Brockett, and Lettie Dutton. In 1995 the women came up with the idea of making a product called "White Trash" for the Merry Marketplace in Odessa, Texas. It was an instant success. The unusual snack blew out of the sales booth faster than a West Texas dust storm. And a new business was born.

Many people are familiar with "Trash" or "Texas Trash." In case you aren't, it is a popular mixture of cereal, pretzels, and other crispy snacks. You've probably seen it served at parties or card games or baby showers.

The three innovative Midland women coated the cereals, pretzels, and pecan halves with white chocolate and came up with the logical name of "White Trash." More than just a cute name, the product is a taste sensation. It is one of those wonderful snacks in which sweet and salty flavors share the spotlight. And if that's not enough, the packaging is brilliant. This crispy blend is sealed in a cello bag packed into a miniature plastic trashcan complete with a lid. Serve the trash straight from the can for an instant party ice-breaker.

The three entrepreneurs are far too creative to stop at one product. Other trashes have popped up, including Cocoa Nut Island Trash, Burgundy Chocolate Drizzle Trash, Uptown Trash, and Chocolate Rocks. Cocoa Nut Island Trash features the original Trash mixed with toasted coconut and drizzled with dark burgundy chocolate. Burgundy Chocolate Drizzle is the original flavor that is also coated with a lacy drizzle of rich dark chocolate. Uptown Trash has 50 percent more nuts. Chocolate Rocks is a gourmet chocolate covered with a thin candy coating that gives it the appearance of a pebble you would find by a stream. What a great gift for the rock hound in your life! All American products have won broad acclaim, and they've racked up numerous awards.

And the trash business has made the three founders celebrities. The women and their unique idea have been featured in newspapers and on television. A *Midland Reporter-Telegram* article jokingly referred to them as "The trash ladies of Midland."

Just who are the three trash ladies? Lexie Kauffman is the trio's public relations guru and the company's "inventive force." Lexie borrowed her sister's recipe to develop the first batch of White Trash. A graduate of the University of Houston, Lexie is a professional educator and owns a patent for a child safety product. She also served as the public relations manager for a dental practice for over fifteen years.

Lettie Dutton is the group's business manager. She is a graduate of Texas Tech University and attended graduate school at the University of Texas Permian Basin. She has won many personal awards (Teacher of the Year is one) and brings patience and dedication to the group.

Sheri Brockett is the company's designer and creative consultant. Her artistic talents range from jewelry making to pottery. She is an active volunteer in the community and a creative force at the company.

Lexie, Lettie, and Sheri seem to be bursting with talent and creativity so it is no surprise that White Trash has made it out of their kitchen and into homes around the country.

Where to Buy. Look for the trash cans at Dillards; Bloomingdales; Henry Bendel; Amen Wardy Home stores in Aspen, Dallas, Las Vegas and Beverly Hills; Trump Plaza in New York City; Sony Plaza in Japan; and other fine department and gift stores. It is especially popular around Christmas. Orders are taken by mail, phone, fax, or the Internet.

⭐ Ashur Products (chocolate tamales)

P.O. Box 280
Pleasanton, Texas 78064
Phone: (830) 281-4200
Internet: www.ashurproducts.com

If the word "tamale" inspires thoughts of pork or veggie, think again. These tamales are chocolate, and they are hot! This novel idea was the brainchild of Catherine Brown as a way to raise funds for mission work in Mexico. She and Tricia Ames are the owners of Ashur Products, which started making the tamales and other innovative items in January 2000.

The company's signature product is the gourmet chocolate tamale, which is available in milk or white chocolate. The rich chocolate is melted and molded in the shape of a tamale, complete with grooves in it to resemble masa. Approximately the size of a chocolate cigar, the tamale is sealed in a cello wrapper, hand wrapped in a cornhusk, and tied with colorful raffia. The company holds the trademark on the confectionery cornhusk wrapper.

The gourmet chocolate tamale is an exquisite dessert to serve after a Mexican dinner. Several colors of raffia are used to tie the cornhusks, forming a rainbow of color when placed together in a basket or on a serving platter. They are in demand by caterers who use them at weddings and other events. Corporations order them in gift sets with their logos or pass them out at conventions. Valentine boxes whimsically proclaim, "You're One Hot Tamale." They can be tied with pink or blue raffia and used as handouts by new parents. The possibilities are endless and the Ashur Products staff is eager to furnish ideas. They will be happy to color coordinate the raffia tie with your needs.

If you are planning a party (or just want to keep some on hand), order in bags of six or twelve.

Chewy cinnamon candies are another Ashur specialty item. The fiery hot candies are shaped like a chile pepper and packaged in a cello bag with the same pepper shape. The candies have a delightful cinnamon flavor and are definitely addictive. What will these two creative women think of next?

Where to Buy. Look for the gourmet chocolate tamales at Dillards in San Antonio (expanding to additional Dillards stores in the future), gift and gourmet shops, gift basket companies, and at Don Pedro's on Military Drive in San Antonio. Visit the Gifts Galore shop in Pleasanton or order by phone or mail. The company is looking into Internet orders. Corporate accounts are welcomed.

A Tasty Visit 📷

Gifts Galore (featuring chocolate tamales)
604 S. Main
Pleasanton, Texas 78064
Phone: (830) 281-4200

Peek through the window of this Pleasanton gourmet shop and watch gourmet chocolate tamales take shape (not much production going on during the summer). Browse the taste tempting selection including Ashur Products' famous chocolate tamales and hot cinnamon candies.

⭐ Atkinson Candy Company

P.O. Box 150220
Lufkin, Texas 75915-0220
Phone: (936) 639-2333
Internet: www.atkinsoncandy.com

Absolute heaven for any child would be going with his or her granddaddy to a candy show and sharing the ride home with a back seat full of candy.

That sweet memory is just one of many recalled by Atkinson Candy's president Eric Atkinson. As a young boy, his grandfather took him to the factory and let him eat as many of the "reject" pieces as he could get down. Reminds me of a scene straight out of *Willy Wonka and the Chocolate Factory.*

Eric's grandfather, B.E. Atkinson founded the company with money he got in return for selling a spare tire. Since then, the company has come a long way and is a sweet story of success.

Basil Atkinson was a lathe operator in a foundry. When he lost his job in the early 1930s, a relative suggested that Basil get into the candy business. This was the Depression Era, but the family member was convinced that in rough times people still bought candy as a cheap way to keep their children happy. Basil was interested, but with a wife, two sons, and no car, starting a business seemed risky if not impossible.

Borrowing a relative's Oldsmobile, Basil took his family for a drive to Houston. There, he spent all his money on candy and sold it to every Mom and Pop store he could find on the way home. The strategy worked, and a candy sales route was established.

The only problem was that he was putting a lot of miles on his relative's car so Basil had to buy one of his own. He went down to the local Chevy and Cadillac dealer one Friday and talked the salesman into letting him have a car for the weekend. He promised to bring in the down payment on Monday. The salesman agreed, and Basil was off to Houston for more candy. (This is where the spare tire comes in.) He sold that tire straight out of the car and used the money to buy candy. On the way back home, he sold the candy and earned enough to make the down payment that Monday.

Now that he had a car, Basil stuck to the candy selling business until about 1938. At that time, he decided to make the candy in his own factory. He moved into a 3,000-square-foot factory and started making a variety of candies including brittle, divinity, mint sticks, and lollipops.

Look at the photo and you will see Basil Atkinson proudly sitting at his desk next to a cabinet stocked with his original candies. The company built its name on using high quality old-fashioned candy recipes, a reputation that has stuck over time.

Atkinson Candy Company remains a family run business, and they are proud to put their name on each label. The company headquarters is still in Lufkin, and now their one hundred seventy employees work in a modern facility. But time hasn't changed the family's commitment to producing fine candies. Top quality ingredients like fresh roasted peanuts, real coconut, and pure sugar go into each tasty piece.

Old Fashion Peanut Brittle was one of the original Atkinson specialties. Today the company continues to make the brittle along with an assortment of other candies.

Chick-o-Stick is a popular Atkinson choice. The peanut buttery candy with just a hint of coconut is a chewy and flavorful treat. Based on an old-fashioned southern recipe, it holds up in the Texas heat and is a good pick-me-up to keep in your purse or pocket. Other favorites include Peanut Butter Bars, Mint Twists, PB Sticks, and Rainbow Coconut.

Where to Buy. Atkinson Candy Company sells their products everywhere. You can find them at retailers around the country including grocery chains, convenience stores, Wal-Mart stores, and just about anywhere candy is sold. Orders are taken through the Internet.

A Tasty Visit

Atkinson Candy Company
1608 Frank Avenue
Lufkin, Texas 75915
Phone: (936) 639-2333
Hours: Monday - Friday 8 a.m. - 4:30 p.m.

Atkinson Candy Company has a retail shop in their lobby. There you can buy bags of candy for around one dollar (give or take). The company is located on the west side of town. Tours are not offered, and be sure to call first to see if the shop is open.

Glazey Days of Yore

Glazed pecans are said to date back to the days before Texas was Texas. Early settlers sold the glazed goodies to travelers who crossed the river from Louisiana. Now that's a sweet Texas-style welcome!

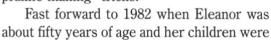

Aunt Aggie De's Pralines

112 N. Sehorn
Sinton, Texas 78737
Toll-Free: (888) 772-5463
Fax: (512) 467-2234
Internet: www.auntaggiede.com

When Eleanor Harren was a child of twelve her Aunt Aggie De taught her the fine southern art of making pralines. Visits to Aunt Aggie De (short for Agnes Dekolb) in San Angelo were a special treat for Eleanor. She fondly recalls her aunt sharing some secret praline-making "tricks."

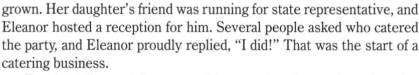

Fast forward to 1982 when Eleanor was about fifty years of age and her children were grown. Her daughter's friend was running for state representative, and Eleanor hosted a reception for him. Several people asked who catered the party, and Eleanor proudly replied, "I did!" That was the start of a catering business.

For about the next five years, Eleanor catered a number of parties where her pralines always took center stage. She still had the original recipe written in Aunt Aggie De's handwriting, and the compliments rolled in as fast as she could make the candies. If she did one party for a client and served pralines, that customer requested pralines for the next event. Eventually, Eleanor decided that making pralines might be a better career than carrying around chafing dishes and silver trays.

Once the praline business idea set in, Eleanor was determined. She made a batch and went on sales calls to three Corpus Christi restaurants. Each one was ready to turn her down so Eleanor made an offer. The restaurants could take the pralines. If they sold them, they could pay her. If not, the pralines were theirs to eat. Needless to say, she was in business.

At first, Eleanor hand wrapped each praline in her kitchen, but as demand grew so did her need for space. (She had been working out of her home, which was approved by the health department because of the catering business.) To gain more space, she moved into 1,200 square feet, which seemed huge compared to her kitchen. She rented for a while and eventually purchased the facility, adding yet another thousand square feet! These days, all production is done in this commercial facility, and she also has a retail shop in Sinton.

Her newest kitchen has a "great big kettle" that can make six hundred pralines in a batch. A staff of twenty-five employees pour and wrap each praline by hand. At full capacity, the company can make 45,000 pralines in a week.

Like Aunt Aggie De herself, Eleanor is picky about ingredients, choosing only top of the line products. She sticks to only Falfurrias butter and believes it is the closest she can get to French style butter. Pralines are temperamental so Aunt Aggie De's "tricks" must be coming in handy because these pralines are consistently delicious. All products are preservative-free.

Aunt Aggie De's pralines are available in Creamy or Chewy varieties. Creamy comes in Original or Belgian Chocolate. The Chewy version is similar in texture to a caramel. The company also makes Pecan Praline Sauce and Hot Fudge Sauce.

Eleanor has come a long way since first selling to the restaurants in Corpus Christi. When a Walgreen's executive tasted her pralines, he loved them so much he put them in hundreds of his stores.

The pralines make an ideal gift item for anyone who wants a chewy taste of Texas. The website offers a variety of gift sets, including a delightful gift tube.

Aunt Aggie De's is a family business. Eleanor is active in every aspect, and her daughter Anne Walls does the accounting.

Where to Buy. Look for Aunt Aggie De's squirrel logo on her pralines at Walgreen's, gift shops, specialty stores, restaurants, the Hickory Farms catalog, Trophy Nut catalog, the New Braunfels Smokehouse catalog, and sometimes in the Williams-Sonoma Christmas catalog. Orders are taken by phone, mail (there is a catalog), fax, and the Internet. Aunt Aggie De's ships to every state and around the world.

A Tasty Visit

Aunt Aggie De's Pralines
121 E. Sinton Street
Sinton, Texas
Phone: (361) 364-2711
Hours: Monday - Friday 9 a.m. - 4 p.m.

Look for the giant squirrel in front of Aunt Aggie De's shop. Inside you'll find a scrumptious assortment of the famous pralines along with other treats made especially for the retail location including English Toffee and Chocolate Dipped Chewy Pralines.

Austinuts

2900 W. Anderson Lane, #8
Austin, Texas 78757
Toll-Free: (800) 404-NUTS
Internet: www.austinuts.com

As a University of Texas graduate student, Ilai Doron missed the taste of fresh roasted nuts. Although he continued his studies and received his degree, an idea was brewing in his mind. He wanted to open a facility where he could roast nuts, offering the freshest possible products.

He opened his store in Austin, hence the name Austinuts, and the little idea in the back of his mind turned into a big success. Today Austinuts has stores in Austin and Plano. And they have a strong wholesale and mail order/Internet business.

According to Doron, there are three things that account for the superb flavor of his products. First, Austinuts uses only the highest-grade nuts. Second, the nuts are dry roasted, which means only heat is used. No oil or butter is involved in the roasting process. Pure dry roasting adds flavor and crunch and also makes the nuts healthier. You can notice the difference in appearance. Nuts roasted in oils are darker, shinier, and greasier than their dry roasted counterparts. Austinuts sells both salted and unsalted varieties. Third, the company roasts small batches every day, five days a week (seven during the holiday season). This means that they are constantly selling fresh products.

In addition to fresh dry roasted nuts, Austinuts offers other delightful snacks including dried fruits, trail mixes, and gourmet chocolates and candies. Unique gift ideas include nuts and other snacks packaged in Texas-shaped clear containers (some dressed with bandanas), wood crates, star baskets and boxes, and other gourmet arrangements. The company has thirty employees, with more added during the Christmas season. They cater to gifts of any size, whether you are an individual with one order a year or a corporate executive with hundreds.

Where to Buy. Austinuts has two retail outlets, in Austin and Plano. They boast a large mail order business, with orders taken by phone, fax, mail, and through their website.

A Tasty Visit 🍴

Austinuts
2900 W. Anderson Lane, #8
Austin, Texas 78757
Toll-Free: (800) 404-NUTS

Enjoy the rich aroma of fresh roasted nuts wafting through the Austinuts store. The shop offers a wide selection of candies, Texas-theme gifts, and of course their famously fresh nuts.

Charlene's Sweets

5711 Westward, #169
Houston, Texas 77081
Phone: (713) 995-4593
Internet: www.realfudgeandmore.com

Take a sweet trip back to Houston, circa 1970. There you would find Charlene Day rolling her candy-filled luggage cart around the downtown streets. Employees of the police department, City Hall, courthouse, and private businesses saw her coming and

Charlene's Sweets
(713) 995-4593
Houston, Texas

pulled out their wallets in savory anticipation of her confections. Customers said her peanut brittle and fudge were the best. Her candies were rich with goodness and so was she. Rather than keeping the proceeds from her sales, Charlene donated it all to churches, charity, and organizations helping the elderly.

Eventually, Charlene parked her candy cart and worked for the airlines and later as a travel agent. But today she is back. No, she's not peddling her candy on the streets. Instead, she is selling it online.

Charlene grew up making candy. Before she could cook, her mother and grandmother needed her help in the kitchen, especially around Christmas. She remembers chopping cherries and helping the two women make divinity and date loaves.

Charlene's Sweets look and taste homemade because, as she explains, they are! Using many of her grandmother's original recipes, Charlene makes a variety of candies to suit every taste. She starts with only the highest quality ingredients, like real butter and whipping cream, to insure that every bite is delicious. Just as she did as a child, Charlene makes her popular Mama's Candy around Christmas, blending the heavenly divinity with cherries, dates, and pecans. She also makes "Santa's Special" that time of year, which is a cross between a candy and a fruitcake. Moist and sticky like candy, it is chock full of dates, coconut, pineapple, cherries, and walnuts.

It is obvious by her web address that fudge is another specialty. Charlene starts by custom blending a few chocolates. With decades of experience, fudge isn't hard for Charlene to make, but she does admit that it is tricky. She gives every batch her personal attention, assuring that it comes out not too hard or too soft, but just right.

Brittles are another Charlene specialty. Choose from Regular, Jalapeño, Cashew, or Pecan. If you see her at one of her booths, she will

Peanut Pattie

The peanut pattie is a popular treat in Texas and other southern states. It may be the original energy bar, packing protein-rich peanuts and energy building sugar into every bite! *(Special thanks to Ron Harbuck from Goodart's Candies)*

no doubt be giving out samples of brittle and fudge. She also offers a line of handmade chocolates and truffles.

Where to Buy. Order from Charlene's website or by phone. Charlene ships throughout the year. She makes the candies by hand as orders are received, assuring that only the freshest products are shipped. A toll-free number is planned, so be sure to check her website for details.

Creative Chocolates

999 E. Basse Road, #138
San Antonio, Texas 78209
Phone: (210) 824-2462
Internet: www.creativechocolates.com

Imagine chocolates in the shape of a Ferris wheel or a bicycle with individually spoked wheels or even wedding bells that swing back and forth. How about an intricately carved chocolate heart? For Richard Berchin, founder and owner of Creative Chocolates, the challenge to sculpt an interesting shape is always a welcome one.

While Richard was growing up, his mother's best friend introduced him to chocolate. A chocolate lover from the first mouthful, it was only later that he discovered his special talent for sculpting with it. Today his chocolates are shipped all over the world.

The possibilities are endless. The brochure features chocolates in the shape of landmarks such as the Statue of Liberty, the Eiffel Tour, and of course, the state of Texas. Another Lone Star favorite is the Alamo, custom designed and sculpted in chocolate by Richard. Sports fans enjoy his chocolate footballs, catcher's mitt (with baseball inside), golf balls, basketballs, and even a bowling pin! Order one sculpted animal or an entire chocolate zoo. Custom orders are welcome.

Creative Chocolates are shipped year round. The solid pieces ship best and are nestled in styrofoam with reusable ice packs.

Where to Buy. The Creative Chocolates retail store is in San Antonio. Phone, mail, and Internet orders are taken. The company's website features a chocolate quiz, which is a fun and entertaining exercise.

A Tasty Visit 🍴

Creative Chocolates
999 E. Basse Road, #138
San Antonio, Texas 78209
Phone: (210) 824-2462
Hours: Tuesday - Saturday 10 a.m. - 6 p.m.

If an Alamo tour or a day at Sea World stirs up a craving for chocolate, stop by the Creative Chocolates shop. Admire Richard Berchin's gourmet creations and satisfy your chocolate urge all at the same time.

Fain's Honey

HC 09 Box 14
Llano, Texas 78643
Phone: (915) 247-4867
Fax: (915) 247-2197

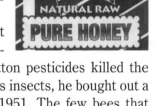

In 1926 farmer H.E. "Horace" Fain started "messin'" with bees. By the next year, he sold more dollars in honey than he did in other farm goods, so he decided to take those bees pretty seriously.

Horace, his family, and the bees went down to the Rio Grande Valley in the mid-thirties, but they eventually found that the cotton pesticides killed the hives. Desperate to save some of the precious insects, he bought out a beekeeper in Llano and relocated there in 1951. The few bees that hadn't yet succumbed to the poison died en route to Llano.

While the new home brought relief from the pesticide problem, Horace was faced with more challenges. The 1950s drought was a huge problem, but he persisted. Today Horace's son Dewey runs Fain's Honey with Erwinna, his wife of over forty years.

Obviously, Dewey grew up around bees. He worked in the family business since age eight and felt comfortable with bees from the start.

There were seven children (Dewey is the youngest son), and he is the only one who stayed in the bee business.

When Dewey and Erwinna began dating in high school, she also started to feel more at home in the company of bees. Over the years, as the kids have grown, Erwinna has taken on a more active beekeeping role.

Dewey has watched his bees change over time. Up until the early nineties, he was able to wear a short-sleeved shirt with no protection. Today's bees are more aggressive, and he covers up to avoid being stung repeatedly each day.

Dewey and Erwinna take a great deal of pride in their products. The bees from their 2,500 hives feed on Texas brush and make a mild-flavored honey, which is sold in bear bottles and one, two, and four pound jars.

The Fains also make a line of honey spreads blended with a creamed honey base and no butter or sugar. The wide selection of farm fresh spreads includes Pecan, Peanut, Amaretto Pecan, Lemon, Cinnamon, Peach, Amaretto Peach, Natural Creamed, Jalapeño, and Almond.

Where to Buy. Look for Fain's Honey products at Whole Foods, Central Market, Sun Harvest, many HEB stores, Callahan's, and produce stands around the state (hint: check the Fredericksburg peach stands). They do some mail order as well.

Goodart's Candy, Inc.

P.O. Box 901
Lubbock, Texas 79408
Phone: (806) 747-2600

Raymond Goodart opened Goodart's Peanut Patties back in the 1940s. Today, about sixteen employees still make these tasty three-inch round pink disks under the direction of peanut pattie pro Ron Harbuck.

GOODART'S
PEANUT PATTIE
LARGEST SELLER
IN
THE SOUTHWEST!

The ingredients are simple. Corn syrup, water, sugar, and peanuts come together to form a Texas favorite. The mixture is cooked at a high temperature and hand poured into rubber molds. Employees who pour are experienced because, even by Texas standards, this stuff gets pretty hot! The patties take shape in the mold, where they cool down and are ready for packaging.

Goodart's Peanut Patties contain a generous dose of Spanish peanuts grown in Texas, mainly in the central part of the state. They make about 20,000 patties a day, as many as 100,000 a week.

Ron Harbuck, who has been in the peanut pattie business for years, says summer is the most popular season for his products. The patties hold up under the intense Texas sun, making them a great warm weather treat. Pour yourself an ice-cold cola, bite into a peanut pattie, and savor the experience. Industrial workers find the peanut patties a great energy booster.

Where to Buy. Goodart's Peanut Patties are sold all over Texas and out of state as well, especially in the South.

A Tasty Visit 🍽

Goodart's Candy, Inc.
Lubbock, Texas
Phone: (806) 747-2600
Hours: Monday - Friday 9 a.m.-4 p.m.

Next time you are in Lubbock, call and arrange a tour of the Goodart's Peanut Pattie plant. Visitors can watch through a glass window as the patties take shape. When you have worked up an appetite for these tasty disks, stop in the gift shop. There, you will find a number of products, including two-pound bags of broken peanut patties (the broken pieces are also sold in Lubbock grocery stores). Call for directions.

⭐ Good Flow Honey & Juice Company

2601 East Cesar Chavez
Austin, Texas 78702
Phone: (512) 472-6714
Fax: (512) 472-6947

In the 1970s, the bee bug stung Tom Crofut. Tom was not literally stung but was struck with a deep interest in the fascinating insects. He read books on beekeeping, talked to beekeepers, and eventually went to work for one in Navasota. There, he learned how to deal with these busy insects. In 1975 he founded Good Flow.

Tom originally kept his bees in Austin, but the threat of bee Africanization and the increase in urbanization sparked his desire to move his hives further away from the city. Today, Tom's bees reside to the south, east, and northeast of Austin. So far, Africanization has not been a problem and he says his bees are "nice ladies." Most of the time Tom does not wear protection. He does get stung here and there, but that hasn't been a problem.

Tom and his son take a great deal of pride in their products (the company has a thriving juice business as well). They heat and filter their honey as little as possible so that the nutritional value is retained, and they offer unheated honey as well.

Good Flow's honey products are available in bears (12 ounce) and one, two, or four pound jars. Some stores carry Good Flow's bulk honey in four-gallon buckets. In addition to the honey made by the family's bees, Tom buys honey from other Texas locations. One that he purchases from an area southwest of San Antonio is very light (Huajillo), and the Clover Honey from up north in the state is a light, low moisture, and sweet product especially good in lemonade and limeade.

Where to Buy. Look for the Good Flow label in Whole Foods (Austin), Sun Harvest (Austin and San Antonio), Central Market (Austin, San Antonio, Houston, and Dallas), Fresh Plus (Austin), some Austin Randalls stores, Wheatsville and Fresh Plus stores in Austin, and some HEB stores. Orders are taken by phone, fax, mail, or email (call for email address).

A Tasty Visit 🍽

Good Flow Honey & Juice Company
2601 East Cesar Chavez
Austin, Texas 78702
Phone: (512) 472-6714
Hours: Monday - Saturday 7 a.m. - mid-afternoon

When in Austin, visit the Good Flow Honey & Juice Company located on the east side of town. You can purchase honey (buy a gallon if you like!) and juices. Call first to make sure they are open.

The Great Texas Pecan Candy Company

870 S. Mason
Katy, Texas 77450
Phone: (281) 395-2500
Toll-Free: (888) 770-1000
Fax: (281) 395-2512
Internet: www.texaspecancandy.com

Home economist Bunny King has the know-how to make great tasting candy. A high school Nutrition and Food Science teacher, she understands the technology behind the technique of candy making.

Her candies, pies, and other sweets begin with native Texas pecans. The most popular candy, a Pecan Roca, is a combination of toffee, pecans, and chocolate made fresh by hand at the store in Katy.

Another favorite is the Pecan Beer Nuts featuring fresh pecans covered with a sweet and slightly salty coating. Other candies include Pecan Brittle, Chocolate Pecans, Poppin' Pecan popcorn, West Texas Fire (hot and spicy pecans), and South Texas Salties (salt, butter, and cinnamon). An assortment of containers are available, including one that is Texas-shaped. Candies are made fresh every day.

In addition to confections, Bunny makes homemade pecan pies and special order desserts. Her freezer is stocked with her creations, and customers often come in to purchase whatever desserts she has on hand. She also prepares boxed lunches for corporations, surprising the recipients with a fresh homemade sandwich, chips, fruit, a mini-dessert selected and made by Bunny, topped off with a sample bag of candy. Now that's a boxed lunch worth opening!

Where to Buy. The Great Texas Pecan Candy Company is located in Katy and accepts orders through the mail, phone, fax, or online.

A Tasty Visit 🍴

The Great Texas Pecan Candy Company
870 S. Mason
Katy, Texas 77450
Phone: (281) 395-2500

Visit the Great Texas Pecan Candy Company in Katy, Texas (near Houston), and savor the pecan confections made fresh daily in the shop. Call for specific directions and hours.

⭐

Harkey's Honey

RR 2, Box 67
San Saba, Texas 76877
Phone: (915) 372-6324
Fax: (915) 372-6377

When Richard Harkey was a high school student, he and his FFA group visited a beekeeper's operation. Richard was immediately struck with how "easy" it was to get honey from a box rather than a tree. After school, Richard shared this new information with his dad, who already had an interest in beekeeping. The two looked at equipment pictured in the Sears Roebuck catalog but were too poor to order it. Instead, Richard's father constructed the boxes and eventually had about ten or fifteen colonies. But at that time (the 1950s) nearby farmers raised cotton, and the pesticide killed the bees.

Richard's fascination with bees was put on hold while he served in the army and pursued a career as a repairman working outdoors. But an incident would occur to change all that.

In 1964 a serious fall at work left Richard in a wheelchair, unable to continue at his job. A skilled repairman, he received training in watch repair. But working at a desk in the corner of a room yielded a longing for the great outdoors.

This desire sparked a renewal of Richard's interest in beekeeping. A buddy from high school allowed Richard and his wife, Floydene, to extract honey from some of his seventy-five colonies. After a few bee stings, Floydene realized that getting stung was not lethal, and she was willing to take an active role in the family beekeeping business.

In the meantime, Richard's father still had some boxes of bees. When he died they were passed on to Richard and Floydene, who also received boxes from acquaintances and through purchases.

That was about thirty years ago. Today the Harkeys remain committed to beekeeping. As they move closer to retirement, their daughter and son-in-law, Pamela and Greg Casco, are taking over the business. The Cascos have five boys, all born in the Dallas area. Floydene and Richard thought their grandsons, ages four to thirteen, would enjoy growing up in the country and were able to convince Pam and Greg to leave the big city.

It has been a refreshing change for the Casco family. The five boys now prefer wide open space over the small backyard they left behind in the Big D. Richard believes his second grandson, Reid, is headed for a career as a naturalist. He loves grasshoppers and other small creatures and of course the bees!

The Harkeys' bees are buzzing all through the year, although occupancy of each box varies with the season. In the springtime and summer, as many as 200,000 bees inhabit a box.

During the summer the family is as busy as bees, extracting honey from the hives. Their Central Texas Wildflower Honey is mild in flavor and a beautiful light amber color. Richard Harkey suggests warming the honey in the microwave ever so slightly to enjoy the fragrance of the wildflowers. He calls the lightly heated honey a "Liquid Bouquet." Even if you live in the city, you can savor a whiff of the country life!

Where to Buy. Look for the 12-ounce Harkey's Honey bear in HEB stores. The Harkeys take orders by phone, fax, or mail.

Flowers & Honey

The color and flavor of honey varies with the types of plants that the bees use for gathering nectar and pollen.

La Chocolatiere

635 W. Campbell Road, # 200
Richardson, Texas 75080
Phone: (972) 690-7209
Toll-Free: (888) 605-6363
Fax: (972) 293-5355
Internet: www.trufflefactory.com

Each piece of La Chocolatiere's chocolate is made by hand, featuring fine Swiss chocolate and fresh cream. And that's just the start.

Making fine chocolate gourmet specialties started as a hobby for the company's founder and owner, Brian McCallister. Over five years later, it is a labor of love. Today his rich chocolate truffles and other candies are popular around the state.

A favorite is Chocolate Rapture, pecan halves resting atop a heavenly chocolate mousse wrap surrounding chocolate mousse fudge and four types of roasted nuts cooked in caramel. La Chocolatiere's best selling truffle is its chocolate raspberry torte creation.

Brian, an environmental engineer by training, has an eye for aesthetics and makes certain that his staff of three to six people possess this quality in addition to good manual dexterity. The end result is a line of confections that look as good as they taste.

Walking in the small Richardson store is just the beginning of the experience. The powerfully rich chocolate aroma seems to capture the senses immediately. Customers gaze wide-eyed at the conveyor belt and mini chocolate waterfall.

Where to Find. La Chocolatiere's products are sold in specialty stores throughout the state. The website contains beautiful product photos and phone order information.

A Tasty Visit

La Chocolatiere
635 Campbell Road, # 200
Richardson, Texas 75080
Phone: (972) 690-7209
Hours: Monday - Saturday 10 a.m. - 6 p.m.

If you need a fix while in Richardson, a visit to La Chocolatiere should help no matter what your level of chocolate addiction. Enjoy the aroma of freshly made chocolate and select from the assortment of gourmet products.

Lammes Candies Since 1885, Inc.
P.O. Box 1885
Austin, Texas 78767
Phone: (512) 310-2223
Toll-Free: (800) 252-1885
Internet: www.lammes.com

The number "1885" is an important one to this Austin-based candy company. That is when it all began, and 1885 is now used in the company's official name as well as its toll-free phone number.

In 1878 William Wirt Lamme founded downtown Austin's Red Front Candy Factory. He lost the business in a poker game in 1885, but his son David Turner Lamme Sr. repaid the debt, and ownership was returned to the family. On July 10, 1885, Lammes Candies officially opened, and over one hundred years later it remains family owned and operated. In the late 1880s, the store moved to a new location, where it stayed until 1956.

In the early years, Lammes sold ice cream and a product called Gem, which was like sherbet. World War II sugar rationing signaled a break in ice cream and Gem making. The products were sold again after the war, until Lammes switched its focus to chocolates in the mid-1960s. They entered this product line with taste, selecting only the highest grade chocolate.

Today Lammes is ninety-five employees strong and is still selling its sweet confections. The Texas Chewie Praline, introduced by David Lamme Sr. in 1893 (after seven years of recipe testing), remains popular, with over two thousand pounds produced each day. The ingredients are the same as they always were: native Texas pecans, corn syrup, sugar, butter, and salt. This praline is a pleasant surprise because of its chewy (hence the name) texture.

Three products make up what the company calls its Texas Trio. They are the Longhorns, Choc a'dillos, and the Cashew Critter. The most popular is the Longhorns, which features a chocolate coating surrounding rich caramel and crunchy pecans. Choc a'dillos have whole roasted almonds nestled into creamy caramel and covered with premium milk chocolate. The Cashew Critter is made from cashews, caramel, and chocolate. The product list now features about one thousand items, so there is sure to be something for every candy lover.

Another favorite is the chocolate-coated strawberry introduced in the late 1970s. Lammes created just a handful at first and gave them to an Austin radio host with instructions to eat them before going on the air. Soon the stores had long lines of customers craving the strawberry sensations. They are available only on very special days, and demand is still strong.

The company's name, obviously, hails from the family. A lamb logo was developed as a cue for properly pronouncing the name, and the store's original sign (in the shape of a lamb) was Austin's first neon sign.

To trace the family history from then until now, remember that David Turner Lamme Sr. saved the day when he repaid his dad's gambling debt. He is also the famous son who developed the Texas Chewie Praline. In 1946 David and his wife sold the business to their children, David Lamme Jr., Lena Lamme, and Evelyn Lamme Teich. In 1965 the children incorporated the business. Nowadays, fifth generation Lammes operate this world-famous confectionary.

Where to Find. Lammes Candies own retail shops throughout Austin, Round Rock, and San Antonio. Call the toll-free number to see if a retailer near you carries their products. Mail, phone, and online orders are welcome.

A Tasty Visit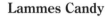

Lammes Candy

Visit Lammes candy stores in Austin, Round Rock, and San Antonio. Walk in and you'll be greeted by a fresh candy aroma. Feast your eyes on the chocolates and other candies available "by the piece" or splurge on a whole box!

LeBlanc Pecans

2032 Highway 90A East
Richmond, Texas 77469
Phone: (281) 342-2101
Toll-Free: (800) 890-1188
Fax: (281) 342-2101
Internet: www.leblancspecancompany.com

Betty and Orville LeBlanc's Fort Bend County shop is a haven for pecan lovers. The store features fresh shelled and unshelled pecans, mostly grown on their fifteen-acre pecan tree orchard. (The ones they don't grow come in fresh from Seguin, Texas.)

Whether you want pecans for yourself or to give as gifts, you are sure to find them here. Pick up some freshly shelled pecans for baking or just nibbling. Or buy a Texas theme gift, such as pecans in a Texas-shaped basket or nestled in a burlap bag with a state emblem. Betty says that everything they do has "Texas" on it in some form, adding Lone Star flavor to any item.

The LeBlancs sell a variety of fresh nuts as well as candies, jams, and other goodies. Be sure to pick up a copy of Betty's reasonably priced cookbook.

Where to Find. Buy LeBlanc pecans at their retail shop in Richmond, Texas, or through phone, fax, and mail orders. The website includes a printable order form.

A Tasty Visit 🎙️

LeBlanc Pecans
2032 Highway 90A East
Richmond, Texas 77469

Pack in some fresh pecans with a visit to LeBlanc Pecans. Browse the nuts, candies, and wide assortment of delectable gifts.

Lone Star Honey Company
(also Walker Apiaries and Walker Honey)

P.O. Box 615
Rogers, Texas 76569
Phone: (254) 983-LONE
Fax/Phone: (254) 983-BEES
Internet: www.walker-honey.com or www.lonestarhoney.com

Clint Walker, owner of Lone Star Honey, Walker Apiaries, and Walker Honey, is from a honey of a family. Clint is a third generation beekeeper, and his family has been in the business since 1930. The Walker brand, a family label for seventy-plus years, is found mainly in Central Texas (primarily the Temple, Bryan/College Station areas), while the Lone Star Honey label is more widely available.

Clint grew up around bees and believes his experience was similar to being raised on any Texas farm or ranch. He points out that bees are like livestock and need to be managed just as cattle, goats, and sheep do. Even as a child, Clint was fascinated with the bees, and getting stung was never a deterrent.

But between childhood and now, Clint had another important career. He received a degree from the seminary and went on to earn a Ph.D. in Theology from Baylor University. He was a pastor in Los Angeles for awhile before he and his wife, Janice, returned to Central Texas in 1993. In 1994 the couple purchased the family business (Walker Apiaries and Walker Honey) and seven years later bought

Lone Star Honey. Today the Walkers' sons are actively involved as fourth-generation beekeepers.

In addition to managing the family business, Clint is active in the industry. He serves as president of the American Beekeeping Federation, a national trade organization. The group supports research and addresses beekeeping issues, such as mites and other threats.

While Clint is busy on many fronts (he's also an avid birder), focusing on the bees is a major priority. The family takes a great deal of pride in their products, which include a wide selection of premium honey varieties. The company's honey is produced by their own bees and purchased from other high-quality suppliers. Their six main honey varieties are Huajillo, Central Texas Wildflower, Clover, Orange Blossom, Tupelo, and Buckwheat.

Of special interest is the Huajillo Honey, a light-colored premium varietal with a mild and characteristically smokey flavor. The only place in the U.S. where it is found is the area extending from the San Antonio area down to near the Rio Grande and across to Uvalde and over to Eagle Pass. Clint markets this honey under both the Walker and Lone Star brands.

The company's selection is so wide that Clint believes they have a honey variety to suit just about anyone's tastes.

Lone Star Honey is also available with the comb, which is said to benefit those with asthma. Clint says many people of the World War II generation prefer this type of honey because they are accustomed to it from their youth. However, he notes a surge in interest due to the studies related to asthma.

Over the years there has been much talk about the health benefits of honey. Clint believes in the value of straining the honey, rather than filtering it heavily. The straining process leaves most of the nutrients intact and does not filter them out.

Where to Buy. Lone Star Honey is available at about five hundred grocery stores, including Central Market, Whole Foods, HEB, Winn Dixie, and Albertson's. The Walker brand is primarily available in farmers' markets and fruit stands in Central Texas, mainly in the Temple and Bryan/College Station areas. Orders are taken by phone and fax, and gift baskets are available.

A Tasty Visit

Lone Star Honey Company

8060 East U.S. Highway 190
Rogers, Texas 76569
Phone: (254) 983-LONE or (254) 983-BEES
Hours: Tuesday - Friday 10 a.m. - 6 p.m.
Saturday 8 a.m. - 2 p.m.
Closed Sunday and Monday

Located off Interstate 35 about ten miles southeast of Temple, the Lone Star Honey Company is a delightful place to visit. Tastefully decorated with antiques, the shop offers interesting exhibits and a wide selection of bee-related products.

Learn about bees by viewing an observation beehive (don't worry, it's behind glass!). See bees in action and watch as they make honey.

And there's more watching to do. Look through the glass into the Packing Room, and view the staff bottling jars of honey.

Honey is just the beginning of what you can buy. In addition to the six varieties of honey available for purchase, the store sells Pecan Honey Butter made with their own honey and Texas pecans, honey candy, hand-rolled beeswax candles, honey-based skin care products, and more. The hours may be expanded, so give 'em a call.

Panhandle Popcorn

1300 South I-27
P.O. Box 878
Plainview, Texas 79072
Phone: (806) 293-4361
Toll-Free: (800) 332-1365
Fax: (806) 293-9557
Internet: www.panhandlepopcorn.com

Things are really popping in the Panhandle! In 1942 Glenn Beard moved there to grow popcorn. And he did much more than just grow the stuff. In addition to establishing a professional association for popcorn growers, he played a key role in setting up Purdue University's Popcorn Institute. And then there are the hybrids...

One of his achievements was developing hull-less popcorn, as well as a number of hybrids that improved the quality of one of America's favorite snacks. Thanks to his research, Panhandle Popcorn is delightfully tender. In 1956 Glenn stopped growing popcorn and went into distribution. Jim Mock, hired as a sales manager in the late 1970s, bought the company in 1987 and moved it from the downtown barn to a location along the interstate. He and his staff of fifteen poppers and packers have quite a following of popcorn lovers. The company has attained national recognition and has been featured in *Southern Living* magazine.

Today the company pops out a line of flavors, its main ones being Caramel, Cheese, Buttery, and Vanilla. If you are wondering about that last flavor, imagine vanilla-coated popcorn mixed with crunchy pecans and almonds. Panhandle Popcorn is top of the line; the Caramel Corn is made from an old recipe with real butter and brown sugar, and the Cheese Corn is smothered with high-quality cheddar. They also sell unpopped corn for those who want theirs straight from the popper or stove top (please, no microwaves).

In 1977 the company was among the first to pack its popcorn in tins. Today a variety of festive tins are offered to commemorate the season. At Christmas choose from designs such as Santa or a beautiful winter scene. Sports fans will flip over the action-packed tin featuring footballs, baseballs, basketballs, and soccer balls mixed with stars and other bright objects. Tins are available in two- or six-and-a-half-gallon sizes. Refill bags allow you to restock your large-sized tins.

If you really—and I mean *really*—love popcorn, choose The Giant Bag. This jumbo plastic bag holds over thirty gallons of buttery popcorn and is certain to make an enormous impression!

Where to Buy. Panhandle Popcorn is sold at a variety of locations, particularly within a three hundred mile radius of the Panhandle. You can munch and crunch it at amusement parks, concession stands, and schools. It is also sold at United Food Stores and Town and Country stores. The plant has a store out front if you happen to be driving through the area. If you cannot find Panhandle Popcorn near you, the company welcomes orders by mail, phone, fax, or online.

A Tasty Visit

Panhandle Popcorn
1300 South I-27
Plainview, Texas 79072
Toll-Free: (800) 332-1365

Pop in for a quick visit to the Panhandle Popcorn plant! Inhale the succulent popcorn-scented air and you will just have to pop for a tin or a bag! The plant, located along Interstate 27 in Plainview, features a store up front so you can grab some for the road.

Quintessential Chocolates

P.O. Box 687
Fredericksburg, Texas 78624
Phone: (830) 990-9382
Toll-Free: (800) 842-3382
Fax: (830) 997-0811
Internet: www.qechocolates.com

Liquor-filled chocolates were once a delicacy only crafted in Europe. Today these fine confections are made in the quaint Texas town of Fredericksburg.

Years ago, when she was working as an architect in Nashville, Lecia Duke traveled to Europe and sampled her first taste of liquor-filled chocolates. A caterer on the side, Lecia enjoyed experimenting with flavor blends. She added chocolate truffles to her catering menu, and their instant success inspired Lecia to learn the European art of making liquor-filled chocolates.

Lecia found a Swiss master chocolatier willing to travel to Nashville to teach her this fine European art. The process dates back two hundred years and is now part of a confectioner's education in Europe. But in this country, things are different. After learning the technique, Lecia faced another hurdle. The specialized equipment needed to make the fine confections is not available in the United States. Shipping it from Europe would be astronomically expensive.

This is where Lecia's architecture background came into play. If an architect can design a building, why not a piece of equipment? Lecia designed and constructed the equipment needed to craft handmade liquor-filled chocolates. The process is similar to sand casting. Put your foot in the sand, remove it, and it leaves an impression. Lecia uses cornstarch to make the molds for the confections. An impression is made in the cornstarch. Obviously, if liquid was poured into the cornstarch it would be absorbed, so the liquor or other filling is suspended in a sugar solution. Lecia is the only person in the country using the European "sugar crust" technique to make these sensational confections.

With equipment in place and the training completed, Lecia was ready to roll. She spoke with a whiskey manufacturer who was enthusiastic about having its spirits featured in the chocolates.

Architects are creative and Lecia Duke is no exception to this rule. When it was time to select a name for her company, she wanted one that would convey the pureness of her products. According to Webster, quintessential is the "pure essence of a substance." The candies have only four ingredients: chocolate, sugar, water, and liquor, and Quintessential was the perfect name.

But Lecia faced another obstacle. The chocolates contain liquor and were fairly new to this country, so there was some confusion regarding their legality in a number of states. Were they candies or alcoholic beverages? Like the other hurdles, Lecia is overcoming this one and her products are now sold in twenty-three states.

Quintessential Chocolates contain only the finest quality liquor like Russian vodka, Canadian blended whiskey, Puerto Rican rum, Cutty Sark whiskey, cabernet wine, high quality cognac, and Australian tawny port. They are also filled with a variety of nonalcohol flavors including Cappuccino, Mocha, Espresso, Peach Nectar, and Cranberry.

Quintessential Chocolates are bite-sized, so most people can slip the entire piece in their mouths. Sink your teeth into the candy, and your mouth becomes saturated with a burst of liquid. The filling is encapsulated in a sugar shell, which lends a pleasant crispiness under the chocolate coating. Once the liquid is swallowed, your tastebuds are left with the outer layer of fine quality chocolate. Eating these confections is an experience that will enliven your senses. It is truly one of life's pleasures.

Quintessential Chocolates are an elegant and unique gift. They are attractively packaged in boxes containing a dozen or half-dozen pieces.

In 1998 Lecia relocated her business to Fredericksburg. The town, with a European influence all its own, welcomed Lecia with a feature in the newspaper. A native Texan, she was thrilled to be back in her home state.

Where to Buy. Purchase Quintessential Chocolates in gourmet food stores and specialty shops as well as liquor stores. When in Fredericksburg, look for them at Texas Wines, Etc. and Judy's Liquors. A partial list of other retailers offering them includes The Orvis Company (Virginia), Chicago News & Gifts (Illinois), Dean & DeLuca (New York), Ritz Carlton Gift Shops (Missouri), Marriott Gift Shops (Texas, California), Gloria Jeans Coffee (New Jersey, Missouri, Wisconsin), and Rocky Mountain Chocolate Factory (Texas, Arkansas, Hawaii, Georgia).

Orders are taken by mail, phone, fax, and the Internet.

A Tasty Visit

Quintessential Chocolates
206A Jack Nixon Road
Fredericksburg, Texas 78624
Phone: (830) 990-9382
Hours: Monday - Friday 8 a.m. - 5 p.m. (closed holidays)

Lecia Duke and her staff can make up to 10,000 pieces of liquid-filled chocolates in one day. Production does not take place every day. Visitors can view a small portion of the production line and are treated to samples and have a chance to purchase.

Sanderson Pecan Company

305 North High
San Saba, Texas 76877
Toll-Free: (800) 443-1355
Fax: (512) 394-0478

Eddie Sanderson got an early start in the pecan business. As a child growing up amidst groves of pecan trees in San Saba, he found early employment. A neighbor owned a lot of land in the area, and Eddie helped him weigh pecans. The child was a good worker and a likable kid, so his neighbor frequently asked him to come over and help him with the pecans.

When Eddie graduated high school, he went on to study Agriculture at Texas A&M University. Today Sanderson Pecan Company is a retail shop in San Saba open

SANDERSON PECAN CO.
"Fancy Shelled Pecans"

SANDERSON
THE NAME TO LOOK FOR WHEN
SELECTING QUALITY PECANS

305 N. High, San Saba, Texas 76877 - (915) 372-5554
"Pecan Capital of the World "

seven days a week from October to January.

The company sells fresh papershell pecans and an assortment of gift boxes. (Eddie has since broadened his agricultural expertise from pecans to tomatoes, onions, peppers, and even mangoes. See Sanderson Specialty Food Company in Chapter 7 for details.)

Where to Buy. Buy Sanderson pecans from the retail shop in San Saba between October and January, or order by phone or mail. Call the toll-free number for a complete price list.

A Tasty Visit 🍽️

Sanderson Pecan Company
305 North High
San Saba, Texas 76877
Toll-Free: (800) 443-1355

Sanderson Pecan Company sells a wide assortment of fresh Texas pecans. Buy some for yourself or select a gift box.

Southeast Texas Honey Company

P.O. Box 176
Vidor, Texas 77670
Phone: (409) 783-2605
Internet: www.texasdrone.com

When Robert Williamson held an indoor office job, he knew there was a better way to make a living. He wanted a

career that allowed him to work outside and enjoy nature. Today his dream has become a reality.

Robert's desire for an outdoorsy career was the reason he answered an ad for a farm hand. At the time he had no idea that it was the start of an entirely different—and satisfying—new venture. It turns out that the farm was a bee farm. Robert took the job and was immediately fascinated with the bees. He spent his off time researching bees, picking up whatever facts he could about the insects. While at work, he asked questions and learned a lot.

In 1995 Robert started Southeast Texas Honey Company, selling honey and related products made in his own hives. He describes the job of a beekeeper as "fascinating." Summer is the busy season, and the bees are constantly in motion, gathering nectar, water, or pollen. Robert thoroughly enjoys the steady hum in the yard as the bees go about their business. For summer protection, he wears a headpiece, but his arms and legs are exposed. Getting stung on the body (not the head) is just part of the job, and Robert is used to it.

Southeast Texas Honey is available in glass jars ranging from one to twelve pounds (one gallon). The company's website (texasdrone.com) is named for the male bee.

Robert continues to research bees and is now a wealth of knowledge on the subject. The company's website buzzes with information and unique products. Robert's wife, Delphine, is active in the family business. Delphine's Candles (check them out on the website) are most unusual. They come in capped jars so they can be kept closed while not in use. Beeswax candles are also available. Delphine's upbringing in France gives the products a European flair.

Robert and Delphine visit her family in France periodically and are struck by the differences in honey overseas. In Europe, honey is often sold in its purest crystalline form and is commonly used in place of sugar.

The Williamsons take a great deal of pride in their products. Their honey is lightly heated and strained so that the nutrients stay in, and

Baby, No Honey for You!

Babies should not be given honey during their first year of life because of the risk of infant botulism.

are not overheated or filtered out. In Europe, honey is touted as a health food, and Robert and Delphine do what they can to make sure their honey is as healthful as possible.

Where to Buy. Find Southeast Texas Honey at flea markets in Winnie, Texas (20 miles west of Beaumont), Livingston, Texas (up Highway 59 from Houston), and Trader's Village northwest of Houston. Orders are taken by phone and through the website.

Susie's South Forty Confections

P.O. Box 4040
Midland, Texas 79704-4040
Phone: (915) 570-4040
Toll-Free: (800) 221-4442
Fax: (915) 682-4040
Internet: www.susiessouthforty.com

When Susie Hitchcock-Hall was ready to start her own confectionary, she looked no farther than the forty-acre pecan grove, South Forty, owned by her friend. Susie combined her love of cooking with a desire to own a business, and opening a candy company seemed like the natural thing to do. Now she and up to forty-three employees (during the busy times) use pecans from the eight hundred South Forty trees to make fresh toffee, pralines, and a host of other sweet treats. Her candies have a loyal following and traveled to Washington, D.C. for the Inauguration, where they were included with other specialties representing President George W. Bush's hometown.

Susie's buttery rich candies start with original recipes and are handmade from scratch. When it comes to pecans, Susie believes that more is better, and her candy reflects this wisdom.

A variety of candies are available, including toffee, pralines, and fudge. The company's most popular product is the Texas Pecan Toffee, which features a blend of homemade toffee and pecans painted with a layer of fine Belgian chocolate. It has a surprisingly light texture, and Susie says the best way to enjoy it is straight from the freezer.

Pralines, called Kickers, are made of real butter and brown sugar heated in a large copper kettle. The finishing touch occurs when a slew of crunchy fresh pecans are added. Be a true Texan, and have yours packaged in a festive red boot box.

Fudge, named Fudge Richey, has a pleasantly intense chocolate flavor. Belgian chocolate lays the foundation for the rich, yet not bitter, chocolate taste. The fudge was originally going to be called "Fudge Rickey" but was changed when the "k" looked like an "h" on a fax copy. Richey may actually be a more accurate description.

The now famous Inauguration candy is called Winners! These rich chocolate morsels feature creamy caramel and crunchy pecans, topped with more pecans, and then coated with rich Belgian chocolate. After eating them, the folks in Washington D.C. surely know just how serious Texans are about their candies!

Susie's South Forty Confections has a website that will make you dream of chocolate and pecans. See the specialties by clicking individual squares of chocolate. Tempting! Detailed product descriptions and beautiful photography answer any questions you might have.

Where to Buy. Susie's South Forty Confections has two stores in Midland. There is the factory at South Forty and another store in the north end of town. And you may see Susie's booth at shows around the state, such as Junior League Christmas bazaars. She takes orders by mail, phone, fax, and online.

A Tasty Visit

Susie's South Forty Confectioners
Midland, Texas 79704-4040
Phone: (915) 570-4040
Toll-Free: (800) 221-4442

Visit Susie's Candy Kitchen and watch through the big glass window as terrific toffee and other treats take shape. The Candy Kitchen is located at the original shop on South Forty, a half mile south of I-20 off Old Lamesa Road. They are open Monday-Thursday year round.

Susie's second store is in the heart of Midland in the Plaza Oaks Shopping Center, at Wadley and Garfield. The store is open Monday-Saturday.

Susie will gladly give you a sample or two, and that's all it will take to convince you to buy some for yourself.

Sweet Taste of Texas

1155 Britmoore, Suite C
Houston, Texas 77043
Phone: (713) 464-5848
Toll-Free: (800) 328-5848
Fax: (713) 464-1943
Internet: www.sweettasteoftexas.com

Oh, the Sweet Taste of Texas! Here pecans, pecans, and still more pecans are the star of the show in confections ranging from pralines to fudge.

Brenda and Tony Wilson first opened their mall retail store in 1985. Today in addition to the mall location, the company's products are featured in other gift shops, and they have a thriving mail order business. The recipe for the sugary nuggets is similar to one used in the days when early Texas settlers first discovered how to sweeten their luscious and plentiful pecans.

The signature product is the Glazed Pecans, available in bags, tins, and jars. The pecans and glaze are cooked together in a copper kettle and cooled on a marble table until they reach the perfectly crunchy stage.

In addition to Glazed Pecans, the candy makers are known for their pralines, fudge, turtles, and cinnamon sugar pecans. The pralines are the chewy sort, made with real cream and fresh pecans. All candies are handmade by the Wilsons and their staff, which grows from twelve to thirty during busy seasons.

State Tree

In 1919 the pecan was named the State Tree by the Texas 36th Legislature.

Where to Buy. Visit the company's store in Houston or order by phone, mail, fax, or online.

A Tasty Visit

Sweet Taste of Texas
Memorial Mall
Houston, Texas

Visit the Sweet Taste of Texas retail shop in Houston's Memorial Mall. There, you can watch pralines, fudge, turtles, and chocolate clusters take shape and may find yourself tempted by a fresh caramel apple.

The Toffee Company

359 N. Post Oak Lane, #126
Houston, Texas 77024
Phone: (713) 688-5531
Fax: (713) 688-7602
Internet: www.toffeeco.com

What's in a name? In the case of The Toffee Company, the name says it all. Ben Burkholder, founder, owner, and chief toffee maker, is a toffee specialist. Using an old family recipe perfected over decades, he has mastered the toffee technique.

His secret? Ben pours his toffee wafer thin, resulting in a candy that is light and easy to bite, yet rich in flavor. The chocolate coating and very generous sprinkling of pecans make this toffee exceptional.

Ben has been making toffee for about forty years, so it is no wonder that he knows what he is doing. He began selling toffee at church bazaars and has expanded to shows throughout Texas. He also has an active mail order business.

The Toffee Company maintains its consistently superb quality because this is a hands-on operation. Ben and his staff, which peaks at five during the busy season, make each batch of toffee by hand, the old-fashioned way. And the proof is in the pudding, or rather, toffee.

Over the years Ben has perfected the art of pouring nearly paper thin toffee. His technique is the basis for a toffee that is easy on the teeth and delightfully rich on the taste buds! And the thin layer of toffee leaves more room for the milk chocolate and pecan coating on both the top and bottom of each piece.

The toffee comes packed in either a classic red or gold tin, with an embossed gold label and festive gold foil encasing the toffee. Decorative holiday tins or Texas-shaped baskets are also available. Peek inside the container and you will be greeted by a tinful of this sinful (but worth it!) dessert. Toffee pieces, some quite large and others small but all consistently thin, greet you, just waiting to be eaten. And trust me, one piece is not enough!

If you are lucky enough to see The Toffee Company's booth at a Christmas bazaar or rodeo, stop by and purchase a small bag of toffee, called a Walkaround. Named by rodeo customers who wanted a small bag to carry around during the event, this item is a big seller. After sampling the Walkaround, you will surely be hooked!

Where to Buy. Look for The Toffee Company booths at the Houston Livestock Show & Rodeo, Junior League Christmas bazaars throughout the state, and on the Internet. Orders for fresh toffee are taken by mail, phone, fax, and online.

Pecan Festival

In September the Groves Chamber of Commerce features this weekend fest. Activities include a Pecan Pie Eating Contest, carnival, arts and crafts, and plenty of food, dancing, and entertainment.

Tyler Candy Company

P.O. Box 6556
Tyler, Texas 75711
Phone: (903) 561-3046

In 1941 Anthony George started making candy. A baker by trade, he found flour too expensive during World War II, so he turned his culinary skills to candy. Candies are sold under the *Dickies* brand, named for Anthony's son. In 1999 the company was sold to Tony Wahl. Mr. George died in 2001 at the age of 90, leaving behind a sweet legacy. He attributed his long life to peanuts, recognized for their health benefits.

Tyler Candy Company is still known for its handmade southern style candies. Machines just can't do what people can when it comes to the art of candy making. The company's signature product is, of course, its peanut pattie. This round confection, sweetened by sugar and fortified with a healthy dose of peanuts, is a staple in Texas.

Tyler Candy Company also makes brittles, pecan rolls, divinity, and peppermint sticks.

Tony Wahl enjoys being Tyler's new "Candy Man." Actively involved with the company, he gives tours to schoolchildren who gaze at the kettles in awe, dreaming of just one taste.

Where to Buy. Dickies brand candies are sold in grocery and convenience stores throughout Texas. Misplaced Texans will be pleased to know that the company accepts individual orders and ships around the country. (They have even shipped their southern confections up to Alaska!)

A Tasty Visit

Tyler Candy Company
Tyler, Texas 75711
Phone: (903) 561-3046

Tours of Tyler Candy Company are available to small groups on a limited basis. After all, those kettles get hot! Monday is a favorite tour day because peppermints are made at the start of the week, and it sure is fun watching those red stripes come to life. Candy makers skillfully pull the confections out of a machine and cut the candy while it is still warm. Then they carefully wrap the red layers around the white ones and there you have it. Peppermint stripes! President Tony Wahl delights in taking schoolchildren and other groups around the facility. And you will be treated to a sample or two!

The company has a candy store in front of the plant. Around Christmas, the shop is known for its freshly made peppermint baskets filled with candy.

Be sure to call to schedule a tour and to find out store hours, as well as directions to the plant.

Chapter 3

Cheese, Ice Cream, Milk, and More

In Texas we are blessed with, among other things, acres of rich dairy land. This makes our cows real happy, and we share in the fun too, enjoying some of the best butter, milk, and cheese around. We spread that creamy joy on fresh biscuits, warm tortillas, and that famous Texas toast. And of course, the Lone Star's littlest folks chug milk by the gallon so they can grow up to be tall Texans.

Then there is the issue of ice cream. Texas summers are long on heat and big on ice cream. In the days of yore, many a back porch was bustling with activity and anticipation as ice creams were cranked out by hand.

There is another important dairy product served across the state. Any way you slice it, cheese is a Lone Star staple. We need something to take the bite out of those jalapeño peppers or to sprinkle on steaming bowls of chili. That's where cheese comes in, which takes us back to being thankful for all the farm fresh dairy land lying within our borders.

Take the delightful land and blend in a dose of true Texas creativity, and you are in for a dairy big treat.

Binasco, Inc.

102 East Austin
Fredericksburg, Texas 78624
Phone: (830) 990-8935
Fax: (830) 990-9076

When a downtown Austin gelato shop closed its doors and the proprietors moved back to Italy, Cornelia Allen, a Fredericksburg, Texas, cookie store owner, bought the specialized Italian equipment,  hired the shop's gelato maker, and relocated the business. Cornelia's cookie shop had featured the gelato, and she was pleased to continue offering it. Today the company's sales go beyond the Fredericksburg shop, and pint-sized tubs of gelato and sorbet are sold in a number of Texas grocery stores.

Romina Dehr, the original shop's gelato maker, hails from the Italian town of Binasco, and the new company was named in honor of her home. Binasco's products are made with Romina's authentic Italian recipes.

Romina eventually moved back to Italy, leaving her talent and recipes behind in the hands of the new owner's daughter, Diane Wilson. Before returning to her homeland, Romina taught Diane the fine art of Italian ice cream making so that the tradition can be carried on.

Enjoy one spoonful of Binasco gelato, and you might think you are with Romina, strolling the cobblestone streets of an Italian village, surrounded by sidewalk cafes and bowls of pasta. You will know that you have tasted something very special.

Diane explains that there are some very real differences between gelato and American ice cream. Gelato is frozen quicker and contains less air. The result is pudding-esque creaminess meant to be savored oh-so-slowly. The flavor is intense, making each mouthful a taste of heaven.

The texture is rich and creamy and—I must admit—it came as a shock that the butterfat content is lower than that of ice cream. And gelato contains no eggs.

Gelato is packed with some of life's culinary pleasures, like milk, heavy cream, and sugar. Fruits and other flavors, such as chocolate, round out the ingredient list.

Diane finds inspiration from the fresh fruits available in Fredericksburg. She enjoys shopping in local markets, searching for seasonal fruits and other fresh ingredients. In a town known for its peaches, Diane adds the freshest picks to her gelato and sorbet. Farm fresh nectarines are also a favorite. Other popular flavors include Tira Misu, Crème Brulee, and Pistachio.

If you would like a refreshing treat with even less fat than a gelato, try one of Binasco's sorbet flavors. This icy-cool concoction contains water, sugar, and fruit and no dairy products. The Binasco sorbet is very creamy with almost an ice cream flavor. Pear and Ginger is popular, and Diane personally selects and hand-peels each succulent pear.

Diane can make about forty different flavors in a day. The Fredericksburg gelato and coffee store offers about sixty flavors, and a wide variety of hand-packed pints are found in grocery store freezers.

Where to Buy. Look for Binasco gelato and sorbet at Central Market, Whole Foods, and a number of Texas delicatessens. Mail orders are taken, but you'll pay a hefty price for shipping. *Can we say very special occasion?*

A Tasty Visit

Austin Street Java & Gelato House
(serving Binasco gelato and sorbet)
102 East Austin
Fredericksburg, Texas 78624
Phone: (830) 990-8935
Hours: Monday - Thursday 7:30 a.m. - 6 p.m.
Friday - Saturday 7:30 a.m. - 9:30 p.m.
Sunday 9 a.m. - 3 p.m.

Choose from a huge selection of gelato and sorbet flavors made right in the store. Peer through a glass window as master Italian gelato/sorbet maker Diane Wilson (the owner's daughter) prepares dozens of creamy concoctions. The shop is a refreshing break when visiting this quaint Hill Country town.

★ Blue Bell Creameries, L.P.

P.O. Box 1807
Brenham, Texas 77834-1807
Phone: (979) 836-7977
Internet: www.bluebell.com

In August 1907 the Brenham Creamery Company opened its doors and began selling butter. That changed quickly, and by 1911 the company was cranking out a few gallons of ice cream a day. Packed in ice and salt, it was delivered around Brenham by horse and wagon. In 1929 the horse and wagon were traded in for a refrigerated horseless carriage, and by 1930 the company was known as Blue Bell Creameries. Today Blue Bell's delivery area has extended beyond Brenham to thirteen southeastern states.

The company takes its products very seriously, closely monitoring production from start to finish. When their ice creams are ready to roll out of Brenham and into our hearts, Blue Bell employees head straight to the stores and place it in the freezers themselves. Maybe you have seen the company trucks heading through your town. Just the sight stirs up a strong desire for a bowl of vanilla.

Speaking of vanilla, Blue Bell's Homemade Vanilla is by far the most popular flavor. President and CEO Howard Kruse created it in 1969 in search of that real home cranked back porch flavor. (His father, E.F. Kruse, was the general manager back in 1919, so Howard obviously knew what he was doing. Howard's brother Ed is also actively involved with the company.)

My friend Dana Joslin grew up near Fort Worth and remembers her family cranking out homemade vanilla ice cream. Today Blue Bell's version offers Dana—and many others I'm sure—a scoop of nostalgia.

Second in flavor favorites is Cookies 'n Cream, an original Blue Bell blend that combines smooth vanilla ice cream with the crunch of chocolate sandwich cookies. Blue Bell uses its own recipe for the cookies, and each tub is generously packed with them.

The company's third favorite flavor is Dutch Chocolate, which has a smooth texture and rich chocolate flavor. Isn't it interesting that all three favorites contain the basics: vanilla, chocolate cookie in vanilla, or pure chocolate?

If you think some Blue Bell flavors seem to come and go, you are exactly right.

The company features a selection of year-round flavors and a host of rotating selections. Some revolving favorites contain fresh fruits, such as peaches, which are not available throughout the year. The rotation assures that the seasonal items can be blended into the ice cream at their peak of freshness. It also adds a bit of excitement to a trip to the grocer's freezer case because you just never know what you might find! The company adds about four or five new flavors each year.

For those who are wondering about the availability of your favorites, here is a list of the year-round half-gallon flavors:

Homemade Vanilla	Strawberry
Cookies 'n Cream	Rocky Road
Buttered Pecan	French Vanilla
Milk Chocolate	Neapolitan
Banana Split	Chocolate Chip
Cherry Vanilla	Country Vanilla
Mint Chocolate Chip	Natural Vanilla Bean
Chocolate Chip Cookie Dough	Pecan Pralines 'n Cream
Strawberries and Homemade Vanilla	Moo-llennium Crunch
Dutch Chocolate	

Check the Blue Bell website for year-round pint-sized flavors, as well as seasonal selections. A "Flavor of the Month" is also presented, giving serious ice cream lovers a reason to click on frequently.

Catering to the calorie conscious and those on special diets, Blue Bell now offers some alternatives to their fully powered ice creams. These include nonfat and lowfat No Sugar Added flavors, as well as yogurt. Individual ice cream and nondairy treats are also sold in your grocer's freezer.

Where to Buy. Blue Bell ice cream is widely distributed in Texas and twelve other southern states. If you live in one of the other states, you can still have your Blue Bell, but it'll cost you. Phone orders are taken, and the ice cream is carefully packed and shipped overnight. The company's website offers the full scoop.

A Tasty Visit

Blue Bell Creamery
Brenham, Texas
Reservations: (800) 327-8135 or (979) 830-2197

Visit Blue Bell Creameries on your next trip through Brenham. The website offers detailed tour information as well as directions.

Tour the plant, see the museum, and watch a few movies on the company's history. On the way out, stop in the Country Store and Ice Cream Parlor for some good old-fashioned ice cream. Tours are offered on weekdays; there is a nominal charge (includes ice cream), and attendance is limited. It is recommended that you call first to make sure that a particular day is not completely booked.

Daisy Brand Sour Cream

12750 Merit Drive, Suite 600
Dallas, Texas 75251
Phone: (972) 726-0800
Toll-Free: (877) 292-9830
Internet: www.daisybrand.com

The word "Daisy" conjures up thoughts of dairy cows, freshness, and creamy foods. It should also bring up the word "knitting" because Daisy Brand sure sticks to its knitting, making only three versions of its signature sour cream. And that is what makes this Dallas company unique.

It all started more than seventy-five years ago with sour cream and a few other dairy products. For the last twenty years, Daisy has focused its efforts on sour cream, now available in Regular, Light, and No Fat. Regular contains sixty calories for two tablespoons, Light contains forty, and No Fat has only twenty calories for the same sized portion.

While Daisy Brand sour cream is creamy in texture and big on flavor, it is short in ingredients. Pick up a tub next time you are in the grocery store, and you will see that the ingredients on the Regular version consist of only "Grade A cultured cream." Period. The Light is a combination of skim milk and cream, and the No-Fat contains skim milk and some additives. Even their packaging is simple and clean looking, with a pure white tub and navy blue and red letters. The "Daisy" logo has its "i" appropriately dotted with a bright red flower.

Where to Buy. In the United States, Daisy Brand is distributed everywhere except the northeast and northwest sections of the country. Look for it in your grocer's refrigerator aisle. Daisy Brand Sour Cream is the only sour cream sold on U.S. military bases around the world.

Hygeia Dairy Company

525 Beaumont
McAllen, Texas 78596
Toll-Free: (800) 879-4561

Back in 1927 Harvey Lee Richards started the Hygeia Dairy Company in Harlingen. In doing so, he made pasteurized milk available in the Rio Grande Valley region of the state. The company's name was inspired by Hygeia, the Greek goddess of health.

Hygeia's milk is uniquely packaged in brightly colored yellow jugs, which protects it from light. In addition to a variety of milk products, the company sells orange juice, and ice cream and cottage cheese in some areas.

Where to Buy. Look for the bright yellow milk jugs in South Texas grocery stores.

Remember the AlaMode!

"A la mode" is a French term meaning "in fashion." And ice cream is a classic that never goes out of style!

Mozzarella Company

2944 Elm Street
Dallas, Texas 75226
Phone: (214) 741-4072
Toll-Free: (800) 798-2954
Fax: (214) 741-4076
Internet: www.mozzco.com

She has been called the "Cheese Wizard," the "Big Cheese," and the "Queen of Mozzarella." She is a community leader, a former schoolteacher, and a renowned cookbook author (*The Cheese Lover's Cookbook & Guide*). Maybe you have seen her in magazines, such as Martha Stewart's *Living*, in newspapers, or even on television. Paula Lambert may seem to appear everywhere, but one thing is certain: Any way you slice it, she is a lover of cheese! Actually, Paula Lambert, founder and owner of the Mozzarella Company, is *passionate* about cheese.

Paula's love affair with cheese began when she moved from her home state of Texas to Italy. There, she was drawn to the region's fresh mozzarella and other flavorful European cheeses. In a land where meals are serious matters, cheese is often the centerpiece. They are fresh, handmade, and full of robust flavor.

When she and her husband moved to Dallas in 1982, Paula found that her favorite fresh Italian cheeses, especially mozzarella, simply were not available. But she is not the type to sit back and settle for something less. Instead, she returned to Italy, this time in pursuit of knowledge. Her mission was to learn to make the fresh Italian cheeses that she sorely missed.

Paula traveled to a town called Umbria in the central region of the boot-shaped country. And by the time her feet were back on Texas soil, she knew how to turn fresh milk into mouth-watering cheese a la Italy. Back in the Big D, with contemporary architecture as a backdrop, Paula

Lambert put old-world techniques into practice, developing cheeses by hand rather than machine. And the Mozzarella Company was born.

Initially Paula focused on selling to restaurants, confident that her cheeses would impress even the most discriminating chefs. Her workday began with a trip to the dairy to pick up fresh milk. From there, she put her knowledge to work, creating fresh mozzarella and other Italian cheeses. As soon as the cheese was ready to use, she hand delivered it to her clients. Word spread and Paula gained national recognition.

In the years since her first cheese-making lesson in Italy, Paula has made additional trips back to learn more. Today dairy fresh milk is still used to make her award-winning cheeses, and they are all made by hand. And years after she found success and gained a following of cheese lovers, she is still passionate and enthusiastic about her products.

Fresh mozzarella, known for its mild, slightly acidic flavor, is available in a choice of flavors and shapes. Choose from Balls, Latte (packed in water), Tubes, or Bocconcini (bite-sized balls). Perhaps you would like Smoked Mozzarella, or Mozzarella Rolls with fillings, or Capriella (goat's milk mozzarella).

In addition to the impressive array of mozzarella, the company offers a wide assortment of both cow's and goat's milk cheeses, about thirty Italian, Mexican, and Southwestern varieties in all. Some have a Texas twist. The Caciotta wheel, for example, is similar to Monterey Jack and comes in Ancho Chile, La Cocina, Texas Basil, or Black Pepper with Garlic, as well as Traditional. A new creation is Deep Ellum Blue, named for the neighborhood where her store is located. The robust cow's milk cheese is semisoft, with a blue mold surface, and is described as "...a blue for people who don't like the blues."

Most of the company's cheeses come in half-pound sizes, but there are exceptions, such as Goat Cheese, Scamorza, and Caciotta wheels. Attractive baskets and "Cheese of the Month" gifts are available.

Where to Buy. The Mozzarella Company has a retail shop in Dallas. Their cheeses are also available in gourmet markets and restaurants. Year-round orders are taken through the catalog, phone, fax, or email.

A Tasty Visit

Mozzarella Company
2944 Elm Street
Dallas, Texas 75226
Phone: (214) 741-4072

Visit Paula Lambert's retail shop in the Deep Ellum section of Dallas. Choose from a variety of fresh mozzarella and many other gourmet cheeses.

Promised Land Dairy

4603 S. Presa
San Antonio, Texas 78223
Phone: (210) 531-3019
Internet: www.promisedlanddairy.com

In 1987 the Promised Land consisted of hundreds of acres first planned as an inland red fish farm. It turned out that the soil was not right for the fish, so the plans changed. More acreage and a herd of Jersey cows turned the Promised Land into an all-natural, unique, and very promising dairy! Today, in addition to a Jersey farm, there is an old-fashioned creamery, deli, and a gift shop.

The creamery was constructed in 1992, and the first Jersey dairy product churned out was a naturally luscious ice cream. Promised Land ice creams are now sold at ice cream shops and restaurants.

Several years later the company brought their creamy milks to market. The fresh Jersey milk is sold in glass bottles to keep the taste clean and the temperature cold. The dairy takes special care of its Jersey cows, controlling the herd, the diet, as well as processing and distribution. Promised Land's Gordon Kuenemann says that the philosophy is to be in control of products "from grass to glass."

Aside from the tender loving care the cows receive, there are a few other reasons Promised Land products taste so good. Jersey milk content is higher in butterfat and nonfat milk solids, giving it a smooth texture and satisfying flavor. The two-percent varieties receive rave reviews because of their whole milk taste and texture. As an added plus, Promised Land milk products are also touted for their higher levels of calcium and protein. And the company's Jerseys are not injected with artificial hormones, so along with no artificial ingredients in their recipes, they provide all-natural products.

Promised Land milk comes in a variety of flavors, such as Chocolate, Strawberry, Banana, Vanilla, Peaches and Cream, and Cappuccino. If you are the adventurous sort, try mixing your own custom blends using two or more flavors, like chocolate and banana. Container sizes vary, depending on the flavor. Eggnogs are available seasonally.

It would only seem natural that the Promised Land Dairy ambassador is a "spokescow." Molly enjoys being petted by happy people who have just had their first ever sip of that rich, creamy Promised Land milk.

Where to Buy. Promised Land Dairy products are sold in major metropolitan areas throughout Texas. The company's distribution avenues are expanding, and their products are available in much of the country. Their website is just waiting to be milked for information!

A Tasty Visit

Promised Land Dairy Tours
2016 State Highway 97W
(Three miles west of Floresville on Hwy. 97W)
Call for reservations: 830-216-7182 ext. 104

Promised Land Dairy tours are available year round, and reservations are required. The nominal entry fee includes a milking parlor demonstration, creamery tour (weekdays only), and ice cream. For a small extra fee, you can enjoy a hayride. Check the website for more details.

The Scoop on Ice Cream Cones

When an ice cream vendor ran out of paper cups at the 1904 World's Fair, he rolled a waffle into a cone shape. And so marked the birth of the ice cream cone.

Pure Luck Texas

101 Twin Oaks Trail
Dripping Springs, Texas 78620
Phone: (512) 858-7034
Toll-Free: (800) 256-8268
Internet: www.purelucktexas.com

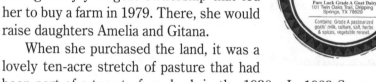

Sara Sweetser Bolton was attracted to the idea of having a family farm animal. It was the lifestyle of living in the country, raising a family surrounded by nature, and experiencing the joy of goat ownership that led her to buy a farm in 1979. There, she would raise daughters Amelia and Gitana.

When she purchased the land, it was a lovely ten-acre stretch of pasture that had been part of a tomato farm back in the 1930s. In 1983 Sara met and married Denny Bolton, who worked at a local plant nursery. The couple had two daughters of their own, Claire and Hope. Today Pure Luck Texas is a pure family business, where everyone has an important role in the three products the family sells: flowers, herbs, and goat cheeses.

Denny is the third generation of a nursery-loving family. His knowledge of plants combined with Sara's desire for a goat farm resulted in their land being one of the first Texas farms recognized as a Certified Organic Farm. All vegetables, herbs, and flowers are grown under tight restrictions with no harmful chemicals. Denny does the marketing, packing, delivering, and customer relations. He talks to garden clubs and other related associations.

Sara's role is production. She spends her time working in the cheese plant or in the fields riding a tractor. Gitana, a University of Texas graduate with a microbiology degree, works part-time on the farm (and has another full-time job). She enjoys making beautiful arrangements with the flowers. Amelia works full-time in the cheese plant, creating some of her own types of cheeses. Her products have brought in rave reviews, high honors, and awards. Claire has helped the family sell eggs and other products. She was featured in the local newspaper for donating some of her earnings to a charity. Hope answers the phone, cuts flowers and herbs, milks goats, arranges flowers, and just plain enjoys life in the country. All family members are committed to their herd of goats and to the beautiful land they occupy.

The goats are also part of the family. They milk about fifty goats in a season, and each one has a name. Each year has a theme for the names. If a goat is born on a special birthday, that goat is named for the birthday person. Freedom, Truth, and Mercy are goats born during the year of the virtue themes. And Frio and Pedernales were born when the river theme was used.

Naming the goats is just the beginning of the pampered life they lead. They are treated gently and with kindness, which has resulted in a tame herd. They enjoy a diet rich in grains and seeds, with no by-products, no animal products, and no prepared seeds. Goats are bred at seven months during the September to January breeding season. They are milked twice a day.

Pure Luck Texas farm has alpine goats, a big, healthy, strong breed. They are good producers of high-quality milk.

The dairy produces a number of fine goat cheeses, including Ste. Maure and French Chevre, for which they have won many awards.

Where to Buy. Buy Pure Luck Texas cheese at Central Market, Wheatsville Co-op, Whole Foods, or Westlake Farmers Market. Orders are taken by phone and the Internet.

Texas Jersey Specialty Cheese Company, Ltd.

3117 Highway 159
La Grange, Texas 78945
Toll-Free: (800) 382-2880
Internet: www.texasjersey.com

What would you do if the wedding gift from your in-laws was a cow?

If you were part of the Frerichs family, you would be delighted with your new acquisition. That was the reaction of Marian and Edgar Frerichs when they married over fifty years ago and received a Jersey cow from the bride's parents. Today Jerseys are the center of the family-run cheese making operation.

The Frerichs family has a long history of dairy farming. It all began about one hundred years ago when Henry Frerichs emigrated from Germany to Texas. He had a dairy farm, which served the family well and provided fresh milk for him and his wife and their three children, Alfred, Edna, and Edgar. When the children grew up, only Edgar stayed on the farm, which is why the Jersey cow was an appropriate gift from his in-laws when he wed Marian.

Edgar and Marian had three children of their own, Helen, Robert, and Ralph, who—as third-generation Frerichs—operate the family-run Texas Jersey Specialty Cheese Company. Ralph's wife, Faith, helps with marketing and tours. The fruits of their labors are some of the best cheeses around and a dairy farm open for visitors year round.

Texas Jersey Specialty Cheese is a farmstead company, which means that the family makes cheese with the milk from its own cows. We're talking deluxe here, since Jersey cows are known for their rich, creamy textured dairy products. "Farm fresh" is taken literally because the Frerichs make sure that the milk goes into cheese production within a day of leaving the cow. Fresh ingredients make the difference between good and great, and these cheeses are no exception.

Jerseys produce flavorful milk, higher in fat and protein than milk from other cows. With a start like this, it is natural that the cheeses are highly desirable both in texture and taste.

Master cheese maker Ralph Frerichs transforms the creamy milk to smooth, delicately flavored cheeses. Cheese making is both an art and a science, and years of experience have taught Ralph to recognize the proper consistency throughout the process. To achieve the clean and pure taste, cheeses are made the old-fashioned way: by hand.

Talent is involved in using the correct temperatures and in determining when the cheese is ready. The complicated procedure involves a series of heating and reheating the curd. If the temperature is off, even by a small amount, the cheese will either be too moist or too dry. Ralph Frerichs keeps a close watch, cutting the cheese carefully and checking its temperature and consistency.

The Texas Jersey Specialty Cheese Company makes products that are a treat for both the palate and the eyes. They are available in small rectangular blocks or in the shape of Texas. Some are plain and pure;

others are spiced with fresh peppers. Varieties include Cheddar, Monterey Jack, Pepper Jack, Jalapeño Cheddar, and Colby.

When the cheeses are aged to perfection, they are hand delivered by members of the Frerichs family, assuring quality control from farm to dairy case.

Because the cheeses have a delicate flavor, they appeal to both children and adults. Their smoothness makes them ideal for serving alone as an appetizer, or enjoying atop a crisp apple slice or a crunchy cracker. Your taste buds will experience a textural treat as the creamy cheese blends with other foods.

Where to Buy. You can find Texas Jersey Specialty Cheese at HEB's Central Market or Whole Foods stores around the state. Or simply order from the company's website, which offers a variety of cheeses and gift baskets.

A Tasty Visit

Texas Jersey Specialty Cheese Company
Dairy Farm Tour

Next time you are near La Grange, you may want your travels to include a visit to the Frerichs' farm. While the cheese-making operation is not open to the public, visitors may stop at the dairy farm year round. Families, school classes, and other groups (even birthday parties) can pet and feed the animals, watch a milking demonstration, and try their hands at milking a cow. Top off your visit with a refreshing hand-dipped ice cream cone and a stop in the unique gift shop. There is an admission fee (check website for information, directions, and hours). For tour reservations, call (409) 249-3406.

Cheese Chatter

Store cheese in the refrigerator at 34 to 40° F. After each use, tightly wrap cheese in fresh, clean plastic. Mold? Scrape it away and enjoy the cheese! *Source: Paula Lambert, the Mozzarella Company*

White Egret Farm

15704 Webberville Road
FM 969
Austin, Texas 78724
Phone: (512) 276-7408
Fax: (512) 276-7489
Internet: www.whiteegretfarm.com

In 1991 Lee Dexter packed up her spirit of adventure and her established herd of dairy goats and headed south, moving from Illinois to Texas. She chose an area southeast of Austin for a variety of reasons. The rolling hills and fertile soil provide rich farmland in an idyllic setting. The region is home to many health conscious individuals, the kind of people attracted to White Egret Farm's products. And the land was home to a rookery of cattle egrets, with 5,000 nesting pairs! Lee was intrigued by these large white birds, which originally came from Africa, and although the birds have moved on, they are remembered in the company's name.

Today White Egret Farm produces natural unprocessed goat milk and cheese, natural beef and pork, and natural free-range turkeys. According to the farm's website, they are "the largest Grade A raw milk goat dairy in Texas."

Goat dairy products are renowned for their gastrointestinal benefits, hypoallergenic quality, and ease of digestion. White Egret Farm's goat milk is naturally homogenized and has a characteristically sweet flavor. Both the goat milk and cheeses meet Texas and USDA cleanliness and safety standards without pasteurization.

White Egret Farm offers a full line of handmade goat cheeses made from the finest goat milk. The processing preserves the nutritional value, resulting in a delightful taste and texture.

The cheeses include Chevre (a mild, sweet cheese), French Pesto Chevre (with French herb pesto from Provence), Garlic and Herb Chevre (dried garlic and herb mix), Gourmet Hot Nacho Dip (with Texas wine, tomatoes, onions, and spices), Farmstead (rich, slightly tangy hard cheese), Garlic-Pepper Farmstead, Gouda (aged washed curd cheese suitable for those with lactose intolerance), Marinated Gouda, Feta, Marinated Feta, Skim Milk Mozzarella (with the characteristic stretchiness), and Skim Milk Cottage Cheese.

Customers rave about White Egret's line of meats. The farm provides its own organically managed pastures, and animals are not given any hormones, steroids, or growth promoters.

White Egret Farm also offers handmade goat milk soap, ideal for the skin and face because of its moisturizing qualities. Like their food products, a great deal of care goes into the soap making process.

Where to Buy. White Egret specializes in individual orders through the company's website. The site is very informative and features detailed product descriptions.

White Mountain Foods

3301 E. 5th Street
Austin, Texas 78702
Phone: (512) 385-4711
Fax: (512) 385-4711
Internet: www.wmfoods.com

In the 1970s the dietary scene underwent a change in this country. More people became vegetarians, and the demand for natural, preservative-free foods was on the rise.

Reed Murray is a vegetarian with experience in the natural foods business. He blended his natural food knowledge with his personal interest in healthy products, and in 1980 he formed White Mountain Foods. Today the company makes a line of natural yogurt, soy, and wheat products.

About ten employees work together to make White Mountain's healthy and flavorful products. The company's signature is its yogurt, which is different from most commercial yogurts because it contains only milk and culture. In place of additives, live bacteria thicken White Mountain yogurt the natural way. The yogurt has no added flavorings and is enjoyed on baked potatoes, in cream sauces, or with honey or maple syrup if added sweetening is desired. It is available in sixteen- and thirty-two-ounce glass containers and plastic gallons.

The soy product line starts with certified organic Texas soybeans, which are then processed into certified organic tofu. The tofu forms the base for a range of deli salads, the most popular being No Egg Salad (i.e., egg-like salad with no egg). Other products include Cottage Tofu Salad, which is a nondairy version of cottage cheese and is an ideal non-dairy ricotta substitute in lasagna. The deli salads are conveniently packaged in reusable plastic containers.

White Mountain's wheat-based products are used as meat substitutes in salads or sandwiches. They are popular in vegetarian versions of fajitas or barbecue, and customers enjoy the high protein and low fat content.

Tamales are another White Mountain wheat product, with their gluten filling nestled inside the traditional cornhusk. The gluten has been ground to achieve a pork-like texture. Again, high protein and low fat are added benefits. Look for the tamales in the freezer section.

Reed Murray remains president and is now joined by his daughter, Lila. In the ever-changing natural food arena, his products have withstood the test of time. He attributes the success of White Mountain Foods to its commitment to producing quality, preservative-free, additive-free foods. He has found that more and more customers want products that are truly free of additives, and his loyal customer base supports his findings.

Where to Buy. White Mountain Foods can be found at grocery and health food stores throughout Texas and outside the state as well.

Chapter 4
Frozen Main Dishes

The fifties was a decade of discovery. American television inched its way into our homes and straight into our hearts. Live TV, timeless sit-coms, and some of the funniest commercials ever made showed up on screens from Texas to Minnesota and New York City to L.A. There is nothing like live television, especially the commercials where even a minor problem could turn a serious script into a belly-breaking comedy.

In the kitchen, separate freezers were a new thing back then. Their predecessor, the icebox, was simply a closed compartment within the refrigerator. Television was an ideal way for manufacturers to let fifties' housewives know about the spacious new freezers. One hilarious commercial of the times featured a woman showing off the new freezer, complete with its very own outer door. The only problem was that the door stuck, and on live television there was nothing a viewer could do but roll on the floor with laughter.

Thanks to reruns, it is as if this era is frozen in time. And why are we talking television in a food book? Well, this all leads up to—you guessed it—frozen meals! Those handy dinner-on-a-tray combos soared into our freezers during the fifties, and since then the industry has had remarkable growth. Microwave ovens have opened the door for a slew of new products. But still, many manufacturers say that their frozen products have a better flavor when baked in conventional ovens just as they were in the fifties.

Since their inception, frozen entrees and appetizers have taken on gourmet qualities. Many of the products available now allow us to enjoy flavorful ethnic foods, which would otherwise be too time consuming to make on a regular basis.

Over the years frozen food companies have rolled their way into Texas. Some like the state's central geographic location, which is convenient for freezer trucks to cart the goods around the country within just a few days. Other companies formed here because their owners are Texans. In any case, the freezer case is a great place to reach your hand into on a hot Texas summer day!

Lana's Enterprises, Inc.

6406 Burleson Road
Austin, Texas 78744
Phone: (512) 385-3235

Lana Lartigue learned to make egg rolls the authentic way. Growing up in Vietnam, her mother said that if she wanted to get married one day, it was important for Lana to learn how to make egg rolls. A self-proclaimed egg roll lover, Lana was a faithful student, carefully following her mother's directions.

When Lana moved to Texas, she took along her mother's recipe and made the authentic egg rolls in her spare time away from her job with a computer company. Friends and co-workers became so addicted to Lana's egg rolls that they ordered them by the case. To keep up with the demand (and the expense), Lana began to charge for the orders, and they kept rolling in.

It all came to a head one day at work when Lana stepped away from her desk and her phone rang. Trying to be helpful, Lana's supervisor answered the phone, but the person at the other end did not have a work-related question. Instead, the caller wanted two cases of egg rolls. Later that day the supervisor said to Lana, "I think I'm going to lose you." She was sad because Lana was a dependable, hard worker. But she was also right. She did lose Lana.

The demand for Lana's egg rolls was too great, and in 1987 she left the computer company to form her own business. Today Lana's Enterprises has grown to about fifteen employees. And the egg rolls are still as delicious and authentic as ever.

Lana attributes her egg rolls' popularity to their thin and crispy wrapper, which does not absorb oil when fried. The egg rolls are all natural and contain no preservatives or MSG. Lana is so particular about her products that she refuses to use any ingredients that she cannot pronounce.

Using fresh vegetables and meats, the egg rolls are made in the morning and frozen in the afternoon. Each crispy cylinder is carefully handmade by Lana and her staff, who can roll out five to ten thousand in one day. They are available in four varieties: Shrimp, Chicken, Pork, and Vegetable. For the best results, Lana recommends frying quickly, in about five or six minutes. Those who avoid fried foods will be happy to know that the egg rolls are also delicious when served hot from the oven.

In addition to frozen egg rolls, Lana's Enterprises makes a line of fresh products such as Breakfast Burritos, Chile Rellenos, and Southwest Egg Rolls. The latter is a thin tortilla filled with vegetables, chicken, beans, seasonings, and spices. These items are delivered fresh to grocery store deli counters.

Where to Buy. Look for Lana's Egg Rolls at Whole Foods stores and other grocery stores in Texas, all the way west to California, and up north to Oklahoma City.

They are also distributed to Chinese restaurants and cafeterias.

Michael Angelo's Gourmet Italian Foods

200 Michael Angelo Way
Austin, Texas 78728
Phone: (512) 218-3500
Toll-Free: (877) ITALIAN (482-5426)
Internet: www.michaelangelos.com

It was 1982 and Michael Angelo Renna had a robust idea. Each night, after closing his small pizzeria near San Diego, California, he moved the dining tables together to form an Italian food making assembly line. His wife and a few friends joined Michael Angelo as he prepared his mother Sara's authentic recipes for lasagna, stuffed shells, eggplant parmesan, and manicotti. In the morning he brought these tasty Italian dishes to local stores, and they were an immediate success!

As demand grew, Michael Angelo broadened his market and moved his company headquarters and production to Austin. Now he is the president of the company, and his five hundred employees are busy at work making Sara's recipes. Sara, now the vice president of Research and Development, is on site every day, overseeing production as well as the creation of new items.

Customers continue to rave about Michael Angelo's homemade taste. The signature product is the Lasagne with Meat Sauce, luscious layers of meat, cheeses, sauce, and pasta. Lasagne is also available in Vegetable, Chicken, Sausage, and Four Cheese. Other entrees include Chicken Parmesan with Spaghetti and Tomato Sauce, Eggplant Parmesan with Tomato Sauce and Mozzarella Cheese, and Manicotti. A line of bulk stuffed pastas includes stuffed shells, cheese or meat ravioli, and stuffed manicotti served with your own sauce. If you would like a meal in a pocket, Italian style, try a Calzone in Pepperoni, Four-Cheese, Meatball, or Sausage. A new item is a snack-sized Mini-Calzone.

Michael Angelo's foods maintain restaurant quality freshness because they use only high quality ingredients (and because they are made from Sara's recipes, of course). Entrees are prepared, frozen, and sent out as fast as you can say "Lasagna with Meat Sauce." Well almost. The company takes pride in its efficient production method. Its trucks pick up ingredients after Michael Angelo's has received grocery stores' orders. When the trucks deliver ingredients back to Michael Angelo's in Austin, the entrees are prepared to meet the orders. Within an hour or two of production, the trucks once again hit the road, this time loaded with entrees and heading for grocery stores. When the plant closes at night, there are no food or ingredients left in stock. Everything is purchased as fresh as possible.

The company's commitment to quality is a serious one. They purchase only top quality ingredients and will not deviate from this philosophy. To bring out the best flavor, they recommend heating their entrees in a conventional oven, although a microwave can be used.

Where to Buy. Michael Angelo's Gourmet Foods are sold at grocery stores around the United States, except in the northeastern area. They are also found in Canada, Mexico, and some Pacific Rim countries. The company's website is colorful and informative.

Night Hawk Frozen Foods, Inc.

P.O. Box 867
Buda, Texas 78610-0867
Phone: (512) 295-4166

Former Austin mayor Harry Akin founded a restaurant in the Capital City on Christmas Eve in 1932. The Night Hawk, located on South Congress Avenue, was like a big coffee shop, catering to the night workers and other late night folks. Back then a "Night Hawker" was a person who was out late at night.

About thirty years later, in the mid-1960s, the Night Hawk restaurants (by then they had more than one location) were known for their delicious charbroiled meats. Customers liked the menu so much they asked if some of the items could be frozen so they could prepare them in their own kitchens. The frozen foods part of the operation took shape, initially located behind the original restaurant.

In 1993 production moved to a modern facility in Buda, Texas, south of Austin. Today some production is automated and the distribution area is huge, but many things have not changed. Steak 'n Taters was a customer favorite in 1967, and it remains on top of the list. The chopped steak and crisp potato rounds have maintained their consistently high level of quality through the years. To add to the convenience, the item comes complete with its own packet of steak sauce.

Night Hawk uses cuts of meat from only steak and roasts, with no soy or other fillers. The meat is charbroiled to maintain its restaurant-quality taste and texture and then placed on trays with other tasty side dishes. Like the popular Steak 'n Taters, several other items have been in production for at least twenty years. Employees frequently fill out surveys so the company can stay in touch with food trends.

The Night Hawk plant has a home kitchen for testing their products. The staff believes that while times have changed since the company's inception, their customers' demand for good taste and texture has remained the same. While their frozen items are suitable for microwaves, they recommend using a conventional oven to achieve the best results with some items, particularly potatoes.

Where to Buy. Night Hawk Frozen Foods are distributed throughout grocery stores in Texas. They can also be found at Wal-Mart Supercenters in the United States, except in the far western reaches of the country.

Chapter 5

Jerky, Turkey, Sausage, and Ham

Texas is the land of milk and honey. Or perhaps I should say meat and plenty. Drive around the state and you can't help but notice cattle ranches stretching across the horizon, with their traditional fencing and brand proudly displayed over the entrance.

With all the ranches in the Lone Star State, things are hot. And I'm not only referring to the summers. Throughout the land, smokehouses are bursting with ham and jerky and sausage and turkey. (Later on you can read about the sauces made for slathering on these fine smoked products.)

After touring and talking to meat processors, I was overwhelmed by their kindness. They are bursting with pride for their meticulously clean facilities. And their products burst with flavor.

Jerky, a dried meat that has been around for centuries, is a low moisture product ideal for traveling those long distances throughout the state. And sausage, largely a reflection of the German influence in Texas, is available in blends to suit anyone's tastes. Jalapeño peppers have found their way into sausage, resulting in new products containing an international medley of spices.

You may want to fire up the grill because the meats described in the pages ahead are sure to inspire a real Texas barbecue.

Bear Creek Smokehouse, Inc.

10857 State Highway 154
Marshall, Texas 75670-8105
Phone: (903) 935-5217
Toll-Free: (800) 950-2327
Fax: (903) 935-2871
Internet: www.bearcreeksmokehouse.com

Back in 1943 Robbie Shoults' granddaddy Hick Shoults was an East Texas cotton grower who was having a rough time making a living. His great uncle, an agriculture teacher, had six hundred turkeys left over after a class project so Hick and his wife, Nellie, took them home. Little did they know this was the start of a new adventure!

Today Bear Creek has two smokehouses, each big enough for five hundred turkeys or about four hundred hams. Ham and turkey take about twelve to eighteen hours to smoke, while pork tenderloin is smoked after about eight hours.

The family stands proud of its products and feels compelled to do things the same way Hick and Nellie did them. They use the identical "smoking secrets" today that they did back in the early days.

While top quality ingredients have been a family philosophy since the beginning, the number of products available has increased dramatically. These days you can order a whole smoked turkey in just about any size, or even a boneless breast. Hickory Smoked Brisket is a lean cut rubbed with a flavorful mix of spices and smoked slowly to perfection. Chopped Barbeque Beef is appropriately referred to as "spreadable brisket." The folks at Bear Creek start with their delicious brisket, chop it up, and mix it with barbecue sauce so that all you have to do is heat it in the microwave and spread it on a bun.

The company's "pride and joy" is its Hickory Smoked Ham, available in Bone-In or Spiral Sliced. Both are ready to eat and come in a choice of sizes so you can feed your family... or the whole block!

Speaking of feeding a group, the Bear Creek Office Party Box is an easy way to satisfy a crowd (and impress the boss). The box is packed with Peppered Pork Tenderloin, Summer Sausage, Cheddar Cheese, crackers, Black-Eyed Pea Relish, and even a paring knife. The Peppered Pork Tenderloin is also sold separately. Just slice it up and display on a platter with crackers and cheese for a delightful meat tray.

The Country Breakfast Box is another hot gift item, featuring Smoked Pork Sausage, Smokehouse Pan Bacon, Biscuit Mix, and Pure East Texas Clover Honey.

A number of other gifts are available, featuring everything from meats to sweets. Items are sealed and shipped in corrugated boxes.

Where to Buy. Shop for Bear Creek Smokehouse products at the plant store, or order by phone, mail, fax, or the Internet. The company has a booth at a number of food shows.

A Tasty Visit

Bear Creek Smokehouse, Inc.
Nine miles northwest of Marshall on Highway 154

Visit the original farm that Hick and Nellie Shoults had back in the forties, which still serves as the company's location. A store on the farm sells Bear Creek's famous smoked products.

Cain's East Texas Meats

600 Highway 64 West
Henderson, Texas 75652
Phone: (903) 655-0786
Internet: www.texascountrymall.com

As a child I recall waiting for my mother while she stood at the meat counter eyeing the roasts, steaks, chops, and chickens as if she were watching a performance. When she parked her grocery cart in front of the meat counter, I knew we wouldn't be leaving anytime soon. I suspect she could spend years at the meat counter in Cain's.

After working for a large grocery chain, Richard Cain bought the shop in 1986. While the meat business has flourished, it hasn't been a completely smooth ride. In 1992 the facility burned and had to be rebuilt. It reopened in 1993.

In addition to fresh meats, a variety of smoked meats and sausages are made and sold by Cain's. The owner's philosophy is to use top quality ingredients in all of his products. His three most popular items are Hot and Spicy, German, and Summer Sausages.

Cain's sausages do not contain any soy, fillers, hearts, chicken, or turkey. Instead, you will find pure Grade A pork and beef. Hot and Spicy is a Cajun recipe that can go straight to the grill or be mixed into jambalaya or red beans and rice. German Sausage is authentic. A mild sausage, it is light on the spice with just a touch of black pepper. The Summer Sausage has won top state honors four years in a row. Cain's also smokes ham, bacon, and turkey.

Where to Buy. Cain's meat products are sold at their store as well as East Texas Wal-Mart stores. They are expanding distribution, so look in other locations. The meats are available for shipment through the Internet address.

A Tasty Visit

Cain's East Texas Meats
600 Highway 64 West
Henderson, Texas 75652
Phone: (903) 655-0786

Visit Cain's East Texas Meats and browse their wide selection of fresh meats and sausages.

Double B Foods, Inc.

P.O. Box A
Schulenberg, Texas 78956
Phone: (979) 725-9444
Fax: (979) 725-9501
Internet: www.doubleb.com

Bill Bucek is the "Double B" behind this company's name. He is proud of the organization he has built and remembers the day it all began.

It was August 4, 1971, when Bill founded Double B Foods, which is based on his philosophy of producing top quality products. Their beef jerky carried out this mission and was among the first in the industry made with solid strips of meat. Today the company has a plant in Schulenberg, Texas, where the beef jerky is naturally smoked, and one in Meridian, Texas, where sausage rolls are made. Double B scores "A plus" grades in the education arena and supplies many school

districts in and out of Texas. The next time you see Sausage Rolls on a school menu, this proud Texas company likely made them.

Prior to that hot August day in 1971 (if it's August in Texas, it has to have been a hot day), Bill was already a food business pro. A strong urge to own his own business and a desire to do things right spawned his first entrepreneurial venture into the pickled pig's feet market. (He kept that business until selling it in the mid-nineties.)

During the thirty-plus years that Double B has been around, quality remains in the forefront. The company's beef jerky is still made of solid strips of beef. Distribution extends around the country, and customers range from snack-eating kids to athletes and hunters. Customers appreciate the 98 percent fat-free quality of Double B Beef Jerky, which comes in flavors such as Original, Teriyaki, and Hot & Spicy. In addition to producing foods under the "Double B" label, the company also serves as a co-packer and prepares items under private labels.

Where to Buy. Look for Double B products at Costco, sporting goods stores such as Academy, convenience stores, duty free shops, and airport retailers. Orders are taken by phone, mail, fax, and the website.

A Fowl Summer

Did you know that June is National Turkey Lovers' month?

Greenberg Smoked Turkeys

P.O. Box 4818
Tyler, Texas 75702
Phone: (903) 595-0725
Fax: (903) 593-8129
Internet: www.gobblegobble.com

Gobble gobble! That is exactly what you will do when you get your hands on a renowned Greenberg Smoked Turkey. These "Holiday Aristocrats" have a reputation for being lip-smacking good.

The company's roots stretch all the way back to Europe. When company founder Sam Greenberg was growing up there, he helped his mother smoke meats. After arriving in the United States, Sam set up a dairy in Tyler. He had a smoker that was small enough to be moved out of the prevailing wind. This little device was used to smoke geese and other meats just as his mother had done.

In 1941 Sam died, and it was up to his son Zelick to take over the responsibility of smoking meats. After Zelick shipped his first order of smoked turkey, it wasn't long before he and his wife, Joyce, could barely keep up with the demand.

Today the company has fourteen smokehouses and a 50,000-square-foot plant. Zelick passed away, and his son Sam (named for Zelick's father) runs the company with his mother, Joyce. Some of the employees have been there for decades.

Greenberg's has been written up in *The Dallas Morning News*, *New York Times*, *Forbes*, and other national publications. Joyce Greenberg is in awe that a Greenberg Turkey article appeared above a Dallas Cowboys story in *The Dallas Morning News*. Now that's talking turkey!

Why are these smoked fowl so famously good? One reason is that the family sticks to the same recipe that Zelick's dad, Sam, used decades ago. They have been using the same turkey supplier for more than twenty years and the same corrugated box company for as long. The fully cooked turkeys are ready to eat when they reach your front door. They are frozen when they leave the plant in a double-walled plastic bag. The turkey should be placed in the refrigerator upon arrival and eaten within six to eight days. If you plan to keep it longer, the instructions say to put it in the freezer. Although the peak season is October through December, the Greenbergs smoke turkeys year round, about every six or eight weeks, and store them in the freezer. Each bird arrives with its own set of instructions in a retro sixties-style brochure. It is clear that when the Greenbergs know they have something good, they don't change it. Thank goodness.

Greenberg Turkeys are extremely popular holiday gifts. They never intend to run out of turkeys during the peak season, but it is best to order early to be sure you get the size you want. (They are available in sizes ranging from six to fifteen pounds.) The family and "like family" staff will gladly insert a gift card. When you call to order, you will be pleasantly surprised by the warm and friendly people at the other end of the phone.

Austinites Sherrie and Bob Frachtman have been giving Greenberg Turkey gifts for years. It all started more than a decade ago when the Frachtmans received a Greenberg Turkey as a gift. Sherrie says that for any occasion, "A Greenberg Turkey is always a welcome gift."

Where to Buy. Gobble gobble gobble, this is a mail order, mail order, mail order company. Orders are taken by phone, fax, or mail. Be sure to order early so you will get the size you want.

Meyer's Elgin Sausage

P.O. Box 940
Elgin, Texas 78621
Toll-Free: (800) MRS-OINK
Fax: (512) 285-3698
Internet: www.elginsmokehouse.citysearch.com

When Henry Meyer came to the United States from Germany, he carried along his treasured sausage recipe. In 1949 his son R.G. (short for Rudolf Karl Georg) used his dad's recipe to make all natural sausages in a small smokehouse. First he sold them locally and then expanded the business to Austin and other Central Texas towns.

In 1959 R.G.'s son F. W. "Buddy" Meyer took over the business. He carried on the family legacy, and the company continued to thrive, growing into a popular sausage name in Texas. After Buddy's untimely death in 1989, his sons Gregg and Gary Meyer took over, and today the brothers are the fourth generation of Meyers to lead the business.

The "not so secret" special ingredient is four generations of tradition. In other words, each sausage has to be just right in order to be labeled with the Meyer family name. With that goal in mind, Gregg and Gary work hard to assure that the sausages are made as close as possible to the way their grandfather made them years ago.

Since R.G.'s time, the equipment used to smoke meats has changed radically, but the company uses the same grind and stuffing as their grandfather did more than fifty years ago. But back then things were a bit different. Smokehouses had dirt floors, which would never be used today. Gregg and Gary Meyer are the proud owners of a modern stainless steel processing oven that gives their sausages a "real good smoke."

The most popular product is the Pork Garlic Sausage. The pork still has its original coarse grind and a lot of flavor when teamed with garlic.

The company makes numerous other products, including Beef Jerky, Turkey Jerky (from breast meat), Beef Snack Sticks, Jalapeño Sausage, Summer Sausage, Smoked Pork Tenderloin, and Smoked Turkey Breast.

Where to Buy. Look for Meyer's Elgin Sausage at nearly all Texas HEB stores and many Albertson's, Randalls, Kroger, Wal-Mart Supercenters, and other grocers and meat markets. It is also sold at the market adjacent to the smokehouse. Order by phone, fax, or online.

A Tasty Visit 🍽

Meyer's Elgin Smokehouse Barbecue Restaurant
188 U.S. 290 (next to McDonald's)
Elgin, Texas
Hours: Sunday - Thursday 10 a.m. - 7 p.m.
Friday - Saturday 10 a.m. - 8 p.m.

Located twenty-four miles east of Austin on Highway 290, Meyer's Elgin Smokehouse offers a bite of real Texas barbecue. Choose from a variety of sausage, brisket, turkey, and rib platters, and hearty sandwiches piled high with your favorite barbecued meats. Save room for a specialty side dish like German potato salad or spicy beans. The regular beef sausage is served, but you can call ahead to reserve the hot, sage, or plain sausage. Fountain drinks are refilled free of charge.

Factory Tours: The Meyer family is happy to give tours to groups, such as schoolchildren. Just call ahead and make a reservation.

✪ New Braunfels Smokehouse

P.O. Box 311159
New Braunfels, Texas 78131
Phone: (830) 625-7316
Toll-Free: (800) 537-6932
Toll-Free Fax: (800) 284-5330
Internet: www.nbsmokehouse.com

Drive along I-35 between San Antonio and San Marcos and you can't miss the New Braunfels Smokehouse Restaurant. The legendary Texas smokehouse has been serving up its barbecue platters for over half a century. Maybe you did not know that

these fine quality smoked meats are also available by mail order.

In 1943 R.K. Dunbar bought an ice plant that eventually became the New Braunfels Smokehouse. Customers could store their ham, turkey, and bacon in the icehouse and have their meats smoked by Benno Schuenemann. In 1951 the Dunbars built a tasting room where they sold their products. In 1969 the family received USDA approval to ship their popular hickory smoked meats nationwide. Susan Dunbar Snyder and her husband, Dudley Snyder, are the second generation of family members to run the business.

Today over 100,000 customers around the country order succulent smoked meats from New Braunfels Smokehouse. The colorful catalog has a huge selection of smoked hams and turkeys of every imaginable size. Order a ham that is Hickory Smoked Spiral Sliced, Hill Country Boneless, Spiral-Sliced Boneless, or Old-Fashioned Hickory Smoked.

Whether you are having a large Thanksgiving dinner or a small family luncheon, there is a turkey for you. Select from Hickory Smoked Smokehouse, Peppered Smoked, Whole Boneless Turkey Breast, Spiral Sliced, Peppered Boneless Breast of Turkey, Spiral Sliced Turkey Breast, and Smoked Breast of Turkey. If you are thinking on a smaller scale, try the Capon Chicken, Golden Smoked Chicken, or Cornish Game Hens. Smoked Brisket and Baby Back Ribs, basted with New Braunfels' special sauce, are also available. (They sell their famous barbecue sauce, too!)

And that is just the beginning. Rocky Tays, New Braunfels Smokehouse assistant general manager, is the smokemaster or "wurstmeister." He has been with the company for over thirty-five years. A descendent of German immigrants, Rocky grew up in a sausage-making family. After receiving his degree in Industrial Technology, he went on to put his talents to work.

Rocky explains that each sausage has its own individual grind. He uses all natural casings and smokes the meaty links in natural smoke from hickory chips. His goal is to consistently produce a top quality product so that a customer's order will taste the same time after time.

Sausages come in a variety of shapes and sizes. Ring style looks like a horseshoe, while rope sausage is a continuous run. Links are about five inches long, and country sausages are still raw and require cooking, usually pan frying or barbecuing.

Rocky and his good buddy Mike Dietert, who is the vice president and general manager of the smokehouse, are meticulous about cleanliness. They believe that any product bearing the company's name must be top quality.

The wide choice of sausages available through New Braunfels Smokehouse reflects a blend of cultures. Although he started out making German sausages, Rocky says that the Mexican influence has found its way into his products. Jalapeño and red peppers are spicing up the delicious sausages he makes today.

Sausage popularity varies with the season. In springtime, the Jalapeño Wurst is a popular choice, while summer brings out the Smoked Pork and Beef Sausage lovers. Applewurst Sausage fills platters around Thanksgiving and Christmas, and like the other sausages it is available year round. Cheddar Wurst is a fairly new sausage that has been lightly smoked and filled with creamy cheese, pork, and beef. The catalog offers a variety of sausages, complete with color photographs and clear descriptions.

Jerky is another house specialty. And Rocky is as picky about his jerky products as he is about the sausage. He uses only lean cuts of meats and natural smoke. Jerky making is a three-day process requiring a great deal of care in the curing. Humidity and temperature levels are constantly monitored so that each batch of jerky has concentrated flavor in every bite.

Jerky, a low-fat snack, is available in Beef, Turkey, and Pork. Bursts of hickory smoked flavor penetrate your taste buds as you chew these flavorful snacks. Beef Jerky comes in four types: Original Peppered, Jalapeño, Mild Beef, and Teriyaki Beef. You can order a Jerky Sampler with a quarter pound of each: Original Beef, Mild Beef, Teriyaki, Jalapeño, Turkey and Pork. Be prepared for how quickly they will disappear!

Smoke Stix are, as Rocky says, a cross between a sausage and a jerky. Available in Beef, Pork, or Turkey, they are packed with hickory smoked flavor and protein from end to end. They are a good addition to your kitchen, lunch box, and sports bag!

For a special occasion, consider the Celebration Box featuring Bismarkian® Sausage Ring, Comal County Sliced Bacon, Smoked Pork and Beef Sausage, Smoked Bratwurst, Canadian-Style Bacon, Salami Chub, Sliced Dried Beef, and Smoked Chicken. Top if off with the condiments and tempting desserts featured in the catalog.

Rocky has gained celebrity status in the sausage industry. He has been featured in the *San Antonio Express-News* and *Houston Chronicle*. For the last thirty years he has been (and continues to be) the resident sausage-maker at the Institute for Texan Cultures festival held in San Antonio every June.

Where to Buy. New Braunfels Smokehouse products are sold at the restaurant, through the mail order catalog, and by phone, fax, or the Internet.

A Tasty Visit 🍽

New Braunfels Smokehouse Restaurant
Original: Corner of Hwy. 46 and I-35 (Exit 189)
New Braunfels, Texas 78130
Phone: (830) 625-2416

Two San Antonio Locations:
6450 N. New Braunfels Avenue (Alamo Heights)
16607 Huebner at Bitters (Deerfield)

In 1951 New Braunfels Smokehouse opened its first "Tastin' Kitchen" so people could sample their hickory smoked meats. Today the original restaurant is a popular dining spot along I-35 between Austin and San Antonio. The restaurant has ample seating and private dining rooms available for parties, meetings, and tour groups. During the warmer months, "The Yard" is open on weekends for those who like to dine outdoors. A "mister system" helps keep you cool.

The restaurant features breakfast, lunch, and dinner items. Breakfast fare, such as Breakfast Tacos, are served until 11 a.m. Sandwiches are made from their own smokehouse meats and come with coleslaw, potato chips, or potato salad. House specialties give you a hearty portion of comfort foods like Chicken and Dumplings, Fredrich's Sausage Platter, and other smoked and barbecued delicacies.

Opa's Smoked Meats

P.O. Box 487
Fredericksburg, Texas 78624
Phone: (830) 997-3358
Toll-Free: (800) 543-6750
Fax: (830) 997-9916
Internet: www.opassmokedmeats.net

Opa's has been smoking meats in the traditional German way since 1947. Schatzie (pronounced "Shot-see") and Ken Wahl continue to bring authentic German specialties through their sandwich shop and packaged meats. (Schatzie, which means "sweetheart" in German, was an adoring nickname given to Mrs. Wahl by her grandfather.) Ken and Schatzie called her dad "Opa," which means "grandfather" in German. When they needed a name for their brand of sausage, Opa was the natural choice.

And Opa's products are a natural choice for sausage fans. They are made in Fredericksburg using only top quality meats. After more than half a century in business, they remain committed to standards that would probably dwarf the Alps.

Their smoked meats are completely cooked and ready to eat. They can be warmed in the oven or placed on the grill. The lean meats form the basis for sausages that have only thirteen grams of fat. After people try Opa's sausages, they are surprised at the high flavor and low fat content.

Their most popular product is the Country Brand Sausage. Choose from Pork and Beef or All Beef. The sausages are delicately spiced, making them ideal for a sizzling breakfast any time of day!

Opa's Cooked Bratwursts are the real thing, a true reflection of the family's German heritage. This authentic sausage, with its classic bratwurst flavor, tastes great straight from the grill. Serve with German potato salad and get ready to dance the polka! Blood Sausage, Liver Sausage, Head Cheese, and Knockwurst are other fine German specialties.

Opa's Jerky products are made from fine cuts of meats and have a pleasing smoky flavor that lasts and lasts.

If you are planning a picnic and want something beyond peanut butter and jelly, Opa's has a full line of convenient gourmet items. Peppered Beef Tenderloin comes completely sealed for easy traveling. Open on the picnic grounds, slice this tender cut of beef thinly, and you've got the makings of a gourmet sandwich with just the right amount of spice to complement the delicate tenderloin flavor. Pork Tenderloin is another gourmet alternative. These items make a glamorous addition to meat and cheese buffet platters.

Other favorites are the Smoked Summer Sausage and Dried Sausage. Slice 'em up for a quick meal or satisfying snack. A California restaurant inspired this appetizer combo that would be an ideal use of Opa's Summer Sausage: Stick cubes of Swiss cheese and sausage on a toothpick and place into a frosted beer mug for a chunk of German heaven on a stick.

Opa's smoked hams are at home at any special occasion. Hickory Smoked Peppered Bone-In Ham and Boneless Peppered Ham are popular choices for large family gatherings and holiday meals.

Their color catalog contains product photos, descriptions, and serving ideas. The website has a whimsical drawing of Opa in his German Alps attire. You can click on this sweet character to enter the site!

When you bring Opa's authentic German products to your home, you can do so with the assurance that your guests will be pleased. Quality is important to Schatzie and Ken Wahl, and they "absolutely refuse" to compromise. After all, Opa's name is on the label.

Where to Buy. Opa's products are sold at most major grocery chains including HEB, Albertson's, independent grocers, and Wal-Mart. They sell a large line of their products through the retail shop in Fredericksburg. Orders are taken by phone, fax, mail, or the Internet. Meats are packed in a cooler so that they arrive fresh and chilled.

A Tasty Visit 🍽

Opa's Smoked Meats
410 S. Washington Street
Fredericksburg, Texas 78624
(830) 997-3358
Hours: Monday - Friday 8 a.m. - 5:30 p.m.
Saturday 8 a.m. - 4 p.m.
Closed Sunday

Located just three blocks from Fredericksburg's Main Street, visit Opa's retail outlet for a selection of authentic German smoked meats and sandwiches. Select from such tasty choices as Opa's Smoked Sausage, Opa's Dry Sausage, Smoked Turkey and Chicken, steaks, cheeses, sauces and salsas, dietz bread, and much more. Chips, dips, cold drinks, cookies, and candies allow you to leave with all the makings for a traditional German picnic. Browse the cookbooks or buy a range of sausage-making supplies while you are there.

Pederson Natural Farms, Inc.

501 McCaleb
Hamilton, Texas 76531
Phone: (254) 675-8713
Fax: (254) 675-4072
Internet: www.healthypork.com

The website name says it all. Healthy pork is not an oxymoron. With Pederson's, people interested in healthier foods can have their bacon and eat it too.

Company president Don Montgomery and sales manager Ejay Roberts explain that, after careful research, Pederson's developed specialized techniques for naturally processing pork. The company opened its doors in 1992.

Pederson's pigs are raised on natural wheat, grains, vitamins, and minerals, are USDA inspected, and are processed with the newest technology. The pork products contain wonderful flavors, but it is what they don't contain that is so intriguing. For example, ingredients such as MSG are missing from their labels.

The company has a line of minimally processed cured bacon, ham, and sausage containing no artificial ingredients. Their line of uncured pork products does not contain nitrites, nitrates, or preservatives.

Pederson's Apple Smoked Bacon is probably its signature product. This smoke-flavored bacon fries up crisp and flavorful. Spiral-sliced ham is also quite popular. In fact, Mayor Ray Sparks proclaimed Pederson's the "Official Ham of Hamilton, Texas." The company has enjoyed other industry publicity as well and is renowned for its remarkably flavorful yet natural pork products.

And the team at Pederson's has a natural ability to overcome adversity. On June 15, 2001, the plant was burned to the ground after lightning sparked a major fire. But they bounced back quickly. Losing only one day of production, the company relocated into temporary quarters while the plant was being rebuilt.

Pederson's offers a wide range of pork products. Hams are available bone-in or boneless, in varieties such as Hickory Smoked, Apple Smoked, Honey, Peppered, Black Forest, Spiral Sliced, and Smoked Ham Shank. Sausage lovers can choose from Sweet German, Jalapeño, and Kielbasa. Bacon is a popular choice and is available in Hickory Smoked, Apple Smoked, Peppered, and Canadian Bacon. Pederson's fresh pork products are also found in the butcher section. Choose from loins, tenderloins, ribs, shoulder, and of course, hams.

Where to Buy. Look for Pederson's natural pork products at Central Market stores in Texas and Whole Foods in Texas, Arizona, California, Colorado, Louisiana, and New Mexico. Mail orders are also taken.

Smokey Denmark Sausage Company

3505 E. 5th Street
Austin, Texas 78702
Phone: (512) 385-0718
Toll-Free: (800) 705-1380
Fax: (512) 385-4843
Internet: www.smokeydenmark.com

When I first heard of Smokey Denmark, I thought it must be a Danish company. I was completely wrong.

Albert Denmark was nicknamed "Smokey" as a child because his hair was sort of a smoky color, kind of blond-gray. His unique hair color earned him the nickname at age five and it stuck throughout his life. By the way, he was not Danish; his heritage was German. Smokey got his sausage making education in Lockhart, a town not too far from Austin.

In 1964 Smokey and his wife, Eloise, moved to Austin and started the Smokey Denmark Sausage Company. (The company still has the original phone number.)

His original plant was about five or six blocks away from where it currently stands east of Austin's downtown area. When the new plant was being built, Smokey became ill and his doctor told him that he'd better stop working if he wanted to live a longer life.

Following his doctor's advice, Smokey put his sausage company up for sale.

Austin attorney Jim McMurtry heard about the company through his brother-in-law, who suggested the two buy it. Jim has an accounting background, so he met with the Denmarks, toured the plant, and looked at the records. Everything appeared to be in good order, so the men took a chance and bought it.

Sometimes it pays to take chances. Modern technology has helped the sausage industry evolve into one combining efficiency with good old-fashioned flavor. Smokey Denmark Sausage Company now makes more sausage before the coffee break on Monday morning than it used to make in a week.

A few years ago Jim's brother-in-law sold his share of the company to Jim's son-in-law Jonathan Pace. Jim and Jonathon work together extremely well. (Jim says that having a family business is delightful. His daughter also works at the company.) Foreman Daniel Lucio has been with the company over thirty-five years.

Every week about 40,000 pounds of sausages take shape at this meticulously clean plant. The company has two stainless steel smokehouses. Heat and humidity are completely controlled, resulting in a consistently premium product. Every piece of equipment has been replaced and updated with the finest available. This is truly high-tech sausage making with good old-fashioned flavor.

Once the sausage meat is ground, it is mixed with the appropriate blend of spices. From there, spiced meat travels through a very fancy computerized machine (called a vacuum stuffer) that is programmed to put the proper amount of filling in the natural casings. Once the casings are stuffed, the sausage moves to one of the stainless steel smokehouses, each of which holds six hundred pounds of links. These "rooms" have a window so staff can peer in and see how the sausages are coming along. An outside control panel resembles that of a 747 flight deck and provides temperature, humidity, and other readings. When the sausage is ready it is showered in the smokehouse to quickly bring down the temperature. The links, still hanging on racks, are then moved to the refrigerator.

Every hickory smoked sausage is of top quality. The Beef and Pork Sausage is the one that made the company famous. Hot Links are another popular choice. Their other sausages include Summer Sausage, Andouille (Cajun), Bratwurst, Chorizo Mexicano, Jalapeño, Pepperwurst, and Polish. They also smoke bacon, brisket, and a variety of other meats. Items such as brisket are smoked in a special oven capable of holding 1,200 pounds at a time.

When Jim McMurtry discusses the sausage company, it is like a proud dad talking about his kids. He is bursting with pride. He is also proud to carry on the traditions established by Smokey Denmark (who has since passed away). Smokey's wife, Eloise, remains a friend of the McMurtry and Pace families, and she still enjoys the sausage made by the company her late husband created.

Where to Buy. Smokey Denmark Sausage Company sells their products to restaurants, hotels, and other food service clients. Their Hot Links are sold at Kroger stores in the Dallas/Fort Worth area, and they plan to expand to other Texas retailers. They take orders by mail, phone, fax, and the Internet.

A Case for Casings

If you've eaten a real Texas sausage, you've experienced the snappy texture of the natural outer casing. Natural casings, usually made from hog's intestines, are there for many good reasons. They allow the smoky flavor to penetrate, they expand without breaking, they add no flavor of their own, and they help the sausage stay juicy as it cooks. Most of all, they add that wonderful snap when you bite into the sausage.

(This information provided by the International Natural Sausage Casing Association website: www.insca.org)

Texas Best Beef Jerky, Inc.

7043 Seymour Highway
Wichita Falls, Texas 76310
Toll-Free: (800) 373-9679
Fax: (940) 691-4217
Internet: www.texasbestbeefjerky.com

Troy Collier's dad was in the cattle business, and his mother always made authentic beef jerky for Christmas and family snacks. Troy experimented with the recipe, started selling it, and now has a USDA-inspected facility.

At his first food show, customers tried the jerky and returned for more saying, "This is the best beef jerky I've ever had!" That night when Troy returned home he knew what to name his company.

That was in the early 1990s. Today Troy makes a variety of Beef Jerky flavors including Mild, Hot, and Extra Hot. The Hot is the most popular choice. He also makes Turkey Jerky, Summer Sausage, and Beef Sticks.

Troy says his products receive rave reviews because of the high quality lean meat he uses along with his marinade and good old-fashioned mesquite smoke. The smoking process takes eight to ten hours. After the jerky is cured, it is vacuum packed and sealed for freshness. Troy also sells his popular marinade so that customers can use it on other meats.

Where to Buy. Look for these products at local stores in the Wichita Falls area, hunting and fishing stores, lodges, convenience stores, and at trade shows. Orders are taken by phone, fax, mail, and the Internet.

Chapter 6

Pickles, Okra, Peppers, Relish...and Tabooley to Boot

Texas is a pickle place. Barbecue joints toss in a stack of pickles with their brisket, beans, and bread. Baseball games and county fairs offer versions almost large enough to use in batting practice. And spicy pickles turn any sandwich into a Texas treat.

Pickled peppers are another favorite. For those who like their jalapeños not quite so hot, pickling seems to do the trick. These sweet-hot rings add zest to soups, stews, or just about anything.

Relishes are an offshoot of pickles. In Texas, relishes have a characteristic twist. Northerners are in for a new experience when they open a jar of authentic Texas mixtures. Hold on to your hat because these aren't your average chunky concoctions.

This chapter is topped off with a blend of Middle Eastern and Texan cultures. Many unusual concoctions are sure to tempt you as you ride through this section of chunky (and funky!) specialties.

Alberto's Food Products, Inc.

4102 Seastone Lane
Houston, Texas 77068
Phone: (281) 893-4776
Toll-Free: (877) 4RELISH
Fax: (281) 895-0983
Internet: www.albertosbrand.com

Albert Habinek used to travel around the country on business trips. During one memorable journey he tried a jalapeño relish unlike any other. Determined to enjoy this unique concoction at home, he experimented until he created something to his liking.

His wife, Sarah, a retired schoolteacher, decided that her husband's special relish was too good to keep it a secret. Before he could say "relish" she booked him into some craft shows and Alberto's Food Products took shape.

Today Alberto's relish is made by Sarah, her husband, and a few helpers in a commercial kitchen. Because it is quite thick, the relish can only be hand packed, so tight quality control goes into every jar. Sarah personally cleans each jalapeño, and her husband and the others bottle up to fifty or sixty cases at a time. Available in Mild, Medium Hot, and Hot, the relish appeals to a variety of spice-loving palates. Mild and Medium Hot are salt-free so they can be enjoyed by those on

Jalapeño Festival

The border town of Laredo heats up every February with this spicy fest. Highlights include the Jalapeño Eating Contest, "Some Like it Hot" recipe contest, and the crowning of Ms. Jalapeño. If you like your foods hot, this is the place to be!

restricted diets. (The salt-free aspect came about when Albert inadvertently left out the salt in his original blend but the concoction was so tasty no one missed it.) The relish goes well on hot dogs, burgers, and any sandwich.

The original relish caught on so well that Sarah and Albert have developed new blends including Corn Relish and Zucchini Relish. The Corn Relish was Albert's mother's recipe, and the Zucchini Relish was created by Sarah for those who do not like jalapeños. Jalapeño Jelly, Jalapeño Mustard, Chili con Queso, and Jalapeño Olives round out this line of hot and zesty condiments. The mustard is designed to go on everything from sandwiches to pretzels. And the Chili con Queso tastes like more than melted cheese. A definite "bite" makes it an ideal way to perk up baked potatoes, dips, enchiladas, tacos, or even macaroni and cheese.

Sarah and Albert are thrilled to be spending their retirement in the culinary world. In fact, they relish their new life!

Where to Buy. Look for Alberto's bright label at Central Market, The Goode Company on Kirby in Houston, Canton First Monday, Dave's Pepper Place in Old Town Spring, and other gift and specialty shops. Order by fax, mail, phone, or through the website.

Blazzin Pickles

6105 N. 32nd
McAllen, Texas 78504
Phone: (956) 630-0733
Toll-Free: (800) 637-0733

Things are ablaze in South Texas! Deep down in McAllen, Craig "Pickleman" Johnson is busy bottling pickles that have an attitude all their own! Craig's mother liked to make pickles, so Craig tweaked her recipe to come with his own blend of fiery sweetness.

In McAllen cucumbers are grown year round, giving Craig constant access to a fresh product. He adds his own special blend of spices and ferments the pickles three to six months. The finished products bring gusto to burgers, potato salads, or anything else that welcomes a pickle. Eat them alone straight from the jar.

The Sweet-Sour-Spicy flavor comes in chips or spears and Dill is available in spears. They have a delicate zing and can be enjoyed by the whole family, including the kids. The special processing brings out the flavor and creates a crisp texture.

The whimsical label features Pancho Pepito, a pickle riding a horse! It is clear that a lot of talent goes into each jar of these crispy zingers.

Where to Buy. Look for the Pancho Pepito pickle riding a horse on Blazzin Pickles bottles in a variety of grocers including Kroger and Tom Thumb stores in the Dallas area. They are in about eight hundred stores, so keep looking and you should find them somewhere near you. If not, order by mail or phone. A number of gift sets are available by mail order.

Carrie Belle Gourmet Foods

P.O. Box 62621
San Angelo, Texas 79606
Phone: (915) 949-9296
Toll-Free: (877) 57-BELLE (23553)
Fax: (915) 223-0200
Internet: www.carriebelle.com

Steve Layman has fond memories of growing up. One of the best-tasting memories he has is of his grandmother, Carrie Belle, and her "tomato sauce." The family lovingly poured this sauce on everything from baked ham to beans.

Carrie Belle was born in Tennessee in 1879 and moved with her family to Bangs, Texas (near Brownwood), around 1900. The recipe for her special sauce dates all the way back to 1910, and it became a traditional part of family meals. Every summer Carrie Belle gave Steve's family some jars of her sauce, and it was considered a very special treat. Thankfully, this is one family recipe that was passed down. When Carrie Belle became too old to cook (she died in 1969), an aunt made the sauce, and in the mid-1990s Steve decided to try his hand at it. When the sauce won a First Prize ribbon in the Tom Green County Livestock Show, he decided to market it. Since that time the sauce has gone on to win numerous awards and honors.

Carrie Belle's Sweet Hot Tomato Relish is still made the natural way with no preservatives. Each jar is packed with tomatoes, fresh onions, fresh peppers, and spices. Sugar and vinegar serve as preservatives, just as they did in 1910. The best way to describe the flavor is, as the label says, sweet and hot! It has a unique blend that tastes great on beans, ham, or other meats. It is also delicious when simply spooned on a cracker.

When it was time to design a label, Steve consulted artist Debra H. Warr. The label is charming, complete with a photo of Carrie Belle and a horned toad, which is another tribute to Steve's grandmother. Carrie Belle loved to tend her garden. When her grandchildren visited, she took them into her yard and showed them the horned toads, which seemed to be everywhere. The memory of playing with toads in Carrie Belle's yard is a special one for Steve.

Carrie Belle's Sweet Hot Tomato Relish is made in Abilene at Disability Resources, Inc. This commercial kitchen is a special place where folks with disabilities use their talents and learn new skills. The unique facility is described in Chapter 10.

Steve continues to rack up major awards for his grandmother's sauce. Carrie Belle would be proud.

Peter Piper's Pickles

Peter Piper picked a peck of pickled peppers. If Peter Piper picked a peck of pickled peppers, how many pickled peppers did Peter Piper pick?

Peter Piper may be busy picking peppers in Texas but he sure isn't *pickling* cucumbers. Texans love pickles with their barbecue, but not too many Texas food companies make pickled cukes.

Where to Buy. Look for Carrie Belle's Sweet Hot Tomato Relish at gourmet shops in and out of Texas. You will find it at Albertson's stores in the Great Plains region of Texas and other areas as distribution expands. Order by fax, phone, mail, and the Internet.

Cherith Valley Gardens, Inc.

P.O. Box 9654
Fort Worth, Texas 76147-2654
Phone: (817) 922-8822
Toll-Free: (800) 610-9813
Fax: (817) 922-8884

Cherith Valley Gardens products are a charming selection of artisan vegetables and relishes. Each jar contains a carefully arranged melody of colors. The beauty of a fresh stalk of dill, red and green peppers, and a plump garlic pod seem to sing with color. This lively arrangement—the company's signature—is a statement

that a great deal of care goes into each hand packed container.

Founders Terri and Alan Werner are meticulous about their products. Their son Scott, daughter Christa, and son-in-law Randall work together harmoniously in this family-run business.

In 1986 Alan was a principal at an independent oil company. The stock market crash of 1987 led to the company's demise and left his family financially devastated. In the midst of the crisis, they were drawn back to the "land" and planted a vegetable garden to save money on food. At Christmas, with little financial resources available for gifts, the family gave away jars of their homegrown specialties. Friends encouraged the Werners to turn their garden into a business. After studying food processing at Texas A&M University, the family was ready to take the big step.

The Werner's first commercial product was prepared on May 8, 1993. Corn relish and jellies were two of the original nine items. Since that spring day, business has grown faster than a well-fed garden. Today the family markets a full line with the motto: "We know you'll enjoy the taste of food produced with the utmost care and finest ingredients." Products are all natural and fat-free. They do not contain any artificial colors or flavors. The Werners even make their own all-natural vinegar. When you put their jars on your shelves, it will bear a strong resemblance to Grandma's pantry.

Their most popular product is Hot n' Spicy Pickled Garlic. Each plump garlic clove is hand-packed with the signature medley of fresh dill and red and green peppers. Enliven your greens by tossing in a few slices or blend into pasta salads. Place into a deli meat sandwich and wake up your taste buds. This award-winning product continues to receive rave reviews and keeps the family busy canning 60,000 pounds of garlic a year! Other Hot n' Spicy Pickled items include Okra, Carrots, Sunburst Squash, Mixed Vegetables, Dill Pickles, Pickled Green Beans, Pickled Mushrooms, and Hearts of Palm.

Spirited Cherries, a spicy melange of whole-pitted cherries, is simmered slowly with fresh stick cinnamon, natural cherry juice, and cherry vinegar. This item adds elegance to a sundae, a batch of homemade cupcakes, or even a flute of champagne. Spirited Peaches sparkle with versatility and flavor. Use as a pie filling or pour over a bowl of vanilla ice cream.

A variety of jellies offer something for every occasion. Exotic flavors such as Passion Papaya add creativity to the breakfast table or appetizer buffet. Mimosa Jelly is a heavenly blend of orange juice and champagne. Use as a taste-rousing glaze over chicken or to add pizzazz to a special brunch.

Cherith Valley salsas burst with fresh flavors. Green Olive Salsa is a spicy concoction just waiting to be spooned into an omelet or scooped up by a crisp tortilla chip. An olive lover's delight! If you are not an olive aficionado, there are many other varieties available.

The company has been featured in *Texas Monthly*, the *Fort Worth Star Telegram*, and on "Good Morning Texas." Their unique array of garden specialties has won numerous honors and awards.

Where to Buy. Cherith Valley Gardens products are sold in over 6,000 specialty shops in all fifty states, Canada, and other countries. Look for them in Central Market, Neiman Marcus, Nordstrom's, Bergdorf Goodman, Williams-Sonoma, Pier One, Dean & DeLuca,

Bass Pro Shops, and other fine stores. Orders are taken by mail, phone, fax, and through some online merchants.

Goldin Pickle Company, Inc.

515 Mills Road
Garland, Texas 75040-6833
Phone: (972) 272-1111
Internet: www.goldinpickle.com

When Steve Collette graduated college in the mid-1970s, he had an opportunity to purchase a pickle company. College graduates need jobs, and this seemed like a good one, so he took the pickle plunge and bought the company from the Goldin family. Steve and his wife, Beverly, are still the proud owners.

In 1923 Jay Goldin made homemade kosher pickles and sold them in his meat market. When they outsold the meats, Jay switched his focus.

Today Goldin Pickles is a big business in a few ways. Steve moved into a new building in Garland with fiberglass tanks, each large enough to ferment 43,000 pounds of pickles. They have to be big because these pickles are huge. At six inches long and two inches wide, they are a mouthful! The dilly delights are the kind you've eaten at ballparks and state fairs.

A Pickle and a Spear (as in Shakespeare!)

The phrase "in a pickle" was coined by William Shakespeare in *The Tempest*, Act V. The meaning hasn't changed and still refers to being in a sorry state.

Pickle making is a slow process, and fermentation takes five or six weeks in the outdoor tanks. This step is necessary to preserve the pickles. Once completed, the pickles move indoors where they are heated, mixed with the tasty Goldin recipe for dills, and packed whole, in slices, or made into pickle relish. The relish flavors are Dill, Sweet, and Sour. If you have eaten potato salad in the Southwest, chances are it was made with the Goldin touch. The company distributes its relishes to a variety of food manufacturers.

Where to Buy. Goldin Pickles sells primarily to distributors, ballparks, schools, and other food service operations. They are also available at Costco and in convenience stores where they are sold either in containers or individually. The two-and-a-half-gallon barrel-shaped jars are a popular choice. People love the pickles and enjoy reusing the container.

Talk O' Texas

1610 Roosevelt Street
San Angelo, Texas 76905
Phone: (915) 655-6077
Toll-Free: (800) 749-6572
Internet: www.talkotexas.com

This West Texas treasure has a history that goes back to the 1940s, when it started in a San Angelo kitchen. The Grimes family founded the company but needed outside financial support. Albert Ricci, an Italian immigrant, came to the rescue and bought company stock. In 1950, when the Grimes' needed financial help a second time, Albert Ricci bought the company and incorporated in 1953.

In addition to the okra business, Albert owned a popular San Angelo beauty salon. Girls would save their money all year so he could do their hair for the prom. When he wasn't styling hair, Albert was busy with his jazz band. He played the French horn, piano, bass fiddle, vibes, and harmonica. If there was a big wedding in San Angelo, people were most likely kicking up their heels to the beat of Albert's band.

Albert Ricci's creativity extended beyond hairdressing and music. He came up with the Talk O' Texas name and label design.

Talk O' Texas continues to flourish as a Ricci family-owned company. Albert's son Larry became the CEO in 1985 and a year later moved the company to a state-of-the-art plant on Roosevelt Street where it remains today. This modern plant assures that the company is capable of meeting the high demand for its top quality products. Larry's daughter Lisa is now a vice president.

Crisp Okra Pickles was the original product, and today the company sells Hot and Mild varieties. They also sell Hickory Flavored Liquid Smoke, a product used to impart a smoky flavor to meats.

During spring, summer, and early fall, there is a flurry of activity at this modern plant. The okra season extends from May to October, and during that time the number of employees swells to seventy-five. Forty-two people carefully hand pack the okra pods one jar at a time, using only the finest ingredients. The hand packing assures that the pods stay intact inside the jars, and this has contributed to the company's standing as the nation's leader in its industry.

Back in the company's early days, San Angelo children brought in okra from their family's gardens. When the demand became greater than the local supply, the company had to get its okra from sources outside the West Texas town. In the heat of production, about 3,500 cases a day are packed.

Okra is a popular southern specialty. Serve it like any other pickle! Many people open a jar and devour the entire thing. Kids like it as a snack. Hosts place it on relish trays. Cheryl Power, who has worked with the company for years, says that one customer wrote in and said that okra is great in place of an olive in a martini.

Where to Buy. Look for the Talk O' Texas Okra Pickles in grocery stores from coast to coast. They are also offered in gift boxes that can be shipped anywhere in the continental U.S. Customers are encouraged to call the toll-free number for assistance finding a nearby store that sells Crisp Okra Pickles. Orders are taken on the Internet as well.

A Tasty Visit

Talk O' Texas Crisp Okra Pickles
1610 Roosevelt Street
San Angelo
(800) 749-6572

Cheryl Power is bursting with enthusiasm about Crisp Okra Pickles, and she enjoys leading plant tours. Kids and adults of all ages tour the plant and hear stories about the company's history and the fascinating crispy pods. Call first to arrange a tour.

Tom's Tabooley

2928 Guadalupe
Austin, Texas 78705
Phone: (512) 479-7337

In the late 1970s Tom and Brigid Abdenoor began selling traditional Middle Eastern specialties from a cart near the campus of the University of Texas. Tom and Brigid, both natives of Peoria, Illinois, enjoyed cooking and used their culinary talents to experiment with new twists on regional favorites.

DILL PEPPERCORN HUMMUS

Tom left the cart business for a while and helped open one of the original Whole Foods stores in Austin. His dream was to own a Middle Eastern shop offering both carryout and eat-in dining. Ultimately his dream came true.

Today the Abdenoors' campus area shop is filled with a variety of Middle Eastern specialties. Succulent aromas drift through the air as the couple and their staff create tasty concoctions. In the late 1980s they expanded to the packaged foods business, making their items available on a retail level. During the quiet after-lunch hours, Tom, Brigid, and their staff are busy cooking and packaging their specialty items.

Tabooley, the national dish of Lebanon, is a garden fresh mixture of green onions, parsley, spearmint, tomatoes, and cucumbers mixed with olive oil and lemon juice. It can be served on a lettuce leaf or eaten by itself with a fork.

Another Tom's Tabooley specialty is Hummus. This tasty ground garbanzo bean spread is available in six flavors: Traditional, Roasted Garlic, Roasted Red Pepper, Calamata Olive, Dill Red Peppercorn, and Southwest, which features fresh roasted jalapeños and is a reflection of Tom's ability to blend cultural specialties with ease.

Clarified butter, called Ghee, is another packaged food offered by Tom's Tabooley. If you have ever shied away from a recipe calling for clarified butter, fear no more. Simply buy some Ghee and pull out the cookbook. Clarified butter is popular because it doesn't burn like regular butter when heated on the stove.

Tom grew up around food in his close-knit family. He watched his mother make Middle Eastern specialties, and he developed a natural culinary talent. Brigid is a talented chef herself. One of her specialties is baklava: sweetened nuts surrounded by forty butter-basted layers of phyllo on the bottom and forty more on the top. Brigid's baklava is unlike any other. A diamond shaped portion is a slice of pure indulgence.

Tom's Tabooley is a family business. Tom and Brigid and their sons pitch in to make sure that every product is of the finest quality. Speaking of pitching, the family is extremely fond of baseball. When not buttering baklava or rolling dolmas (stuffed grape leaves), they can often be found on the field rooting for their son's team or cheering for their favorite Major League Baseball clubs.

Where to Buy. Purchase Tom's Tabooley products at Central Market or Whole Foods.

State Pepper

In 1995, the 74th Texas Legislature proclaimed that the jalapeño is the State Pepper.

A Tasty Visit

Tom's Tabooley
2928 Guadalupe
Austin
Hours: Tuesday - Thursday 7 a.m. - 7 p.m.
Friday: 7 a.m. - 3 p.m.
Saturday 11 a.m. - 6 p.m.

When in Austin, head to the campus area for a Middle Eastern feast. Tom's Tabooley sells a complete menu of authentic specialties based on recipes from Tom's mother. Choose from Falafel, Dolmas, Tabooley/Hummus Wrap, and much more. A huge selection of salads and ala carte items is available. Top off your meal with a slice of Brigid's heavenly baklava. And don't share dessert. The baklava is so out-of-this-world good (buttery, but not overwhelmingly rich), you will want the whole slice to yourself! Wash it down with a mocha latte, espresso, cappuccino, or other coffee favorite. A small area in front allows you to dine on the premises. Have fun browsing the specialty candies and other unique items.

Two Women Cooking
P.O. Box 162285
Austin, Texas 78716
Phone/Fax: (512) 263-2984

Gail Calder has been dubbed the "Queen of Condiments." Before moving to Austin in 1992, Gail lived in Dallas where she was known for giving jars of homemade relish as Christmas gifts. For

years her friends said they wished they could buy her spicy blend.

When Gail relocated to Austin, she gave a friend some relish and the two decided to embark on a new career. (Gail later bought her partner out and is now the sole owner.) Central Market staff took one look (and bite) of the product and immediately put it on their shelves.

Today Gail's company makes four products: Hell of a Relish, Hotter than Hell of a Relish, Heavenly Relish, and Purgatory Barbecue Sauce. Notice a theme?

Hell of a Relish was an easy name to come up with because people who sampled it proclaimed, "It's a hell of a relish!" Gail said the Hotter than Hell of a Relish name came naturally. Hell of a Relish is a blend of carrot, jalapeño, red bell pepper, sugar, vinegar, and spices. The Hotter version is the same with habaneros instead of jalapeños. Gail describes it as a hot sweet pickled relish.

Most people start out using it as an appetizer with cream cheese and crackers. Then they find that it enlivens eggs, potatoes, tuna salad, hot dogs, burgers, and just about anything else. For years Gail has been getting a stream of letters, from as far away as Taiwan, suggesting new uses.

On a heat scale of one to ten, the regular version is a four, and the hot version is about a six or seven. Although Gail likes "heat," it is important to her that fire does not mask flavor. Every jar is carefully hand packed, assuring top quality control.

Heavenly Relish is a corn relish that Gail originally created as a dip. It contains corn, carrot, diced tomato, red onion, and garlic. This mixture creates a harmony of colors that make a pretty presentation. Add to beans or soups (like tortilla soup), or spoon onto steamed fish.

The Purgatory Barbecue Sauce is another hot and sweet taste temptation containing "the relish." Pomegranate gives it a touch of the exotic. The sauce is super with meats, portobello mushrooms, or mixed with cream cheese and eaten on a cracker. Add to mayonnaise for a zippy sandwich spread, or make into a flavorful dressing.

State Native Pepper

In 1997, the 75th Texas Legislature proclaimed that the chiltepin is the State Native Pepper.

Gail is also a co-owner of Austin Kitchens, Inc. (see Chapter 7), an Austin commercial kitchen that prepares a variety of foods.

Where to Buy. Purchase Two Women Cooking products at major grocery stores throughout Texas, such as Albertson's, HEB, Randalls, Central Market, and Whole Foods. They are available around the country at specialty gourmet shops.

★ West Texas Pepper Traders

P.O. Box 1246
Abilene, Texas 79604-1246
Phone: (915) 692-8300
Toll-Free: (888) 440-WTPT (9878)
Internet: www.peppertraders.com

It wasn't an April Fools' joke that Tony Spradlin and Scott Bridges were pickling peppers. But it was April 1, 1999, when they started their company.

The two West Texans were inspired by an old recipe for making pickled rings out of jalapeño peppers. They made a few batches, much to the delight of family and friends who were fortunate enough to serve as taste testers.

Today the Bread 'N' Butter Jalapeños are made at Disability Resources, Inc. (see Chapter 10 for details on this very special non-profit organization), a commercial kitchen in Abilene.

Demand for these spicy rounds is quite strong, and the company uses five tons of fresh jalapeños a month! The peppers are cleaned, hand sliced one at a time, and blended with fresh onions and other spices before being heated to almost two hundred degrees. The mixture of spices and sugar takes some heat from the jalapeño but retains the pepper's distinct flavor.

When customers started raving about the juice, the company started bottling it alone as a marinade (an award-winning marinade!).

The peppers are similar to bread and butter pickles, except they are jalapeños and not cucumbers! They taste great with almost anything. Pop a few in a bowl of soup to perk it up, layer on sandwiches, cook in an omelet, spread over burgers, add to cornbread, the list could go on. They are mild enough to eat out of the jar. Even the brightly colored label is a work of art.

The April 1 endeavor has been a great one, and the product has racked up some prestigious awards.

Where to Buy. Look for the Original Bread 'N' Butter Jalapeño at Texas HEB stores, United, IGA, Albertson's in the Dallas/Fort Worth area, and Albertson's in Oklahoma, Tennessee, Iowa, Kansas, and Mississippi. The product is distributed to over seven hundred grocery stores. Orders are taken by mail, phone, and the Internet.

Chapter 7

Salsas, Sauces, and even some Jellies!

This category is as big as Texas. There are a lot of fresh ingredients grown under the sunny Texas skies. Large quantities of these seedy wonders find their way into glass jars in the form of salsas, sauces, and even jellies.

In the past it was essential to make your own if you wanted a salsa or sauce that was a bit different. Today Texas food companies offer many unique options. Chipotle steak sauce is one. Mango salsa is another. Really, the sky is the limit. And as we know, Texas has a big sky!

Austin Kitchen, Inc.

807 Josephine
Austin, Texas 78704
Phone: (512) 326-2526
Fax: (512) 326-2561

In the world of food manufacturing, *co-packer* is a popular term. Suppose you have a salsa you would like to sell, but you don't have access to a commercial kitchen. You could contract with a co-packer to cook and package your product.

A co-packer is a commercial kitchen that prepares and packages food items for a variety of food companies. Austin Kitchen is mentioned as an example of such (and they have their own line of red

Red Sauce

and green salsas). If you happen to have a recipe you'd like to take to market, a co-packer might be your pot of gold at the end of the recipe rainbow.

Gail Calder and Kathy O'Kelley have owned Austin Kitchen for several years. Gail also owns Two Women Cooking (see Chapter 6), which makes a line of relishes. When Austin Kitchen's previous owner was going to close it, Gail and Kathy bought it and became certified food manufacturers.

The kitchen now serves a number of companies. They began making only salsas, and now they prepare a variety of sauces and dressings as well.

If a company is interested in using them as a co-packer, one of the first steps is to have Austin Kitchen prepare their food item to see if it comes out just right. After all, when quantities are multiplied some ingredients may need adjusting. This isn't a free service, so companies pay a fee. Once the recipe is correct and an agreement is signed, Austin Kitchen will cook the products, bottle and label them, and put them on pallets. It is up to each individual company to arrange distribution.

Austin Kitchen has five full-time and three part-time employees, plus the two owners.

Where to Buy. Purchase Austin Kitchen salsas at Sun Harvest and Fresh Plus stores.

★ Austin Slow Burn

P.O. Box 150042
Austin, Texas 78715-0042
Phone: (512) 282-7140
Toll-Free: (877) 513-3192
Fax: (512) 282-7140

What would you do if you had a large crop of friends who wanted your salsa and an even larger crop of habanero peppers?

If you were Jill Lewis, you just might start a business. In the mid-1990s that is just what this Austin entrepreneur did. Friends who said the sauces had a

delayed effect inspired the brand name. Today the company's three employees turn out six saucy items.

The Southwest Pasta Sauce blends Southwestern spice with a traditional Italian sauce. The red sandia chile adds fiery flair to fresh tomatoes and Italian spices. On a hotness scale of ten, it's about a three, making it suitable for the entire family. Serve it as the sauce for spaghetti and meatballs or in lasagna or chicken parmesan. The red sandia chile adds body so that the sauce adheres nicely to the pasta.

The Jamaican Jerk Marinade combines tropical juices with habanero peppers, garlic, and spices to create a bold, exotic flavor. Soak your chicken, pork, beef, seafood, or veggies in Jamaican Jerk and your meals will have added zest. Use your imagination—this marinade will enhance anything you put on the grill. The label contains specific directions for marinating or for using as a dressing.

If you like food ala New Orleans, try the Creole Sauce. A blend of tomatoes, vegetables, and herbs, this Cajun specialty makes a quick meal out of chicken, seafood, sausage, or vegetables. You can even use it in your meatloaf. If you close your eyes while enjoying this sauce, you might just think you are in New Orleans!

Where to Buy. Look for Austin Slow Burn products at Central Market, Whole Foods, and gift shops throughout Texas, the U.S., and Canada. The Southwest Pasta Sauce and Creole Sauce can be found in Central and South Texas HEB stores. Rice Epicurean carries the salsa and jellies. You can order by phone if you'd like a case or more.

Austin Spice Company

P.O. Box 202003
Austin, Texas 78720
Phone: (512) 360-5589
Fax: (512) 360-5589
Internet: www.austinspice.com

Craig Barton loves to cook. In 1995 he and his wife entered some dry spices and salsa in the Fiery Foods Show. They won awards and Austin Spice Company was born. And today they say, "Austin's hot and we're smokin'!" And smokin' they are, roasting their own chiles in the heart of Texas! (And to the heart's delight of many a Texan.)

The company now offers a large selection of salsas, a Bloody Mary mix, a marinade, and a few dry seasonings. The products are known for their natural mesquite roasting.

The Chile Ancho Salsa is a mild and chunky salsa that goes great with chips or in cooking. With its medium level of heat it is a crowd pleaser even for those new to chile eating.

Smoky Hill is a line of salsas and barbecue sauces offering something for everyone. Smoky Hill Salsa "Hot" is loaded with jalapeño peppers that have been fire-roasted over mesquite. This is the original award-winning salsa. Smoky Hill Salsa "Medium" is a toned down version (in terms of heat) of the "Hot." Smoky Hill Salsa Verde blends tomatillos with peppers that have been fire roasted over mesquite. Heat is medium and flavor is top notch! Smoky Hill Barbeque Salsa is a unique blend of mesquite-roasted peppers and spices.

Green Chile Salsa uses those famous Hatch, New Mexico green chiles that have been roasted. If you have not tried the Hatch chiles, you are in for a real treat. (When they are in season, Central Market has been known to set up a storefront grill and sell fresh roasted Hatches. Their Hatch hamburger buns are sensational, too.)

Campfire Corn and Bean Salsa is a great side dish or dip, with its zesty mixture of corn, black beans, and peppers that have been roasted over mesquite.

Steak and Fajita Marinade is ideal for any cut of meat. Simply marinate for four to eight hours or overnight, and get ready for some sizzle.

Austin Spice Company has two dry seasonings. Texas Red Lemon Pepper adds zest to chicken, pork, fish, and blackened recipes. Or try it

Spicy in Any Language!

"Salsa" means "sauce" in Spanish.

on French fries. Texas #202 Beef Seasoning makes a brisket to brag about and tastes great on other meats as well.

The Hare of the Dawg Bloody Mary Mix is another award-winning product. Austin Spice Company has racked up over seventy national awards. See their website for details. The website also has recipes and other useful information.

The company sells gift packs that combine several products into one nifty set. The Texas Mega contains the company's most popular salsas and two dry rubs. What a hot gift! For Christmas, Austin Spice Company will concoct custom gift boxes.

And if you think Craig Barton's name sounds familiar, maybe you've seen him on television or as a guest chef at a food show.

Where to Buy. Austin Spice Company products are sold throughout Texas and many other states, including Alaska (they need all the heat they can get up there!). In Texas, their products can be found at a variety of locations including Central Market, HEB, Fiesta, Randalls, Krogers, Whole Foods, Sun Harvest, Wheatsville Co-op, Guitars and Cadillacs, and Pecan Flats (in Spring). Orders are taken by phone, fax, or online. The website has ordering details.

⭐ Austin's Own

P.O. Box 200395
Austin, Texas 78720-0395
Phone: (512) 452-2179
Fax: (512) 419-1775

If you are from Amarillo, you may remember a barbecue restaurant called The Hickory Hut. Open for lunch and dinner, this popular spot had lines stretching out the door. In the dead of winter, with snow blowing sideways and temperatures well below freezing, the lines were long.

The meat was juicy and flavorful, but it was the barbecue sauce that became a legend. Yet this legend didn't end in Amarillo. You can still get your hands on some of the original barbecue sauce. And you won't even have to wait in line. In fact, you can serve it at your own family barbecues. The sauce has a new name and a new hometown, but it still has the same great taste.

Sharon and Joe Cayton are the proud owners of Austin's Own barbecue sauce. Joe's dad owned The Hickory Hut and eventually closed down the Amarillo restaurant when he got older. The recipe landed gently in the hands of Sharon and Joe, who moved from Amarillo to Austin in 1984.

Sharon kept the original barbecue sauce recipe close to her heart. Actually, she stored it in her hip pocket, knowing that she was holding on to a real Texas treasure. When her in-laws' friends wanted Sharon to sell them some sauce, an idea was sparked and Austin's Own Barbecue Sauce hit the shelves. The couple lovingly named it for the hometown where they first made the sauce available to the public.

The first jar went to market in 1986. Back then, Sharon and Joe distributed the sauce themselves, reaching the grocery stores at the crack of dawn along with the bread and milk trucks. Skaggs Alpha Beta in Austin was the first store to carry it. Joe had taken a sample to the manager who happened to be from Amarillo. Then Tom Thumb ordered some. Eventually, Albertson's entered the picture when they bought Skagg's, so the product was introduced to many of their stores. Then HEB wanted some. Demand grew, and Sharon and Joe knew they had reached a turning point. They found a distributor, and now their products are widely available. (Sharon and Joe no longer deliver it themselves.)

Austin's Own makes three sauces in a commercial kitchen. Flavors include Original, Border Edition, and Chipotle. The Original is a mild sauce using The Hickory Hut recipe. The other two sauces are hotter versions of the Original. The Border Edition, with four different peppers including a touch of habanero, was created for those who really like some kick.

Sharon and Joe enjoy watching people react to their sauces, and they do all in-store promotions themselves. If you see people giving away samples of Austin's Own, it's likely to be Sharon and Joe Cayton. If you don't see the couple handing out sauce samples, maybe you'll catch them on television. Sharon has already had the pleasure of cooking with Bobby Flay. The two appeared on a Food Network show featuring Texas barbecue. Austin's Own has come a long way since it was served at The Hickory Hut. Joe's parents would be proud.

Where to Buy. You can find Austin's Own at most grocery stores in Texas, as well as specialty stores such as Central Market. Discount stores, such as Sam's and Costco, sell it in larger half-gallon jars.

Billy Beans

3602 North Clack
Abilene, Texas 79601
Phone: (915) 690-9521
Toll-Free: (888) TEX-BEAN (839-2326)
Fax: (915) 673-7829
Internet: www.billybeans.com

Tony Dry, the Head Bean at Billy Beans, is a cowboy who is "too blessed to be stressed." His enthusiasm for life, charity, and faith is enough to fill zillions of jars of Billy Beans salsas and sauces. In fact, Tony himself is actually overflowing with zest. So you can only imagine how great his products taste.

It was either "Mama Bonnie" or "Daddy Koot" who came up with the original salsa recipe for Billy Beans I "Scream" Sauce. Why the "Scream" you might ask. Because it is loudly flavorful! You might also ask how Tony Dry wrangled up the name Billy Beans for his brand of spicy sensations.

Well, it all goes back to a joke and here it is:

Billy Bean from Abilene likes to brag about all the famous people he knows. So it's 1985, and during a round of golf on a nice Abilene day, Billy's two friends doubt that Billy Bean really knows so many celebrities. They are, in fact, so skeptical that they say to Billy Bean, "We'll bet you fifty thousand dollars that you don't know President Reagan."

Billy Bean gets a big old grin on his face. "Oh darn," he says, "I knew Ronnie when he was shootin' movies in Hollywood." So Billy Bean and his two Abilene buddies fly on Billy's private jet to Washington. While touring the White House, Billy Bean steps to the side and says to the secret service agent, "I'm Billy Bean from Abilene. I'd like to see the president."

So they knock on the door of the Oval Office, and when it is opened President Reagan looks up from his desk and shouts, "Billy Bean from Abilene, you get right in here ole buddy!"

Obviously, Billy Bean's friends are stunned. They're also fifty thousand dollars poorer.

A few weeks later Billy Bean and his two friends are out golfing again. And his friends want their money back.

"Hey Billy," they say, "We want our money back so this time we'll double it and bet you one hundred thousand dollars that you don't know the Pope."

Billy Bean says, "I knew the Pope when he was a priest in Poland." So Billy and his friends fly to the Vatican. A Cardinal answers the door, and Billy says, "I'm Billy Bean from Abilene, and I'd like to see the Pope. And my friends want to see him, too."

The Cardinal explains that because of tight security the Pope can't see all three of them. Only Billy Bean is allowed in, and he tells his friends to go around and watch because he and the Pope will appear together on the veranda of the Vatican.

So the two friends walk around to the front where a crowd has gathered. Sure enough, Billy Bean and the Pope come out on the veranda standing arm in arm. The two friends ask the man next to them if that's really the Pope in the white robe.

The man says, "Well it sure looks like him, but you see that ole boy standing next to him, that's ole Billy Bean from Abilene!"

Now that you've got a smile on your face, let's get back to Billy Bean, salsa-maker because this is serious business. Billy Beans I "Scream" Sauce is a salsa, an award-winning one at that. On a heat scale of one to ten, it's a seven. As Tony says, "We give you some flavor, but we don't set you on fire." And this Head Bean knows his stuff. An oilman for twenty-three years, Tony has always loved the art of cooking. And the closest he gets to oil nowadays is safflower oil.

Tony didn't stop with salsa. Billy Beans Down Right Incredible Bar-B-Que Sauce is another crowd pleaser. It is not only good, it's good for you. In fact, a serving has only one gram of sugar so people on special diets, such as those with diabetes, can slather it on more freely.

When it comes to making these great products, Tony assures that they are made with pride. I mentioned that he is excited about charity work. He puts his products where his beliefs are and has them made at a wonderful place in Abilene called Disability Resources, Inc. Here, folks with disabilities find gainful employment and learn new skills. Chapter 10 has more details on this organization, and Tony's enthusiasm for the group is contagious.

Billy Beans products are award winners, and the company's wonderful website has the full details. The site is also a celebrity forum, featuring letters from the Bushes (Dubya and Laura), General Chuck Yeager, and many more famous folks. Seems that Billy Bean really is well known, even among the celebs! The salsa also appears in a movie, *The Pretender,* and is a big hit at the Academy of Country Music Awards.

Family is a key to Billy Beans' success. Tony, his wife, and his cousin Gary Dry work together with shared enthusiasm for this fantastic line of products.

Where to Buy. Look for the screaming chile pepper on Billy Beans labels at a variety of stores throughout Texas including all Albertson's in the DFW area, over eighty HEB stores, Super S grocers, all Brookshires, all United Supermarkets, an Austin airport shop, Jethro Pugh's Paradies Shops in the DFW and Midland airports, and at other specialty stores. Outside of Texas, Billy Beans is sold at all the Albertson's stores in Nebraska, Iowa, Kansas, Oklahoma, Arkansas, and Tennessee. You can also order by phone, fax, mail, or online.

Texas Fiery Foods Show

Austin is fiery hot in August. The Texas Fiery Foods Show starts with the Dash of Pepper 5K race. The main event is alive with spicy foods and related items of art, clothing, kitchen accessories, and more!

Brazos Country Foods

700 S. Bryan
Bryan, Texas 77803-3928
Phone: (979) 775-1611
Toll-Free: (800) 8-SAUCES
Fax: (979) 775-1917
Internet: www.brazoscf.com or www.texasredeye.com

Craig Conlee's family lived in Texas before it was a state. Both his great-grandfather and grandfather were Brazos County sheriffs, and his father was the mayor of Bryan. His grandmother's cooking was famous throughout the county. In fact, she served some of the outlaws sent to prison by her husband.

A love of the land and a passion for good Texas cooking served as the inspiration for Brazos Country Foods, which Craig founded in 1985. Raised with square dances and home style Sunday dinners, Craig and his family always loved great food. Today that love and a hearty dose of true Texan culture can be found in every product the company makes.

Before we take a peek inside the jars of fiery hot salsas and sauces, you have to understand the power behind the whole enchilada. Craig Conlee is a Texas legend himself. His hand-stitched Western boots and ten-gallon hat (complete with a turkey feather in the brim) give an outer appearance that just says "Proud Texan." Craig is a Lone Star legend through and through. He and his wife, Carol, had a uniquely Texas wedding, which was featured in the January 2000 issue of *Insite Brazos Valley* magazine. The event was a reflection of the commitment and love Carol and Craig feel for the Brazos County land.

Let's flash back to 1986. A Neiman Marcus buyer asked Craig to create a Bloody Mary mix different from the rest. The result was a thick, vibrant mix containing jalapeño peppers. It was a huge success, and the company's beverage mixes have grown even hotter with ingredients like habanero peppers and horseradish.

When the late 1980s rolled around, the company rolled out a line of salsas. Since that time Brazos Country Foods has launched a stampede of new products. The Bryan-based company now has a 15,000-square-foot facility and markets a variety of sauces, salsas, and beverage mixes.

The company's Brazos Legends brand is pure Texan. It's no surprise that this line was inspired by Craig's deep Texas roots and strong regard for the land. The label has a rustic appeal that would surely bring a grin to Craig's granddaddies, Sheriffs Jeff and John D. Conlee.

Brazos Legends pours a hearty dose of Texas pride into its salsas, dips, sauces, and beverage mixers. The tasty concoctions boast names as bold as any Texan. Single Shot Salsa is for those who like their salsa mild, yet robust. And for those who want a bigger kick, there is Rawhide Burning Salsa. The name says it all! El Queso Grande and Chuckbox Spicy Cheese Dip have big cheese flavor in every drop.

The Brazos Legend line also features salsas flavored with Indian Corn, Wild Peach, Prickly Pear, and Big Garlic. Be sure to note the "Big" in the Garlic. This wonderful concoction is bursting with chunks of real garlic.

Brazos Legends has sauces that do everything from flavoring your barbecue to marinating your fajitas. Side Saddle Sopping Sauce just begs to be "sopped" over your grilled chicken, ribs, or shrimp. You can toss away the barbecue brush because the folks at Brazos want you to just use a rag and sop it on!

Mercado Mexican Sauce, a gravy-type concoction, is flavored with chili peppers. Serve over enchiladas, tamales, steak, or whatever you'd like. The secret for this sauce comes from an authentic Mexican café.

The Brazos Legends label also adorns hot sauces and chili mixes. Cowboy Cayenne and Habanero Hot Sauce are two pepper sauces sure to make your dishes themselves come alive!

There is so much to choose from in the Brazos Legends line you might just want to order a gift set. Gift packs are made up in Texas style: cardboard box with the bold Brazos Legends label and a window for peeking in at the jars. A variety of gifts are available featuring something for everyone.

Beverage mixes are sold under the company's RED EYE™ label. Originally created for Neiman Marcus, RED EYE mixes are made from 96 percent tomato solids. In other words, think thick! The mixes will spice up more than just beverages. To try them in cooking, simply substitute the same amount of RED EYE into any recipe using tomato paste and water.

Brazos Country Foods has won many awards for their products. Check the website for details.

Where to Buy. Purchase Brazos Country Foods' products at upscale grocers, such as Central Market, Whole Foods, or Rice Epicurean Markets. The RED EYE™ Bloody Mary Mix is more widely available in larger grocery stores.

Bronco Bob's Specialty Foods

151 Regal Row, Suite 118
Dallas, Texas 75247
Phone: (214) 630-9101
Toll-Free: (800) 552-8006
Fax: (215) 630-7360
Internet: www.ladywalton.com

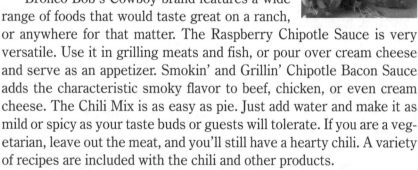

In 1994 Susan Walton (of Lady Walton's cookie fame—see Chapter 1) introduced Bronco Bob's Cowboy brand named for her father. An avid horseman and rancher, Robert's equestrian talent has been passed on through this family of highly ranked polo players. It seemed natural to name the sauce for him.

Bronco Bob's Cowboy brand features a wide range of foods that would taste great on a ranch, or anywhere for that matter. The Raspberry Chipotle Sauce is very versatile. Use it in grilling meats and fish, or pour over cream cheese and serve as an appetizer. Smokin' and Grillin' Chipotle Bacon Sauce adds the characteristic smoky flavor to beef, chicken, or even cream cheese. The Chili Mix is as easy as pie. Just add water and make it as mild or spicy as your taste buds or guests will tolerate. If you are a vegetarian, leave out the meat, and you'll still have a hearty chili. A variety of recipes are included with the chili and other products.

Cowboy Crunch is a snack mix that gives you that satisfying sound when you munch on it. It is a sweet and salty mix of peanuts, spices, pecans, sesame cheddar, and garlic sesame sticks.

Where to Buy. Lasso in some of Bronco Bob's products when you shop at specialty and gourmet stores, including Neiman Marcus. Orders are taken by phone or fax.

★ El Fenix Corporation

P.O. Box 29437
Dallas, Texas 75229
Phone: (972) 241-2171
Toll-Free: (877) 591-1918
Fax: (972) 241-3031
Internet: www.elfenixtexmex.com

On September 15, 1918, Mike Martinez made Texas a hotter place. He is considered the pioneer of Tex-Mex foods, a style of eating that is now bigger than the Lone Star State. The company's motto is "Where the Mexican Food Revolution Started."

The El Fenix founder, Mike Martinez, was born in Old Mexico in 1890. Working for only pennies a week, he drove a string of burros to and from some nearby mines when he was just seven years old. At age fifteen he worked for those mines to support himself and his mother. When she died Mike left his homeland and moved to the United States and ultimately settled in Dallas. There, he eventually took a job washing dishes at the old Oriental Hotel across the street from the now famous Adolphus Hotel in downtown Dallas. Mike had a keen interest in cooking and watched closely as meals were prepared. Later he moved up the ranks to cook's helper, all the while grasping on to whatever knowledge he could obtain about the food business. He learned so much that on that infamous day in 1918 he opened his own restaurant in a Dallas neighborhood then called Little Mexico.

Originally El Fenix served only American specialties while Mike fixed his native foods just for himself. Soon the diners began to ask what he was eating. It smelled great, looked delicious, and they said, "We want what he's having!"

Mike began to serve traditional Mexican food and then created some dishes of his own. He took chili, an old-time Texas favorite, and wrapped it in a tortilla to become an enchilada. Eventually, chips and hot sauce flew onto the tables as fast as customers could crunch them.

As interesting as Mike's background is, you would expect there to be a story behind the restaurant's name, and there is. The name was inspired by the legend of the phoenix, the mythological bird that never died. According to the tale, every five hundred years the phoenix voluntarily flew into a fire and burned to ashes. The bird would emerge with more energy and drive than before. Mike Martinez identified with that story because of his own practice of working hard and not giving up.

His family says he was similar to the phoenix bird because he "seemed to be burning up in his zeal to achieve." Today a colorful bird appears on the company's packaging.

Mike's high standards earned his restaurant a fine reputation, and eventually he had to move to a larger place. All the while, Mike and his wife, Faustina, raised their children in the midst of the busy restaurant business. The boys learned to cook and serve the meals, and Mike, although hesitant, allowed his daughters to work as cashiers, hostesses, and in the business area.

Then World War II hit and the Martinez boys served in the U.S. armed forces. When they returned, Mike retired and gave his children the opportunity to carry forth his dreams. Today El Fenix has sixteen restaurants in the Dallas/Fort Worth area. Susan Martinez, Mike's granddaughter, is the vice president for Advertising and Marketing. She and seven other family members, including her dad who is the president, run the business with the same pride and enthusiasm that Mike had for his work.

When the restaurant staff heard requests that customers wanted to use El Fenix products at home, they entered the packaged foods business. Now their hot sauce, margarita mix, and pralines can be found in grocery stores or ordered directly from the company. Their popular tortilla chips can be special ordered.

The hot sauce is the company's most popular packaged food item. It has been shipped as far away as Hawaii and Alaska and to soldiers all over the world. When one Martinez family member went to college, he couldn't leave his hot sauce on the counter or his roommates would devour it. As you can imagine, the Martinez family is very particular about its sauce. In order for a jar to be put on the shelf, it has to pass the family test of tasting "exceptional."

Pralines are another popular item, and again the family has strict quality control. They are a caramel type praline available in Chewy or Regular. The Regular pralines have a characteristic maple sugar texture.

El Fenix has a festive line of gifts, including t-shirts, caps, a six-pack of hot sauce in a soft cooler, Dip Duo (two jars of hot sauce and a decorative bowl), a margarita mix and glasses (just add tequila), and a Party Pak with hot sauce, margarita mix, and pralines. With eight Martinez family members at the helm of the organization and others holding a variety of posts, you just know the quality is, as they would say, "exceptional."

Where to Buy. El Fenix products are sold at grocery stores such as Kroger, Tom Thumb, Central Market, and others. Order products by the case or select a gift pack by mail, phone, fax, or online.

A Tasty Visit

El Fenix Restaurants
Dallas/Fort Worth Area

If you have a chance to visit any of the El Fenix restaurants, you can have a taste of the Martinez family specialties. There are sixteen locations in the Dallas/Fort Worth area. The restaurants feature authentic Tex-Mex food and interior Mexican specialties. They are renowned for their chips, hot sauce, and margaritas, as well as many other dishes. Stop in on a Wednesday night for the Enchilada Dinner Special.

The El Paso Chile Company

909 Texas Avenue
El Paso, Texas 79901
Phone: (915) 544-3434
Toll-Free: (888) 4-SALSAS
Fax: (915) 544-1552
Internet: www.elpasochile.com

In 1980, when El Paso native Park Kerr moved back home after college, the last thing he wanted was a job that required wearing a business suit. This fun-loving, innovative man was cut out for something beyond a regular desk job. He did, however, need a job.

He returned to his family's El Paso home, unsure of what the future would hold. It was a short jaunt over to New Mexico that actually set off a career spark. There, Park noticed hordes of Texans buying ristras (strands of dried chile peppers). He loaded up his trunk with the decorative strands and headed back to El Paso to set up a stand on the side of the road. His ristras sold out in just a few hours.

Park's mother, Norma Kerr, was thinking about starting a business at the time, and she was impressed with her son's ristra discovery. She and Park set up a booth called the El Paso Chile Company at the 1982 Dallas gift show. Ristras were an instant hit, and the mother and son team captured $2,000 worth of orders in just a day.

Norma and Park became official business partners. Their next pitch was to Neiman Marcus and the Horchow Collection. To their delight, both prestigious retailers featured the ristras on their catalog covers. Business was heating up but there was one glitch: ristras were a seasonal item. What would they do the rest of the year?

They took the next logical step, or rather giant leap, and created a line of fiery food items. Norma gathered up some recipes so that the company could create a symphony of sauces, salsas, and dips. The growth was well orchestrated and met with rapid success among prestigious retailers such as New York's renowned Dean & DeLuca shop.

As salsas swept the nation in popularity, The El Paso Chile Company's growth continued. Today this El Paso company is thriving under the family's leadership. W. Park Kerr is the co-founder and chairman and "Ambassador of Border Cuisine," and Norma is co-founder and "Mother Superior." Park's sister Monica Henschel is the personnel director and heads up the catalog and retail store operations. Her husband, Sean, is president and chief financial officer. With about thirty employees, they call themselves a "big small company."

The group is known for innovation. This is apparent the moment you feast your eyes on a jar of their products. Names like Snakebite Salsa and Chipotle Cha Cha Cha are attention grabbers. Snakebite Salsa is a thick and chunky blend of West Texas jalapeños, New Mexican cilantro and red chile pods, and other fiery flavors ready to explode in your mouth!

While Park is pleased with the creative names the company develops, he makes it clear that it is what's inside the bottle that really counts. He believes that being innovative sometimes means being more authentic. Many items are based on traditional products found in various regions of Mexico or the Southwest.

Park is also adamant that his products emphasize big flavor over heat. Sure, some are spicy, but his first goal is for the flavor to come through without being masked by the heat.

The El Paso Chile Company has numerous products and a few different brand names. They make many salsas, sauces, and dips with a wide variety of flavor blends. Each product has its own flavor profile so it stands out boldly from the others. The El Paso Chile line primarily consists of upscale, artisan salsas. They are made by hand in small kettle batches, using fresh ingredients and no additives. A lot of care, including hand roasting the chiles, is poured into each jar.

Desert Pepper Trading Company is the name for the company's line of salsas, dips, and drink mixes containing fresh, all-natural ingredients produced on a larger scale. Park has recently found inspiration from abroad and has created a new line of Mediterranean and Italian items.

In 1999 Park proudly turned his golden palate toward something silver. Tequila Nacional is a Mexican estate-grown silver tequila especially distilled for margaritas. He calls Nacional "bottled liquid Mexican sunshine." Alive with the flavor of the agave with hints of lime, it is a crisp, bright tequila. The label is also alive, featuring designs based on Socialist posters circa 1940s Mexico.

While innovation and excitement encompass The El Paso Chile Company's products, they have taken innovation to the next level with their unusual gift sets. A favorite is the Burro Piñata, a festive donkey packed with Tostados Tipicos, Salsa Loca, Chipotle Honey Orange BBQ Sauce, Salsa Borracho, Sweet Texas Fire, and Spicy Black Bean Dip.

Products burst with the enthusiasm Park displays toward his work. He and his family are so strict about quality that no product leaves the plant without their approval.

The company has received numerous awards for their fiery sensations, and Park has attained celebrity status. A renowned cookbook author, he is also the food editor at El Paso's ABC affiliate, KVIA-TV. He hosts a brief cooking and food news segment called "Let's Get Cooking," which is a three-time nominee for the James Beard Foundation "Best Local Television Cooking Segment" award. Maybe you have seen him on national television shows such as "Good Morning America," "Live! With Regis and Kathy Lee," "CBS This Morning," "The Home Show," or on the food channel.

Where to Buy. The El Paso Chile Company's products are sold at a variety of retail outlets. The El Paso line is sold in upscale grocery chains and specialty food shops. Desert Pepper Trading Company products are available at most grocery stores and at Sam's. Orders are taken through the company's colorful catalog by mail, phone, fax, or online.

A Tasty Visit 🍽️

The El Paso Chile Company Chile Shop
909 Texas Avenue
El Paso, Texas 79901
Hours: Monday - Friday 10 a.m. - 5 p.m.
Saturday 10 a.m. - 2 p.m.
Closed Sunday

When in El Paso, be sure and visit this shop owned by The El Paso Chile Company. Surround yourself with an array of artisan salsas, sauces, dips, and more. Feast your eyes on the imported Talavera pottery. The shop offers a pleasing selection of unique items.

Fischer & Wieser Specialty Foods

411 S. Lincoln
Fredericksburg, Texas 78624
Toll-Free: (800) 369-9257
Fax: (830) 997-0455
Internet: www.jelly.com

If you have driven through Fredericksburg during the summertime you have seen the colorful peach stands lining the main highways. People come from all over to bite into those fresh, sweet, and succulent Fredericksburg peaches. If you drove through the area back in 1969, you might have stopped at a roadside peach stand owned by Mark Wieser and his family.

THE ORIGINAL ROASTED RASPBERRY CHIPOTLE SAUCE
Handcrafted One Jar at a Time.
Net Wt. 15.75 Oz. (446g)

The Wieser's peach business was a popular one, and eventually the family bought a log cabin situated on a farm. Total cost was one hundred forty dollars, plus ten dollars for some rocks on the property! That location was and still is called Das Peach Haus, which sits on sixty-five acres of beautiful Hill Country land. In Das Peach Haus, Mark's mother made her delicious peach preserves.

In 1979, while still in high school, another Fredericksburg boy named Case Fischer began working for Mark Wieser. Case later studied food and fiber marketing at Texas A&M and ultimately joined Mark (also an Aggie) in the business. Fischer & Wieser Specialty Foods is now a popular company. Mark Wieser is the chairman, and Case Fischer is the CEO. Dr. Ginny Wieser, a niece of Mark's, is the chief operating officer, and other family members play active roles as well.

Fischer & Wieser's first product was—take a guess—peach preserves. The company has ripened faster than peaches in the summer, offering over one hundred products made in their modern 32,000-square-foot production facility. A test kitchen is the hub of experimentation where new products get their start. The owners are inspired by everything from restaurant chefs to everyday consumers and believe that innovation is important...and fun!

Fischer & Wieser's products reflect a deep knowledge of foods and a refinement of flavors. Their most popular item, Roasted Raspberry

Chipotle Sauce, has received rave reviews and top honors. When it was introduced in 1997, consumers were immediately drawn to the distinctive pepper-raspberry combination with its unique sweet and smoky flavor. A versatile sauce, it can be blended with cream cheese and served as an hors d'oeuvres or brushed onto beef tenderloin, pork, or fish.

The FW Gourmet line features a range of distinctive sauces giving any home a gourmet touch. Specialty items include cooking sauces, unique preserves, mustards, salsas, and soups. The line includes products such as Whole Lemon Fig Marmalade, Seville-Orange Cranberry Horseradish Sauce, Sweet Sour and Smokey Mustard Sauce, and Jalapeño Sauce.

Like the sauces, each jar of Fischer & Wieser salsa is filled with quality and a touch of the gourmet. Salsa Verde Ranchera and Salsa a la Charra are a way to add elegant heat to any Mexican dish, or to a crunchy assortment of tortilla chips.

For those who like mustard with a twist—a big twist—there is the Smokey Mesquite Mustard. This blend of mesquite smoked flavor and whole grain mustard seed is a tangy addition to potato salads, pork and beef tenderloin, or even a ham sandwich.

Fischer & Wieser sells a gourmet specialty based on a traditional southern snack. The Old Chisholm Trail Cheese Straws are a bold blend of sharp cheddar and a dash of cayenne. In true Fischer & Wieser style, this gourmet item comes in an assortment of flavors that extend well beyond the original. They are: Garlic & Basil, Jalapeño, Roasted Chipotle & Cheddar, Rootin' Tootin' Chili Pistachio, Peanut Butter, and Lemon Shortbread. Enjoy as a snack or serve as an appetizer. In any case, get ready to eat more than one! The colorful tin makes a rustic, yet elegant, gift presentation.

Speaking of gift giving, Fischer & Wieser offers a number of delightful sets. Like their products, a lot of thought and creativity goes into developing them. Gift sets are available in the FW Gourmet or a Classic line. The latter has a black and white label on an old-fashioned half-pint jar. A three-pack of half-pints is nestled in a straw-filled wooden crate.

Fischer & Wieser's innovative products have received many high honors. Their website has more information on the company's awards.

Where to Buy. Fischer & Wieser products are sold at upscale grocery stores such as Central Market, Rice Epicurean, Whole Foods, and other specialty shops. They can be ordered by phone, fax, mail, or online.

A Tasty Visit

Fischer & Wieser
Fredericksburg, Texas

When in Fredericksburg, stop by Fischer & Wieser's production facility, their Epicurean Shop, or the original Das Peach Haus.

Fischer & Wieser Production Facility & Company Store

The facility and store are two blocks off Main Street in an historic warehouse. Call in advance to schedule a tour. The store is open during regular weekday business hours, 8 a.m.-5 p.m.

Fischer & Wieser Epicurean Shop

This specialty shop is located on Fredericksburg's Main Street. There you will find an array of gourmet products from around the world, including all of the Fischer & Wieser items, and of course, some samples!

Fischer & Wieser Das Peach Haus

See the original location from 1969! This old-fashioned building houses a country store and roadside market. It is open seasonally in the summer and on most weekends year round.

Hell on the Red, Inc.

Rt. 1-Box 8K
Telephone, Texas 75488
Phone: (903) 664-2573
Fax: (903) 664-2301
Internet: http://home.texoma.net/~fcec0704

When a small Fannin County town needed a name, a shop owner's suggestions kept getting rejected. Finally, he submitted "Telephone" because his store had the town's only phone. That name obviously rung some bells because

it was accepted. There is also a Texas town named Telegraph, but that's another story.

Back to Telephone. This town is abuzz with heat because it just happens to be the home of a company called Hell on the Red. The history of this sauce goes back about twenty years, when a group of hunters had a serious discussion about hot sauce. Red Baugh boasted to his buddies that his hot sauce was better than the one they were eating at the time. They challenged him to prove his point. And he did!

Hell on the Red products are so good that customers become hooked after just one taste. Red's daughter, Lisa Hamilton, has boxes of letters from satisfied customers.

Hell on the Red makes salsas (Hot and Mild), Hot & Spicy Cheese Dip, and Chili Fixins. The Mild salsa has bits of onions and peppers and a whole lot of flavor. It has some kick, but you won't fall over. In fact, kids like it too. The salsas, packed in sixteen-ounce jars, are called Party Dips. While they are sure to liven up any gathering, they will also bring to life a dish of eggs or even a burger.

The Hot & Spicy Cheese Dip is queso loaded with hot peppers and tomatoes. A popular item, it has a bold flavor.

The Chili Fixins is a starter for your own chili. You can add meat and nothing else, or let your imagination run wild.

The name, Hell on the Red, was inspired by a few things. First, there is the founder. Red was a childhood nickname—based on hair color. And Telephone is close to the Red River. You can only guess what "Hell" represents. One taste and you'll have this riddle solved. The bold name does get people's attention, and once they try the sauce they brag about it just like Red did with his huntin' pals.

Quality is important to the family, and every ingredient is picked with care and pride. The company's six employees can make around four hundred cases a day, packing each jar by hand. They grind jalapeños, mix in the tomatoes and other ingredients, and heat in a commercial eighty-gallon kettle. Fans of the products extend way beyond the Red River, all the way down to Puerto Rico and up to Alaska.

Where to Buy. Look for Hell on the Red Party Dips and other products at most major grocery stores in Texas, as well as Wal-Mart. Order by fax, phone, or mail or print out the online ordering form.

Hudson's on the Bend

3509 RR 620 North
Austin, Texas 78734
Phone: (512) 266-1462
Toll-Free: (800) 996-7655
Fax: (512) 266-3518
Internet: www.cookingfearlessly.com or www.hudsonsonthebend.com

Jeff Blank takes Texas food and transforms it into haute cuisine. He can make anything—including rattlesnake—suitable for the gourmet palate. It has even been said, by Dan Rather no less, that Jeff and his wife, Shanny Lott, could make a horseshoe taste good. I think you get the picture.

Jeff Blank is the owner of Hudson's on the Bend restaurant on the edge of Austin near Lake Travis. The renowned restaurant is known for its quality ingredients, remarkable cuisine, and rustic, yet elegant, limestone ranch setting. The menu features a wide range of items that bring bold flavor to even bolder combinations. A Hudson's on the Bend meal is a passionate dining experience.

In the mid-1990s, after many customer requests, Hudson's on the Bend began selling a line of gourmet sauces and dips. This is a boutique sauce line, using only the best ingredients made in small quantities. Jeff hand packs each jar at the restaurant.

Take a look at some of these extraordinary items. As they say, "Eat dessert first," so we will start with a glimpse of Hudson's one and only dessert sauce. Bourbon Vanilla Praline Sauce has pure butter, Texas pecans, brown sugar, vanilla, some flavorings, and spices. The restaurant serves it warm over cheesecake. It is heavenly when drizzled on a bowl of vanilla ice cream or a dish of homemade apple pie. This rich and wonderful sauce can be heated, but the label warns that if you overheat you will have "bourbon-vanilla pralines." And is that a problem?

Now that we've finished dessert, we will move on to the Mexican Marigold Mint Honey Mustard. I told you this group is known for their extraordinary combinations! It turns out that Mexican Marigold Mint is a substitute for tarragon, which does not grow well in Texas. The herbs placed into this and other sauces are fresh from the restaurant's garden.

Another unique item is Champagne Herb Vinegar, which contains restaurant-grown begonias and herbs like basil, pink peppercorn, and a fresh hot pepper.

Apple Cider Brandy complements pork, chicken, lamb, or turkey and game birds. Chipotle BBQ Sauce brings new life to barbecue with the smoky addition of chipotle peppers. Orange Ginger BBQ Sauce adds tang to grilled foods. The owners have a delightful recipe using this sauce in baby back ribs. Strawberry/Raspberry Sauce can be served with pheasant, chicken, turkey, or even pork loins. Tomatillo White Chocolate Sauce is a versatile blend that can be used on everything from eggs to enchiladas. Or chill it and serve with tortilla chips. Even though it contains Belgian white chocolate, it is not considered a sweet sauce, but is more like a molé. Also choose from Guava Sour Cherry or Mango Jalapeño.

The Hudson's Mixed Gift pack is an epicurean extravaganza featuring these sauces resting in a decorative wooden crate: Tomatillo Chile Chocolate, Mango Jalapeño, Mexican Marigold Mint Mustard, and Bourbon Vanilla Praline. The BBQ Gift Crate is a collection of Chipotle and Orange Ginger BBQ sauces also packed in a wooden crate.

These sauces are sure to bring out the supernatural cooking powers within every person who opens a jar. The tasty concoctions are just waiting to be stirred, drizzled, spooned, or slathered onto many home cooked items. You can find more unique cooking ideas in *Cooking Fearlessly* by Jeff Blank and Jay Moore, with Deborah Harter. This colorful cookbook is as beautiful as it is inspiring. Glorious photography by Laurie Smith does a great job of showing off the enticing recipes. Hudson's sauces are featured in a number of recipes, such as Coca-Cola® Baby Back Ribs and Bourbon Vanilla Praline Sweet Potatoes. Even if you do not want to try the recipes—and I can't imagine that—this book is a treasure for any collection. Shanny Lott's chef paintings are featured throughout, adding even more style and a touch of whimsy.

One of my mother's favorite phrases was, "Never say never." This saying is also featured in the book. It is clear to me that when the folks at Hudson's on the Bend are developing new concoctions, they never say never.

Where to Buy. Hudson's on the Bend sauces are available at Central Market, some HEB and Randalls stores, Breed & Company in Austin, and other specialty or gourmet shops. You can order them by mail, phone, fax, or on the Internet.

A Tasty Visit

Hudson's on the Bend Restaurant
3509 Ranch Road 620
Austin, Texas 78734
Reservations: (512) 266-1369
Open for dinner only, seven days a week.

If you want a unique and elegant dining experience in Austin, visit Hudson's on the Bend restaurant. Specialties include wild game, pheasant, rabbit, fish (wonderful fish), rattlesnake cakes (instead of crab cakes), vegetarian items, and more. This is a popular spot, so plan ahead and book a reservation.

Jardine Foods

#1 Chisholm Trail
Buda, Texas 78601
Phone: (512) 295-4600
Toll-Free: (800) 544-1880
Fax: (512) 295-3020
Internet: www.jardinefoods.com

Back in 1979 the Jardine family used their old ranch recipes and began selling salsas, chili mixes, barbecue sauces, hot sauces, seasonings, and much more. Their products caught on and became popular in and out of the Lone Star State. The company was sold to new owners in 1998, but the old ranch recipes live on, and hot new items are wrangled up all the time.

The company owners love to try out new recipes. As a result, the Jardine label has over one hundred products. They also make a few hundred other items for other companies. In other words, that ranch kitchen is doin' some serious cookin'.

And a ranch kitchen it is. The production facility is located on a thirty-acre ranch in Buda, which is south of Austin. Longhorn cattle and other wildlife roam the grounds.

The products have a characteristically fresh flavor because they are made in small batches by many of the same cooks who have worked there for years. Jardine products are preservative-free, and tight quality control assures that those ranch recipes are followed.

Chief operating officer John Trube says the company enjoys innovation, basing many new ideas on some old ranch favorites. A few of their new items include an artichoke dip and a parmesan pesto salad dressing. Employees are encouraged to bring in their ideas, and new recipes are tested in small batches.

Some of the most popular items include Peach Salsa, Salsa Bobos, Raspberry Chardonnay Salsa, Queso Loco, and Texas Champagne (hot sauce). Peach Salsa combines the sweetness of a sun-ripened peach with the heat of a jalapeño. Salsa Bobos is a flavorful blend of black beans, corn, bell pepper, spices, and just a touch of jalapeño. Queso Loco, which is medium in heat (try Queso Caliente if you like it hotter), is a versatile item that can be eaten straight from the jar or warmed up and drizzled over everything from tortilla chips to a baked potato. Wake up your taste buds by using it in macaroni and cheese. Texas Champagne is a pepper seasoning that can be added to soups, cocktails, eggs, seafood...the list goes on. Whether you like your sauces mild, medium, or triple hot, Jardine has a product for you!

Their gift packages are fun and creative, and the Jardine folks are constantly coming up with new gift ideas. Their boxes travel well and are sure to please any former or future Texans up north. Here is a quick look at some of the sets.

The Bar-B-Q Sauce Sampler 4-Pack has four popular barbecue sauces including 5-Star, Killer Hot, Mesquite, and Chik'n Lik'n. The sauces are packed in an attractive, rustic cardboard box.

Blazin' Saddle Pepper Sauce Sampler is for serious spice lovers. It contains a three-pack of Habanero XXX Hot Pepper Sauce, Spicy Wooster Sauce, and Texapeppa Jalapeño Pepper Hot Sauce. This is truly a gift with a Texas kick!

The Round-Up Cowboy Collection will inspire a number of ranch style meals. It contains Chili Fixins, Steak Seasoning, Texas Champagne Hot Pepper Sauce, 5-Star BBQ Sauce, Queso Loco Cheese Dip,

Bronco Jalapeño Mustard, Salsa Bobos, and Texas Caviar Jalapeño Stuffed Olives.

There are many more gift items available in a variety of sizes and prices. Whether you want to send a small thank-you gift or welcome a new neighbor in a big Texas way, you are sure to find a Jardine gift pack that does the job.

Where to Buy. Look for Jardine products at higher end grocery stores, Central Market, Whole Foods, airport stores (for those last min-ute gifts), Guitars & Cadillacs, and other specialty shops. Jardine accepts orders by phone, fax, mail, or online.

A Tasty Visit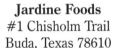

Jardine Foods
#1 Chisholm Trail
Buda, Texas 78610

Visit the thirty-acre ranch site where Jardine products are made. Walk the grounds and admire the longhorn cattle, donkeys, and ponies. The production facility has a window so you can watch products as they are prepared. A General Store sells Jardine items at factory direct prices offering deep discounts. Buy a few products and enjoy lunch on the ranch's picnic grounds. Or try your luck in the horseshoe pit. A Salsa Bar (salsa, as in food) is located in the old stone ranch house. Enjoy salsa and shop for souvenirs in this rustic setting.

Poteet Strawberry Festival

Poteet, the "Strawberry Capital of Texas," is the place to be for this gigantic fest in April. Children's activities, music, dancing, and a wide assortment of food and wine booths add to the fun.

Jimmy O's Texas Marinades

P.O. Box 4233
Bergheim, Texas 78004
Phone: (830) 336-2708
Toll-Free: (888) 282-2216
Fax: (830) 336-3773
Internet: www.jimmyos.com

What happens when you take a cattle rancher, add in a college degree and a few decades of restaurant experience, and let him loose in the kitchen? You get marinades so robust that you may have to lasso yourself a few cases of them.

Jimmy O's marinades take great cuts of meat, fish, and chicken to new levels of taste. And they do it in award-winning style, with a variety of flavors to please any Texas palate. It all started in 1991 when Jimmy O'Brien returned to Bergheim, Texas, with a big dose of restaurant expertise and a hearty knack for cooking. A cattle rancher, Jimmy knows that the best cuts of meat deserve only top rated marinades. He originally came up with a marinade for jerky and now offers a complete line of marinades, sauces, and spicy rubs.

The original product, Texas Mesquite, works well as a marinade for jerky or just about anything else. A twelve-ounce bottle is all you need to make fifteen pounds of beef, turkey, or venison into a tasty jerky.

The Tangy Teriyaki flavor peps up your palate with ginger, garlic, horseradish, and sweet onions carefully mixed with soy sauce, red wine, and just a splash of balsamic vinegar. This bold blend (remember, it does contain horseradish!) can be used as a marinade or a table condiment in place of steak sauce or barbecue sauce.

Peach & Pepper marinade brings together ripe Texas Hill Country peaches, roasted bell peppers, and a slew of fresh herbs and spices. The result is a versatile marinade ideal for all meats and vegetables. Mix it with cream cheese and add zip to any cracker or vegetable.

Peach Habanero Sauce is a fiery blend of the Peach & Pepper Sauce and the hottest of peppers, the infamous habanero. Pour it on next time you want to add some real kick to barbecue, burgers, tacos, and even shrimp.

Garlic Pesto marinade combines fresh herbs and spices, like garlic, basil, parsley, and peppermint with lime juice, white wine, balsamic vinegar, and olive oil. This pleasant combination can be poured over vegetables and salads, adding only about half the calories of butter, margarine, or salad dressings.

Jimmy O's line is completed with Texas Spicy Rub and Texas Roasting & Rotisserie Blend, which are sure to shake up your kitchen.

The marinades and rubs have won numerous honors, including twenty-six national awards. And Jimmy puts his restaurant background to work, offering a range of recipes and serving suggestions. While his marinades are high in flavor, they are free of fat and contain no MSG or preservatives.

Where to Buy. Look for Jimmy O's award-winning products at HEB, Whole Foods, and Sun Harvest. You can also order individual bottles or cases by mail, phone, or fax. The website has online ordering details.

Mother Teresa's Fine Food, Inc.

5010 Highway 288B
Clute, Texas 77531
Phone: (979) 265-7429
Toll-Free: (888) 265-7429
Fax: (979) 297-0932
Internet: www.italianfoodmot-teresas.com

When Teresa Polimeno married and moved to Houston over forty years ago, she brought along an authentic taste of Italy.

Teresa grew up in San Vito, a town located in the Calabria region of southern Italy. She fondly remembers the sweet aromas that filled the family's modest home. Her parents, two sets of  grandparents, and nine brothers and sisters lived under one roof.

Everyone did their part in the kitchen and on the grounds, harvesting tomatoes and other vegetables so that the family could enjoy canned vegetables and relishes year round. In authentic Italian style, the meals were made entirely from scratch. The family had their own recipes for everything from sauce to pasta to homemade wine. Sunday was the exception. Only on that day of the week would Teresa's mother purchase pasta.

The family's modest two-story home had no central heat and was warmed by the fireplace on each floor. Her mother cooked sauces and rich espresso on a small butane stove. The family staple was homemade pasta, made from fresh eggs and hand ground flour. Bread was baked in a dome oven big enough to hold a dozen loaves. Robust tomato sauces brimming with fresh herbs and spices simmered in large pots while fragrant homemade bread baked in the oven and fresh pasta dried on racks. Imagine the aromas!

Love was the only power strong enough to take Teresa from her home across the ocean. Although her husband was from a nearby Italian town, he found a job in Houston so Teresa left her idyllic home and embarked on a new adventure. After her arrival in Houston, she worked in the kitchen of a daycare, where the small children called her "Mama T," or "Mother Teresa." She loved the chance to give them a cookie and bring a smile to their young faces.

In the late 1980s Teresa opened her own restaurant and served authentic Italian cuisine. Her fresh tomato sauces and dressings left customers pleading for the chance to buy jars for their homes. A family member convinced Teresa to take her sauces to a food show, where they were an instant success.

Today Teresa's products are as authentically Italian as she is. They are prepared in a commercial kitchen near Houston but taste like they could have come from her childhood home in San Vito. Although Teresa has spent over four decades in this country, her accent is as thick as her marinara. She speaks with pride as she explains that her sauces contain only ingredients she could grow in a garden. You won't find any preservatives or artificial flavorings in Mother Teresa's products. This is Italian cooking in the purest form, with top quality olive oil and a low salt content (a serving of pasta sauce has only twenty milligrams of sodium).

The Marinara Sauce is bursting with large tomato chunks, mush-rooms, and fresh herbs. Pour it over pasta, pop in an Italian opera CD, and you might think you are in Italy, or at least in the home of an authentic Italian cook.

While Marinara Sauce is Mother Teresa's most popular item, there are a host of other products as well, including Pasta Sauce (regular or extra spicy), Italian and Balsamic dressings, and other specialties. Mediterranean Caponata is a flavorful blend of eggplant, celery, garden vegetables, marinara sauce, Italian dressing, and spices. It is delightful on salads, antipasti, and hors d'oeuvres. Mediterranean Mushrooms is a mixture of mushrooms bathed in Italian dressing and a fragrant blend of pepper, garlic, herbs, and spices. Mediterranean Garlic is soaked in wine vinegar and a blend of spices. Mediterranean Giardinera is a gar-den in a jar. Mushrooms, cauliflower, bell peppers, and other vegetables are steeped in Mother Teresa's Italian Dressing.

The product labels have a picture of the Italian hillside in Mother Teresa's hometown, along with a vintage photograph of Teresa herself. Each label clearly states "Original Family Recipe."

Where to Buy. Look for Mother Teresa's authentic Italian items at Central Market, some HEB stores, Kroger, food shows around the state, and garden shows (such as the one at Moody Gardens). Orders are taken by mail, phone, fax, or you can visit the website for ordering instructions. There, you will also find a host of specialty gift baskets and crates.

New Canaan Farms, Inc.

P.O. Box 386
Dripping Springs, Texas 78620
Phone: (512) 858-7669
Toll-Free: (800) 727-5267
Fax: (512) 858-7513
Internet: www.newcanaanfarms.com

New Canaan Farms began back in 1979 the way many food companies do. The Tingle family gave jellies to friends around Christmas. One year they decided to set up a booth (actually a card table) at Wimberley Market Days. Their jellies and jams promptly sold out. More craft and food shows followed, and their products sold like a peach. They put all profits into a healthy chunk of land, which they called New Canaan.

Today New Canaan Farms is owned by Cindy Figer and her husband, who knew the original owners. The company has grown, and now the 6,000-square-foot production facility sits on ten acres located seven miles west of Dripping Springs.

Cindy is a natural at running the business. Her husband is a CPA, and she has an accounting background and degree. When New Canaan was owned by the Tingles, Cindy helped with the business. She answered phones and did consulting, spending more and more hours there. When the owners decided to sell in 1997, it was natural for Cindy and her husband to purchase it. Now she spends her days actively involved in New Canaan Farms, and she is thrilled with her new career.

The company has expanded its product line to include a variety of jellies, salsas, sauces, and dips. A favorite jelly is Jalapeño, which is beautiful and festive in appearance and has a delightful flavor. It can be blended with cream cheese, melted in a crock-pot and served with sausage or chicken, or slathered on grilled meats.

The Peach Amaretto & Pecan Jam has all the goodness of a sunny Texas day packed in a bottle. Spread it on toast or use as a glaze for chicken. For a scrumptious dessert, warm it in the microwave and spoon over a bowl of Blue Bell Homemade Vanilla Ice Cream.

When it comes to New Canaan Farm's salsas, it is no surprise that Peach Salsa tops the list of requested items. The peaches are grown in nearby Fredericksburg, a town where people come *just for the peaches!* Speaking of fresh fruit, New Canaan Farms is picky about produce. They buy blueberries grown in East Texas and blackberries from a few Texas locales including Wimberley, East Texas, and the Brazos River region.

New Canaan makes a line of sauces including Shrimp Sauce, Raspberry Chipotle, and Jalapeño Mustard. This spicy mustard is a joyous blend of sweet and heat. It livens up any sandwich, especially ham, turkey, and even hot dogs. It also adds zest to deviled eggs.

A variety of dry dips round out the company's offerings and include Garlic-Onion, Spinach, and Jalapeño. Mix with sour cream and mayonnaise or add to a basic bread mix to make herb breads. Blend with oil and vinegar and serve over pasta. Or stir into your mashed potatoes for extra gusto. The dips also work well in burgers and meatloaf or anything that needs a flavor boost.

If you want to give a gift that says "Texas," New Canaan Farms is a good place to check. The jars are labeled with beautiful color photography featuring Texas scenes such as landscapes, hillsides, and bluebonnets next to a black-and-white photo of a child dressed in cowboy get-up. Charming is the only way to describe this unique blend of color and black-and-white photography. Proudly shown on the Jalapeño Jelly label is the owners' son Andrew, dressed in his cowboy hat and grinning ear to ear. The photo was taken when Andrew was about four years old. Today he is a bright and good-natured college student.

When you give a New Canaan product as a gift, you are sure to please friends and family. If you would like to give more than a jar, a number of gift baskets are available. The baskets are custom made and contain Lone Star favorites such as Jalapeño Jelly and salsas.

Where to Buy. Find New Canaan Farms items at upscale grocery stores such as Central Market and Whole Foods, as well as other specialty shops. They are sold at Canton First Monday, the Dallas World Trade Center, and gourmet food shows. Order by mail, phone, fax, or the Internet.

A Tasty Visit

New Canaan Farms
Hours: Monday - Saturday, 10 a.m. - 5 p.m.
(Open Sundays between Thanksgiving and Christmas)

Drive out Highway 290, seven miles west of Dripping Springs and visit the factory's gift shop. Munch on samples and quench your thirst with complimentary coffee or fresh squeezed lemonade. There are always chips and crackers set out and waiting for you to spread on some jelly or salsa. Enjoy the gourmet treats and buy some wonderful and unique gifts.

The Original Habanero Company

P.O. Box 700010
San Antonio, Texas 78270
Phone: (210) 651-HEAT (4328)
Toll-Free: (800) 946-9401
Fax: (210) 651-4378
Internet: www.HabaneroCo.com

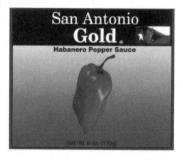

It all started with an overzealous crop of habaneros. Jean Vanderhider and her friend Jay Davis knew how to grow these hot peppers. In fact, they harvested so many they tried to give them away until a friend suggested they make something out of them.

Jean and Jay took the challenge. Every Friday night for a year-and-a-half, the two heated up Jay's kitchen with fiery concoctions. The pot was so big that Jean had to stand on stacks of phone books so she could see inside. Three blenders and food processors later, Jean, Jay, and their friends agreed they had made gold.

San Antonio Gold, a carrot-based hot sauce was the first fiery product to pass the test and hit the market. This sunny and mild blend of carrots and habaneros is a versatile hot sauce ready to add a hint of fire to a variety of foods.

Friends loved San Antonio Gold but challenged Jean and Jay to make something hotter. The pair headed back to the kitchen, and Texas Heat Wave was the next item to blow into the markets. Texas Heat Wave is a hotter version of San Antonio Gold. Both products contain no preservatives, MSG, salt, or fat. You can have your fire (hot or mild) and eat it guilt-free! People who love peppers but find tomato products irritating have found their pot of gold in these unique items.

Both the mild version (San Antonio Gold) and the hot (Texas Heat Wave) are versatile sauces that go well with a variety of foods. Creating a balanced flavor that breaks through the heat was important for the two culinary creators. Add to soups and stews for a touch of spice. Use as a marinade for shrimp, fish, or chicken before placing on the grill.

Blend with butter and sauté for a sizzling steak sauce. Mix with mayonnaise for a succulent sandwich spread. The possibilities are endless. These are the types of sauces that will do more than just sit on the refrigerator shelf. They are destined to become household staples.

The product line now has expanded to ten bold items. Texas Snake Bite is a premium steak sauce that tastes great on smoked turkey or any other meat. Texas Six Shooter Salsa, available in Mild, Medium, or Hot, is a blend of flavors mixed with the company's signature habaneros. Like their other products, it is all natural, with no preservatives or MSG. Texas Stampede is a barbecue sauce thick enough to stay put when you slather it on meats during grilling or at the table.

If you like olives, try Texas Single Shot, habanero stuffed olives. Use as a fiery appetizer, in cooking, or in a genuine Texas Martini!

The company makes a line of jellies under the Jean's Pepper Garden label. Natural ingredients and no food colorings or dyes make these products stand out. Use in cooking or spread on toast. Mix with barbecue sauce for a delightful chicken glaze. Or add a new twist to sweet and sour meatballs.

One dry seasoning rounds out the line of innovative products. West Texas DUST, available in Regular or Salt Free, is an ideal way to spice up everything from potatoes to popcorn. Top off with a cold beverage and if you are not a Texan, you may start to feel like one.

These days The Original Habanero Company's products are made in a commercial kitchen in San Antonio. Jean no longer has to stand on phone books, but she and Jay are committed to packing their boldly flavored products with all natural ingredients. When they do food demonstrations, customers are often surprised that their products do not contain MSG.

Where to Buy. Look for some Texas heat in a variety of grocery stores including HEB, Whole Foods, Sun Harvest, and specialty gift shops. They are also sold at military bases. Order by mail, phone, fax, or the Internet.

Renfro Foods, Inc.

P.O. Box 321
Fort Worth, Texas 76101-0321
Phone: (817) 336-9961
Fax: (817) 336-7910
Internet: www.renfrofoods.com

In 1940 Fort Worth resident George Renfro lost his job after an appendicitis attack. Needing an income, he started a one-truck food distributorship. In 1948 George expanded to the manufacturing side of the food business and bought a syrup company. He made the syrup and delivered it through his own distributing company. In 1951 he bought another company and bottled his wife's original Chow Chow, a popular southern relish. The concoction is a flavoring for beans and can also be used on hot dogs, burgers, and in potato salads. More than fifty years later, Renfro is still making their Chow Chow under Mrs. Renfro's label, named for the founder's wife.

George Renfro continued his business through the 1960s and expanded in 1971 when he purchased a small hot sauce manufacturing company. He started out making taco sauce and later developed a selection of picante sauces. Today Mrs. Renfro's has a complete line of salsas including Green Salsa, Habanero, Peach, Chipotle, and Black Bean. The Green Salsa made a cameo appearance in the Robert Rodriguez film *Spy Kids.*

Currently, second and third generation Renfros are active in this family-owned business. All but one company officer is a Renfro. A staff of twenty-five people works at the Fort Worth organization where its products are still made. Bill Renfro, who is the son of the founder, takes pride in the company's achievements.

Three of the most popular products are its Nacho-sized Jalapeños, Habanero Salsa, and Green Salsa. The family and employees are proud of the company's consistently tasty products. They use only top quality ingredients and strive to maintain the quality standards set by the founders. After all, they have the Renfro name on their jars!

Where to Buy. Look for Mrs. Renfro's jars in most Texas supermarkets. They also sell Chow Chow in other southern states under the Dixieland label. Some mail and Internet orders are taken, and gift sets are available.

Riba Foods, Inc.

3735 Arc
Houston, Texas 77063
Phone: (713) 975-7001
Toll-Free: (800) 327-7422
Fax: (713) 975-7036
Internet: www.ribafoods.com

Start with the freshest tomatoes and peppers, and roast and grill them to bring out the natural flavors. That's how salsas are made in the traditional Mexican method. Actually, that's Arriba!®

And that's what Riba Foods calls its products. Riba Foods set up shop in 1988  and pioneered the fire-roasting process used in large commercial kitchens. Riba roasts and grills fresh tomatoes and peppers to smoky perfection. This age-old process brings out the natural flavor, resulting in a salsa or sauce exploding with robust flavor and chunky texture.

The Arriba! line is as big as it is bold. Choose from a variety of red and green salsas, dips, exotic pepper sauces, and Bloody Mary mixes. The fire-roasted salsas are packed with tomatoes and peppers in a flavorful blend of spices. The process keeps the tomatoes plump so the salsas have both body and smoked flavor.

Salsas are available in red and green varieties. Choose Fire-Roasted Mexican Red Salsa in Mild, Medium, Hot, or Chipotle. The bold red color and chunky texture make these salsas ideal for munching with crisp tortillas. The thick texture means more salsa stays on your chip, making each bite a texture and flavor sensation. The salsas add gusto to eggs, tacos, enchiladas, and even a good old-fashioned juicy American burger. A hot product in terms of popularity is Chipotle Salsa, which has the characteristic flavor of smoked jalapeño peppers.

Fire-Roasted Mexican Green Salsa comes in Mild, Medium, or Hot. The tomatillo is featured in this tasty blend. This fruit adds a tart flavor and an even thicker texture to the salsa.

The Chile Con Queso and Bean Dips are other Arriba! favorites. Queso, available in both Mild and Hot, has a rich cheddar cheese flavor blended with fresh tomatoes and jalapeño peppers. Bean dips are cooked slowly with fresh vegetables and mixed with the fire-roasted salsas for a unique and complex flavor.

Exotic is the appropriate word for the company's pepper sauces. The Riba Foods' chefs looked south of Mexico to create combinations using exotic fruits and peppers from Central and South America. Flavors include: Mango Pepper, Pineapple Pepper, Chipotle Pepper, Garlic Pepper, and Verde Pepper, which contains roasted manzana peppers and tomatillos. These unusual pepper sauces are a bold complement to soups, stews, fish, poultry, hors d'oeuvres, and vegetables.

Bloody Mary mixes come in two thick and rich flavors bursting with fire-roasted goodness with or without the vodka. Fire-Roasted Blood Mary mix contains the Arriba! Medium Red Salsa, while the Chipotle Blood Mary mix blends the smoky chipotles with Arriba! Medium-Hot Chipotle Salsa. Slice up a few crisp celery sticks and enjoy the aroma as you stir the thick and zesty mixes.

Pride runs thick at Arriba!, and when company executives like John Wall describe the texture and taste of their products, you just have to run to the nearest grocery store and try some! There is reason to be proud. The products are full of body and flavor and contain all natural ingredients. They have received a number of awards and honors.

The Norteña Arriba!® line features traditional regional Mexican products made with a variety of chiles such as juanita, habanero, and guajillo. The peppers are blended with other fine ingredients into salsas, enchilada sauces, and cheese dips. The distinct spicy flavor blends well with many home-cooked foods. Try something different and pour Norteña Arriba! sauce on your roast at the start of cooking for a meat dish that bursts with flavor.

If you are a serious "chile head," you will love the Norteña Arriba! Habanero Heat Salsa. The label warns that the item is "for the brave." Habaneros appear in the top three ingredients, a sure sign that the heat inside is the real thing. The salsa is blended with spices to bring out the fruity habanero flavor.

And now for something almost completely different, Riba Foods also owns the Texas Pepper Works. In other words, they have been packing pickles and peppers in blends that just might create an inner mouth explosion. Candy Krisp Pickles are sliced sour pickles blended with spicy marinades sweetened with sugar. Bite into one and you will put your taste buds to work. The label proudly proclaims, "Not too sweet, not too sour." Rather, it's a pleasing blend of both.

Candy Krisp Jalapeños are pepper rings bathing in a blend of sweetness and heat. Mix with cheddar and other ingredients for a tasty cheese ball. The label features an adorable snake and proclaims, "Nice bite. Not too hot, not too sweet."

Where to Buy. The Arriba!® line of salsas, sauces, dips, and Bloody Mary mixes is available at all major grocery chains in Texas. Norteña Arriba!® products can be found at a number of HEB stores. Orders are taken by mail, phone, fax, and the Internet.

Sanderson Specialty Food Company

305 North High
San Saba, Texas 76877
Toll-Free: (800) 443-1355
Fax: (512) 394-0478
Internet: www.texasfoodsdirect.com

Sanderson Specialty Food Company's history is a heartwarming story of family togetherness, respect, and ultimately success. Eddie Sanderson's background in foods and agriculture extends all the way back to his childhood. He turned his love for the land into an agriculture degree, running a pecan business with his wife Brunhilde and sons Sean and Brian. Family has always been the core of the Sandersons' life, and they hold a strong mutual respect for one another. Hearing about this

family-run business is as refreshing as a cold glass of tea on a hot summer day.

It is no surprise that it was Eddie's family who gave him some tasty ideas in the early 1990s. While Eddie was thinking of branching out from the pecan business, it was sons Sean and Brian who led him to where he is today.

Both college graduates spoke enthusiastically about the salsa business and suggested their dad apply his agricultural background to this growing industry. After all, they told him, salsas are a mix of three important agricultural products: tomatoes, onions, and peppers. And they convinced him that making salsas would be just plain fun. Salsas are a party food, so wouldn't it be great to create a robust blend that would make people enjoy their events even more?

Eddie researched the world of salsas, and believe me, that is a big world to study! He read about salsas, blended salsas, and finally made the decision to take the big salsa step. After developing the recipe (you have to understand that Eddie Sanderson is a perfectionist so the recipe had to be just right), Eddie thought he was ready to market it. But the next step was a board meeting. The Sanderson family gathered around the kitchen table, eating salsa of course, and decided to go for it.

Eddie's eye and palate for perfection was on target, and his salsas instantly received rave reviews. He proudly recalls seeing them displayed on the grocery shelves for the very first time. It was probably similar to watching your child perform on stage or on the ball field. Brings tears to the eyes.

Speaking of being teary eyed, the Sanderson Texas-Texas brand salsas are available in heat levels for everyone: Mild, Medium, and Hot. These three products were the company's mainstay for over two years. Then Eddie took his wife Brunhilde on a visit to Germany, which is her birthplace. Always the researcher, Eddie noticed that the German markets were filled with a variety of sauces designed to flavor meats. This sparked an idea.

Eddie's inspiration and determination came together to create a sensational new product. Texas-Texas Chipotle Steak Sauce took a year to perfect. Brunhilde watched Eddie blend jar after jar of the concoction. Finally he thought he had created the perfect sauce. Again it was time for a kitchen table board meeting, this time featuring Chipotle Steak Sauce. It was an instant hit with his family and later with consumers. This fabulous product has caught on in a serious way and is served on steaks, chicken, pork, and fish. Try it on a baked potato instead of butter. And be sure to put it on eggs. The versatile sauce has a delicate smoky flavor that enhances a wide range of foods. It appeals to a wide range of palates, and kids love it too.

Eddie is having as much fun in the salsa business as his sons said he would. He has taken the plunge into more exotic salsa blends like Mango Almond and Peach Pecan. Like the other Texas-Texas products, these salsas have fresh ingredients such as native Texas pecans from the family's pecan business. The Sandersons are a health-conscious family, and they use apple cider vinegar in their salsas.

Eddie's agriculture background comes into play when each bottle of salsa is commercially prepared. He is aware that one crop of tomatoes or peppers may vary from the next. Every batch is tested and tasted so that it is as consistently delicious as the batches before and after it. He is also knowledgeable about the chemistry behind food preparation and the need for stringent quality control. Eddie personally checks all products before they leave for the grocery shelves.

Sanderson Specialty Foods has introduced a line of items sold exclusively on the company's website. The Texas Legends products consist of red salsas (Mild, Medium, and Hot), fruit salsas, and a steak sauce. The line brings to life a fascinating tale about the lost San Saba Silver Mine. The website is a treasure in itself, featuring the entire legend told by a ninety-plus-year-old San Saba native who spent time looking for the lost mine.

From his kitchen board meetings to popular salsas and that incredible Chipotle Steak Sauce, Eddie Sanderson is guided by personal integrity and strong family bonds. To gain a true sense of what family means to the Sandersons, read the poem Eddie wrote in the 1970s:

Our Family
by Eddie Sanderson

We cry when things are sad,
We laugh when things are funny,
We play together and call Mother, Mommie.

We share our values with each other,
We find happiness in being together,

We like to touch and share emotions with our brother.

We experience joy with the simple things of nature,
We believe in maintaining high moral stature,
We like to dream and practice the philosophy of our faith.

We believe and trust in God Almighty,
We express and distribute our love evenly,
We act respectfully and enjoy being a family.

The family shares pride in their achievements, which include many awards for their quality products. The Texas-Texas labels boldly state "Premium Salsa," an appropriate title for products from this premium Texas family.

Where to Buy. Look for Texas-Texas products at Albertsons, Central Market, HEB, Randalls, Wheatsville, Wal-Mart, and Whole Foods as well as other fine food stores. Sanderson's products are also available by mail, phone, fax, or Internet orders. A variety of gift sets are featured on the company's website.

Sgt. Pepper's Hot Sauce

P.O. Box 49565
Austin, Texas 78765
Phone: (512) 280-2727

When J.P. Hayes entered a hot sauce contest in 1991, he may not have realized he was entering more than a contest. He was entering the world of commercially made food items. His combination of hot sauce and habaneros created an instant sensation.

Today Sgt. Pepper's makes a wide range of products including seven sauces, seven pestos, and six spices. A line of spice rubs is sold under the Ancho Mama and Chipotle Del Sol labels.

The original blend, Tejas Tears, continues to be very warmly received. In three words: "It is hot!" One hot sauce collector ranked it as the eighth hottest he had ever tasted. But J.P. is careful not to cover up the taste with heat. He brews first for flavor, and second for heat. The sauce adds kick to foods like tacos, burgers, Italian dressing, chicken (as a marinade), or Yucatan-style Mexican items like pork and shrimp.

Chipotle Del Sol Smokin' Hot Sauce carries a medium level of heat. The chipotle has an inherently smoky flavor, and the heat slowly creeps up after taking the first bite. For that reason, J.P. calls it the "sneaky hot sauce." A key ingredient is balsamic vinegar, which adds a sweet flavor without the use of sugar. The sauce can be brushed on anything you put on the grill. Try it on chicken or pork tenderloin, or use as a marinade. The Chipotle Grilling Glaze is similar to the hot sauce, but it is more of a finishing sauce to be added toward the end of the grilling time. Because it is a glaze it contains more sugar than the hot sauce.

Tropical Tears adds an island flavor through the use of fresh mango and ginger.

A chile connoisseur, chef, and food stylist, this Austin entrepreneur knows his peppers. He blends the sauces himself, using ancho (mild), chipotle (medium), and habanero (hot) peppers. The sauces are brewed in small batches and hand packed. J.P. seeks out chiles that emphasize flavor rather than mask it. He is continually experimenting with ideas and introducing new products.

J.P. has taught the art of chile cooking at the renowned Central Market Cooking School. His recipes have been published in a variety of cookbooks. And it is no surprise that J.P.'s products are also hot when it comes to awards and high honors.

Where to Buy. Shop for Sgt. Pepper's products in Central Market, Fiesta Gourmet of Texas in San Antonio, O'Shucks/Tears of Joy in Austin, Dave's Pepper Palace in Old Town Spring, Blum Street Cellars in San Antonio (near the Alamo), and other specialty shops. Online orders are taken at the Tears of Joy/O'Shucks website (www.oshucks.com).

Sisters & Brothers, Inc.

P.O. Box 33131
Austin, Texas 78764
Phone: (512) 326-3304

In 1987 twin sisters Lauri and Carol Raymond and their friend Celeste Seay (whose nickname is "Sister") began marketing a unique and versatile line of fresh dressings.

The Raymond sisters have brothers (not working with them), and they also have male staff members, and thus the name "Sisters & Brothers" evolved. By 1990 Celeste was unable to stay with the company, so the Raymond sisters bought her out, and the women still remain close friends. Today Sisters & Brothers has five employees who work together to hand pack their popular dressings using the SASS label.

How did they get from Sisters & Brothers to SASS? They were first interested in the name "Splash" because their dressings can be splashed on just about anything, but research showed that the name was already taken. SASS was chosen because their products are sassy. The original dressing was first named Eureka Garlic SASS. Eventually the name was changed to Sesame-Garlic SASS. And SASS has become their clever acronym for "Season All Stuff Sauce." Season all stuff is quite appropriate for their line of versatile products. Sister and brother, these are more than just dressings!

But before we get into the individual products, here is some insight into the SASS philosophy: natural, natural, natural. The products do not contain any additives, thickeners, colors, stabilizers, MSG, or preservatives. They are designed to be both nutritious and flavorful. The oil used is expeller pressed canola, a term meaning that no solvents are used to extract the oil. It is simply pushed out the old-fashioned way, with force!

SASS products are made and bottled by hand in Austin. After the sauces are blended in a non-cooking method, they are refrigerated. Products leave the kitchen and head for the stores in a refrigerated truck within five days of production. Once they reach the stores, they are commonly placed in the refrigerated produce section. Each item has been professionally tested for stability over time and is guaranteed to have a twelve-week shelf life if stored at forty degrees (refrigeration temperature).

Lauri and Carol bring a great deal of enthusiasm to the company, and this is reflected in their bold and zesty products. Fresh, vibrant flavors are important to them, and their goal is to offer products that people can use to make sensational meals without all the fuss. Their motto says it all: "Fresh. All Natural. Gourmet Convenience."

The bold line of dressings includes Sesame-Garlic, Tomato-Basil, Bombay-Ginger, Rancho-Grande, and Lemon-Song.

Sesame-Garlic was a success from the start and still tops their popularity charts. Each jar is hand packed with a healthy dose of fresh garlic, giving this sauce a big garlic flavor. Garlic is an integral part of all SASS blends and is used in every product except Bombay-Ginger, which is bursting with fresh ginger.

In 1990 Tomato-Basil was added. Like its predecessor Sesame-Garlic, Tomato-Basil is a versatile item. Stir into pasta or spread on pizza crust. Mix it into beans or stews. Or use as a dressing!

Bombay-Ginger was added in 1995. This sauce makes an excellent addition to stir-fry. Simply add toward the end of cooking, heat for a few minutes while the vegetables soften in it and serve over rice. Try it on mashed potatoes, steamed vegetables, or as a marinade for chicken or vegetable kabobs.

Rancho-Grande and Lemon-Song were the most recent additions to the SASS product line. Rancho-Grande was created for customers who craved the bold SASS flavors but wanted a low-fat alternative. The addition of chipotle peppers makes this dressing a healthy twist to many southwestern dishes including dips, meats, salads, and sides. Lemon-Song blends fresh lemon juice, fresh garlic, and Asian spices into a delicate concoction that complements a variety of soups, salads, pastas, and stir-fries.

These sassy blends burst with flavor and zest. With enthusiastic creators like Lauri and Carol, who would expect anything less?

Where to Buy. SASS products are available in Dallas/Fort Worth, Houston, San Antonio, and Austin supermarkets, such as HEB and Randalls, Central Market, Whole Foods, as well as health food stores.

HEB may add them to additional stores upon customer request. In most stores, the SASS products are located in the refrigerated produce section.

⭐ Stubb's Legendary Kitchen, Inc.

P.O. Box 40220
Austin, Texas 78704
Phone: (512) 480-0203
Toll-Free: (800) BARBCUE
Fax: (512) 476-3425
Internet: www.stubbsbbq.citysearch.com

C.B. "Stubb" Stubblefield said his parents were "real good cooks." When his family moved to Lubbock to pick cotton in the 1930s, Stubb himself tried his hand in the kitchen. He worked in area restaurants and hotels until leaving Texas for the Korean War. A staff sergeant in the last all-black army infantry, Stubb was well liked and respected by those around him. While at war, he managed meal production, furthering his culinary talents and preparing for his next real adventure.

After his military duty, Stubb returned to Lubbock and in 1968 opened his first restaurant. While the tangy aroma of barbecue filled the air, the jukebox blared with Stubb's favorite blues tunes. An avid music lover, Stubb welcomed to his restaurant the likes of Joe Ely, Stevie Ray Vaughn, Willie Nelson, Johnny Cash, Linda Ronstadt, the Fabulous Thunderbirds, and many more talents. Some would sing for a meal, and everyone had a great time.

In the meantime, Eddie Patterson was growing up in Lubbock and recalls his parents eating at Stubb's restaurant. Eventually Eddie left West Texas to take a job in New York City. During his years in the Big Apple, Eddie missed Texas, and he especially missed Stubb's ribs slathered with the famous barbecue sauce. Stubb sent Eddie some products, and in return Eddie helped market them. This marketing "hobby" became a full-time business, and Eddie ultimately headed back to Texas.

Today Eddie Patterson and Scott Jenson run the food business, while a third Texas friend, John Scott, is involved with the restaurant. They all share Stubb's dreams and ideals and are proud to carry on his legacy. When Stubb died in 1995, Eddie felt like he had lost a grandfather.

The men know they have big shoes to fill when selling products that carry the Stubbs label. Before his death, Stubb saw the men establish the food business and the restaurant in Austin. They knew him well enough to understand how important it was for blues and barbecue to stay connected. Stubb cooked for dignitaries and plain folk. He crossed a lot of boundaries and barriers, and today his products do the same. Even in areas outside of Texas, where barbecue has its own local flavor, Stubb's products receive rave reviews.

What makes Stubb's barbecue sauce taste different is that it has a tomato-vinegar base, giving it a smooth, balanced flavor. It has a consistency thin enough to penetrate the meat during cooking, imparting its taste throughout the ribs or brisket or whatever is sizzling on the grill. While Stubb used to cook his sauces in a fifty-gallon drum, today they are made in a commercial kitchen using his recipes. Each bottle is labeled with a photo of Stubb and this quote: "Ladies and Gentlemen, I'm a Cook."

Stubb's Bar-B-Q Sauce comes in Original, Mild, and Spicy. Moppin' Sauce Bar-B-Q Baste was designed for brushing on meats as they cook. There are two marinades, Beef and Chicken and Wicked Chicken Wing Sauce.

The barbecue sauce labels suggest a three-step grilling method, which includes rubbing before cooking, basting during cooking and pouring on prior to serving. Stubb would be mighty proud.

Where to Buy. Look for Stubb's big grin on sauce jars at major grocery stores in Texas and beyond. Orders are taken by phone and fax. See the online catalog for product information.

A Tasty Visit

Stubb's Bar-B-Q Restaurant
801 Red River, Austin
Phone: (512) 480-8341
Hours: Tuesday - Wednesday 11 a.m. - 10 p.m.
Thursday - Saturday 11 a.m. - 11 p.m.
Sunday 11 a.m. - 9 p.m.
Closed Mondays
Nightclub open till 2 a.m. Tuesday - Saturday

Sink your teeth into Stubb's legendary barbecue. Choose from a huge selection of appetizers (like thick battered onions spiced with their own seasoning), barbecue plates, sandwiches, and sides. For a special treat, enjoy the Sunday Gospel Brunch (reserve ahead). Stubb built his name on blues and barbecue, and the restaurant continues the legend. Check the website for band schedules.

Tears of Joy

618 E. 6th St.
Austin, Texas 78701
Phone: (512) 499-0766
Fax: (512) 499-0766
Internet: www.oshucks.com

O'Shucks Tamales is described in Chapter 9. Owners Brian Rush and his mom, Joy, also own Tears of Joy. When the two aren't busy making tamales, you just might find them making their one-of-a-kind hot sauce.

Tears of Joy, a name that Brian created in honor of his mother, is a tomato-based hot sauce with fresh lime juice. (Brian and Joy actually squeeze the limes themselves.) In addition to the lime, Tears of Joy has another surprise ingredient: tequila!

This specialty hot sauce is used to make everything from a Bloody Mary to a marinade. The tequila adds a unique flavor to this award-winning handmade and hand packed blend. Restaurants use it in their Bloody Mary drinks, and you can buy a jar, too!

Where to Buy. Pick up some Tears of Joy at the store by the same name in Austin, as well as other specialty shops. Orders are taken by mail, fax, phone, and online.

A Tasty Visit

Tears of Joy/O'Shucks

Visit the O'Shucks Tamales section in Chapter 9 for details on this spicy shop on Austin's historic Sixth Street.

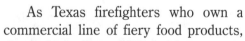

Texas Firehouse Chili & Salsas

1908-D South Padre Island Drive
Corpus Christi, Texas 78416
Phone: (361) 852-FIRE (3473)
Toll-Free: (800) 347-3431
Internet: www.texasfirehouse.com

J.C. Dykes, Scott Rasmusson, and Eddie Saenz are familiar with intense heat. As firefighters, their job is usually to cool things down. But their award-winning sauces are a sure-fire way to make foods sizzle.

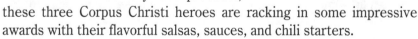

As Texas firefighters who own a commercial line of fiery food products, these three Corpus Christi heroes are racking in some impressive awards with their flavorful salsas, sauces, and chili starters.

Speaking of starters, it all began in 1993 when J.C. Dykes was given a picante sauce recipe his dad had been making and selling in Seguin, Texas, for fifteen years. J.C. decided it was time to market it beyond the borders of Seguin.

He and his buddies created several salsas based on the original recipe. The names are a unique blend of firefighter lingo and pepper talk. Salsa is available in Mild, Medium, Hot, and Blazing Hot (habanero). The salsa has a delightfully chunky texture and fresh robust flavor.

Perch it on a chip and enjoy. Jalapeño Flashover is a zesty combination of jalapeño peppers, onion, and garlic.

A line of barbecue sauces is available in three blends: Back Draft Mesquite Barbecue, Chipotle, and Texas Firehouse Three Pepper. A meat marinade is appropriately called Surround and Drown, and the meat rub is Resuscitation Rub with the subhead "Bring your meat back to life with Texas fire."

The trio is also renowned for its Search and Rescue Chili Mix. The label says, "For those of you who have been searching for that perfect pot of chili, you've just been rescued." The liquid mix (you add the meat) is a blend of tomato sauce, chili powder, cumin, and spices. It comes in a sixteen-ounce jar, which is enough to make a half-gallon of authentic Texas chili in just thirty minutes.

Texas Firehouse gift sets are really hot! The Emergency Survival Kit is as creative as it is tasty. The rectangular carton resembles a fire extinguisher box. Made from heavy-duty cardboard with a large opening in front, the kit contains a jar of each: salsa, Jalapeño Flashover, and barbecue sauce. The large front opening (or window) is surrounded by an illustration of flames and two axes. The label proclaims: "In Case of Emergency Open Jar." The set is a fabulous gift for just about any-one—teachers, doctors, nurses, neighbors, and friends in other states with a desire for some authentic Texas heat.

When they are not making sauces (or coming up with those cre-ative names), the three men are busy firefighters and paramedics. J.C. has worked at the Corpus Christi Fire Department for fifteen years, while Scott and Eddie have each been there thirteen years. J.C.'s wife Jane is a full-time employee of the food company, keeping things rolling while the men are out fighting real fires.

You will know if you see them at a food show because they will be the only food manufacturers dressed in bunker pants and helmets! Their display is outfitted with red flashing lights, hoses, and axes. A genuine fire truck adds a huge burst of authenticity to their display. On a serious note, their skills have come in handy in the food arena. While they were handing out samples at an Austin show, a woman ran up to them and said a small infant was choking. They ran to the baby who was already purple in color and dislodged a piece of apple from the infant's tiny throat.

If the story of these three firefighter-food makers sounds familiar to you, maybe you have seen them on television. Bob Phillips did a *Texas Country Reporter* segment on Texas Firehouse, and they have appeared on the Food Network (that's their flashing red light on the 911 Food Emergency show).

Awards have rolled in faster than you can say "911." Texas Firehouse products are adorned with seals of honor from a variety of highly acclaimed authorities and contests. They're heroes and they're winners—cool guys making some hot products.

Where to Buy. If you'd like to add some firefighters' heat to your cooking, look for their products at a number of HEB stores in Corpus Christi, San Antonio, and Austin and gift shops in Corpus Christi, Port Aransas, and around the state. Orders are taken by phone or the Internet, and the website has details on the unique gift sets.

Salsa vs. Ketchup

Salsa is a popular condiment (more popular than ketchup, I hear). It goes with everything from soup to nuts.

Chapter 8

Soups, Spices, and Great Bowls of Red (Chili, that is!)

Texans are shaking from the coast to the Panhandle and the Piney Woods to the desert. It's not an earthquake; it's the spice phenomenon. Throughout the state, people are shaking their favorite blends onto meats, soups, stews, salads, and just about anything else.

There is a lot of heat being ground up in Texas and made into savory spices, soup mixes, and fiery bowls of red.

Dry seasonings have a very versatile role in the kitchen. They can be used in rubs, dips, marinades, stews, sauces, soups, and the list goes on. There may be as many uses for them as there are counties in Texas.

This chapter is sprinkled with charming stories of old family recipes that have become Texas legends. It seems as if these entrepreneurs have had as much fun naming their spice blends as they have had creating them. I never knew there could be so many ways to say, "This is hot!" In any case, the soup, spices, and chili mixes made in Texas are a hot phenomenon!

Ant Hill Production

(Bertrand's Pepper Seasoning)
708 Hillebrandt Acres
Beaumont, Texas 77705
Phone: (409) 796-1963
Internet: www.pepperseasoning.com

Down in Southeast Texas, the land is fertile for growing a variety of peppers, the hotter the better. The moderate spring temperature quickly heats the ground, encouraging those peppers to pop up. If a pepper appears on a small plant, it needs to be picked so the plant can use its energy toward growing. Raising peppers requires frequent picking so that the plants grow big and tall. John Bertrand is a pepper expert.

In 1995, when friends made their own deer sausage, they knew they could count on John for some fiery seasonings from his garden. Always glad to add some spice, he dried and ground home grown peppers for the sausage. His small favor for friends sparked a new business.

John began with a dehydrator and quickly advanced to a commercial one that holds about twelve pounds of peppers. He is the company's sole pepper picker, washer, cleaner, dryer, and grinder. He has an entire building devoted to the processing and is meticulous about each step, especially cleaning them. Donning a suit that looks like something worn in a scientific lab, he carefully moves the plants through the process from whole pepper to dry spice.

The result is a ground seasoning that is ready to eat on sandwiches, eggs, bacon, hot dogs, chili, salads, or anything else your heart desires. Some people love to barbecue with it, and others, like John's buddies, use it in their sausage. It comes in two sizes, Chef (2.5 ounces) or Kitchen (1.1 ounce). This versatile seasoning is all natural and contains just pure pepper and no salt. Shake on freely or carefully, depending on how much heat you want.

John's farm is located outside of Beaumont, which by the way was named because it is French for "beautiful hill." In this idyllic pepper paradise, John has plenty of room to grow and process his hot pods. Gardening is a passion, and customers are passionate about his peppers. He gets letters, emails, and phone calls from people wanting, needing, and craving more Bertrand's Seasoning.

Where to Buy. Bertrand's is available in Beaumont area delis and cafés and stores such as Pure Cajun and Seafood Lover, or at Butcher's Korner and Eagon Meats in Nederland, Texas. Orders are taken by mail, phone, and the Internet. Buy a jar and you will become a "Preferred Customer" and receive a free jar of seasoning for every $15 purchase.

Baldy's Seasoning

6502 Sharpview, Suite B
Houston, Texas 77074
Phone: (713) 988-1548
Fax: (713) 981-0688
Internet: www.baldysseasoning.com

Stewart "Baldy" LuPau never liked bland foods, and even as a child he preferred bold flavors. When he was just nine years old, his dad taught him how to cook. Soon the adventurous child began concocting his own spice blends.

Baldy's love of adventure has carried over to his adult years, and he lives by the motto: "Nothing ventured, nothing gained." This spirited philosophy guided him when friends suggested that he put his unique seasoning blends on the market. Armed with experience as a professional meat cutter since 1970, Baldy was already familiar with the intricacies of the food business. In 1987 he began making seasonings commercially and incorporated a year later.

Every business needs a name, and it was the label artist who came up with the Baldy's idea. A smiling sketch of Baldy is proudly displayed on the brightly colored labels.

While the label has a striking design, it's what's inside that counts, and Baldy's seasonings score high. They are available in three flavors: Original, Cajun, and BBQ Style. Called "All-Purpose Seasoning," these tasty blends add concentrated bursts of flavor anywhere you sprinkle them. Shake them into salads (trust me, you won't need to use dressing) or use in stews, soups, and eggs. Because the spices are granulated, the flavor comes out faster so they can be used in quick-cooking grilled meats like steaks and chicken. The BBQ Style flavor is especially good on these items.

Baldy's seasonings are labeled "Health Smart" because they are all natural, contain no MSG, and are 80 percent salt free, with less than one gram of salt per half tablespoon. Each flavor is a delicious blend of twenty herbs and spices, garlic, light brown sugar, lemon peel, onion, and salt.

Baldy's expertise with meat is sprinkled into each jar. The varied texture of his spice blends and their piquant taste add zest to meats without drowning the natural flavor. All three spices have tantalizing aromas and flavors that appeal to kids as well as adults. The Original and BBQ Style blends are not too hot, and they have a pleasant peppery-garlicky flavor. The BBQ Seasoning starts with the same delicious ingredients as the Original and also contains a touch of cloves and cayenne pepper. The Cajun is hot! You might want to start with a quarter teaspoon and slowly work your way up from there. This N'Orleans style blend begins with the Original enlivened with cayenne pepper for a bold flavor. Baldy suggests serving ice cream for dessert when using the Cajun! (Fear not: even the hot Cajun spice lets the flavor penetrate the heat.)

You can substitute Baldy's as the spice in a casserole, salad, creole, soup, stew, or other favorite dish. The website offers a page of cooking tips, including meat-trimming facts.

Baldy's Seasonings are available in 4.75-ounce bottles and one- or four-pound bags. Baldy's baseball caps are a fun gift item available through the website. Maybe you know someone who would enjoy wearing a "Baldy's" cap.

Where to Buy. Orders are taken from everywhere, in and out of the country! You can order Baldy's by phone, fax, mail, or online.

Bolner's Fiesta Products, Inc.

426 Menchaca
San Antonio, Texas 78207
Phone: (210) 734-6404
Fax: (210) 734-7866
Internet: www.fiestaspices.com

Clifton Bolner learned the ropes of the food industry when he worked at the family's grocery. The store, which Clif's grandfather had proudly opened in 1906, was a fine way for a young man to learn about the complex business of running a food company.

In 1955 Clif, who was married with one child and another on the way, founded Bolner's Fiesta Products. Those grocery store years provided the know-how to design products that met customers' needs. One of the company's first products, fresh garlic, is still on the market today. Clif knew that customers selected garlic pods by appearance. Based on this, he developed clear-wrapped boxes so people could see the garlic they were buying. The product is still a top seller.

Today Clif's son Michael is the sales manager, and other family members are active on the management and marketing teams. Packaging is available to suit a variety of customers, from large institutional accounts to individuals. Sizes range from gigantic two hundred pound drums to jars small enough for a spice rack.

San Antonio is home base for Bolner's Fiesta. Spices travel from sixty countries to the Alamo City where they are inspected, re-cleaned, ground, blended, and packaged.

Many people know the company for its Fajita Seasonings. This product line emerged in the 1980s and gained notoriety as fajita popularity soared. Fajita Seasonings are available in a wide choice of flavors including Fajita, Chicken, Mesquite, and No-Salt. They combine Fiesta's zesty spices with meat tenderizer. These blends appeal to a wide range of tastes, and their uses extend beyond fajitas.

Steak Seasoning is another popular item, especially in Texas. The flavors of the Southwest team up in a blend designed especially for a juicy steak. For a robust flavor, keep adding seasoning throughout the cooking process.

It comes as no surprise that this seasoning company would offer two chili blends. Regular Chili Mix is designed for flavor release during slow cooking. Quick Chili Mix has a higher concentration of flavors and tenderizers and is designed for those times when you want chili and you want it fast!

The Bolner's Fiesta product line is enormous, with over six hundred traditional Mexican items. Choose from a wide range of authentic blends such as Enchilada Seasoning, Carne Guisada Seasoning, and the Tamale Kit.

The Bolner family takes pride in all of its products and has years of experience purchasing from quality growers, storing properly, and developing blends that allow customers to bring out a variety of robust flavors in their own kitchens.

Where to Buy. Look for the festive Bolner's Fiesta label on their products in chain stores throughout Texas, states bordering Texas, and certain other areas scattered around the nation. The products are sold online or by mail, phone, and fax.

Bubba's Spice Company

P.O. Box 801854
Houston, Texas 77280-1854
Phone: (713) 461-4261
Toll-Free: (888) 461-4261
Fax: (713) 461-5245

For several decades Brad Jones had been using his special blend of spices to flavor the meats that sizzled at fajita cookoffs. His fajitas were so popular that people asked where they could buy his seasoning.

Much to the delight of many, Brad took the suggestions seriously, and Bubba's Red Dust is a hot choice for fajita lovers. Customers as far away as Alaska and South Africa enjoy receiving Red Dust by mail.

Not too salty or spicy, Bubba's Red Dust is a versatile blend that was created to enhance the flavor of beef, pork, poultry, and fish. The label suggests that you dust it on the meat and sit back and wait while the seasoning penetrates. This message is proudly conveyed on each label, which features a cowboy relaxing in his rocking chair. What an easy way to poke some flavors into your meats. This medium hot spice is available in a six-ounce jar.

Where to Buy. You can find Bubba's Red Dust at Houston area meat markets, such as Witty's, Poncho's, and Ting Meat Market. Order by mail, phone, or fax.

Carmie's Kitchen

210 Windco Circle
Wylie, Texas 75098
Phone: (972) 442-1337
Toll-Free: (800) 337-1337
Fax: (972) 442-5279
Internet: www.peppersprings.com

Carmie Randack has several claims to fame. First, she is J.R.'s wife *and* mother. Second, you can buy her seasoning on the South Fork Ranch. And third, she can whip up a spice blend that tastes great today and even better mañana!

In 1989 Carmie featured a product at an arts and crafts show held in a home. People said she needed to market the spicy dip, which was gathering up rave reviews.

Carmie decided to try it, and at the end of a year she expanded from one to four products. Today she makes about fifty dips, soups, and bread mixes in her own 3,100-square-foot commercial facility with equipment that bags 1,200 seasoning packets an hour.

Offering the ultimate in convenience, Carmie's Kitchen seasoning blends are available in single-use packets. The mixes contain no MSG or preservatives and are sealed for freshness in a cello bag. Each blend has a colorful label with mixing instructions and a whimsical product name. All items are easy to prepare. Simply mix with sour cream and mayonnaise or just sour cream. (Carmie also includes instructions for low-fat dips.) Chill for a few hours before serving.

Mexican Mañana Dip is one of Carmie's most popular products. A native of New Mexico, Carmie was familiar with southwestern flavors. When she decided to blend her own spicy dip, she mixed it with sour cream and sampled it a few hours later. Initially she was disappointed that it didn't have more kick, so she stuck it back in the refrigerator wondering what she should do differently. The next morning she tried it again, and this time—ZING—it was really hot! A friend suggested the name "Mañana Mexican Dip."

The red pepper adds color and heat to this zesty appetizer dip. Serve with tortilla chips, crackers, or veggies and watch your guests smile when they take the first bite.

Customers rave about Carmie's Fiesta Spinach Dip. If you are looking for an easy and quick way to make a great tasting spinach dip, here it is! Freeze dried spinach shares the spotlight with flavorful spices in this palate-pleasing blend. Serve with rounds of bread, and even Popeye will be surprised at the fresh spinach flavor.

Another zesty blend is Country Cucumber Dip. Before a chip-full of this concoction reaches your mouth, your nose will capture the distinct cucumber aroma. Serve with fresh veggies, or use as a refreshing filling for finger sandwiches. Mix with cream cheese, thin just a bit, and make pinwheel sandwiches.

Dilliest Dill Dip Mix is another favorite. Made with dill weed, the dip is a festive blend of green and white. J.R.'s Ranch Dip is named for the two J.R.'s in Carmie's family: her husband and eldest son! This perky mixture of coarse ground black pepper, garlic, and other spices is quite versatile. Make it into a dip or spoon a dollop onto a steaming hot baked potato or use as a base for salad dressing. Would you expect anything less than versatility from J.R.?

Carmie's Kitchen also makes soups, including her famous Border Town Tortilla mix. This easy-to-prepare soup mix makes two quarts in about fifteen minutes. Add the water, top with some of your own crunchy tortilla chips, and serve. If you'd like to add chicken, the instructions tell you how to do that, too. Other creatively named soup mixes include Bunkhouse Broccoli, Campfire Bean, and Pepper Pete's.

Complement the soup with one of Carmie's bread mixes designed for machine-made loaves (cornbread can be made in a regular oven). Carmie puts added effort into her products to assure that customers have an easy time making them. Her blends are packed with flavor, so all you have to do is mix and enjoy!

Carmie's cookbook contains recipes using her mixes, as well as recipes from her mother, grandmother, and a friend.

Where to Buy. Purchase Carmie's Kitchen dip, soup, and bread mixes in specialty shops throughout the United States. Texas stores include Guitars and Cadillacs, Austinuts, Marriott on the San Antonio River Walk, Longhorn General Stores, Fredericksburg area gift shops, and gift basket companies. A number of airport stores sell her products, including Parodies in Dallas/Fort Worth and Wine and Roses in San Antonio. Carmie has booths at Junior League Christmas bazaars around the state. Her products are also available by phone, fax, or mail. The web address provides additional information.

Hot as a Habanero!

In 1912 Wilbur Scoville developed a scale to measure the level of heat in chile peppers. The Scoville Scale is the most popular pepper heat chart. Hotter peppers have more Scoville units. Habaneros top the list with 300,000 Scoville units (give or take some). Serranos have about 5,000-25,000 units. Jalapeño and chipotle peppers are found toward the bottom with 2,500-10,000 units. Poblano peppers can be in the 1,000-2,500 range.

Company's Comin'

202 Magnolia
Hearne, Texas 77859
Phone: (979) 279-2607
Fax: (979) 279-2901
Internet: www.companyscomin.com

For years Hal Mossberger dreamed of being in the food business. In 1992 he decided to stop dreaming and take action. He started small, and the business has snowballed (or should I say cheeseballed?) into something big.

LONE STAR
TORTILLA SOUP

He makes a line of dry mixes that are designed to make anything from dips to soups or even a meal! All of the recipes were originally developed in the family's kitchen, with Hal's wife Gladys, the "Number One Chef," at the helm. Their daughter Shannon is also active in the family business.

Hal and the rest of the family take great pride in the Company's Comin' Mexican soups: Chicken Enchilada, Tortilla, Beef Enchilada, and Old Mexico. Just add water and milk and your choice of cheese or chicken. The Lone Star Tortilla Soup mix resembles a Texas sunset with its array of orange and red powdered seasonings. Old Mexico Cheese Soup is a spicy red and white mixture with instructions for making with milk, beer, or a blend of the two. This spicy soup is a textural treat when you toss in some crushed tortilla chips.

Branching out from Mexican soups is the Red River Rice Soup, to which you can add water, instant rice, and chicken for a Louisiana gumbo.

Company's Comin' offers a variety of dips broad enough to fill any Texas buffet table. Texas Fire Dip is a "very spicy" blend of jalapeño, onion, garlic, mesquite, and spices. Selma's B.L.T. (Bacon, Leek & Tomato) Dip is a chunky and colorful mixture of bacon bits and veggies. Mix with sour cream, wait thirty minutes, and serve.

You can make a meal out of Rosita's Beef Enchiladas mix. The packet contains all the spice you need for five or six servings of meaty enchiladas. Add a pound of ground beef or turkey, water, cheese, sour cream, and corn tortillas for a delicious enchilada feast.

Each Company's Comin' mix has a label with a charming checked border. Blends are conveniently packaged in single-use plastic bags. The family offers a huge selection of products, including thirty-five soups and twelve dips (some are low fat). If you keep them on your shelf, you will certainly be prepared when Company's Comin'!

Where to Buy. Look for the quaint Company's Comin' checked packages at Junior League bazaars throughout Texas, the Houston Nutcracker Market, and shows around the nation. Their products are also available at a wide range of specialty shops. Orders are taken by mail, phone, fax, and the Internet.

A Tasty Visit

Hoyt's Pharmacy
202 Magnolia
Hearne, Texas 77859
Phone: (979) 279-2607
Hours: Monday-Friday 8 a.m.-5 p.m.
Saturday 10 a.m.-2 p.m.

The makers of Company's Comin' dips and spices have a store housed in the old Hoyt's Pharmacy in downtown Hearne. It is an old-time drugstore with an authentic soda fountain (just for show) and old-fashioned sized cola drinks.

EZ Fixin's Spice Company

P.O. Box 154115
Waco, Texas 76715
Phone: (254) 714-1744
Internet: www.ezfixins.com

The name for this unique company says it all. Russell Ritchey's EZ Fixin's seasoning and accompanying cookbook make fiery foods just a few sprinklins' away.

EZ Fixin's makes one seasoning, called Tex-Mex, a tasty blend that is like

having a complete spice rack in one jar. It is made from a countdown formula, going from nine teaspoons of chili pepper down to one teaspoon of cayenne with seven spices in between. In other words, there are nine teaspoons of chili pepper, eight teaspoons of paprika, leading all the way down to the one teaspoon of cayenne. The spices come together to make a blend that adds concentrated bursts of flavor to a variety of foods.

Russell Ritchey is bursting with enthusiasm for Tex-Mex seasoning and with ideas to make it easier to use. A mechanical engineer, Russell has designed a product that literally has built-in conveniences. The cookbook is a binder filled with recipes printed on cards. And now for something trés chic, the spine of the cookbook has a clip so that the spice bottle hooks right onto it. There you have it: a cookbook with recipes using Tex-Mex spice and a jar of the spice right there at your fingertips! Only an engineer would be so practical and clever.

How did this talented engineer end up creating a spice blend? Russell was raised in the chili cookoff circuit by parents who took their bowls of red quite seriously. His mom, dad, and sister-in-law have won numerous cooking awards.

Around 1997 Russell caught chili fever and wanted to develop his own spice blend. He loves spicy foods, so he didn't mind cooking and experimenting and eating all that chili. In the meantime he had the engineering job and his family to keep him busy, but creating a blend was always on the back burner. Finally he developed the mix that worked, and he knew he had a product others would like. Tex-Mex seasoning is spicy but balanced and full of flavor. Once he got the mix down, he stirred and simmered and sautéed and baked until he had a whole range of recipes using the one Tex-Mex spice blend.

Then came the idea for recipe cards, and of course, the infamous clip hooking the bottle to the cookbook! The book contains about fifty recipes in these categories: appetizers, main dishes, side dishes, condiments, and breads. Blank cards provide space for your own creations. But you won't have to do much innovating as Russell has done it for you. The cookbook features yummy recipes that are a cinch to make (with the attached spice blend) and appeal to the whole family. The names are fun as well. Texas Cannonballs are sure to spice up a cocktail hour. "The Way 2-EZ Chili" is a quick way to make a good bowl of red.

"QUESO" is posted on the cover as an acronym for "Quick-Unique-Easy-Simple-Ordinary." This is one talented engineer!

Russell enjoys testing his recipes, and there is no end to his ideas. Tex-Mex is so versatile that you can use it as a table spice to enliven whatever fills your plate. An engineer with culinary expertise is truly a winning combination.

Where to Buy. Tex-Mex is sold at a few sites around Waco, including a store called Salsa in the River Square Center, and Griff's in China Spring. It is also available through the EZ Fixin's website.

Gordon Specialty Foods, Inc.

P.O. Box 6488
Katy, Texas 77491-6488
Phone: (281) 347-4782
Fax: (281) 347-4783
Toll-Free: (888) GRUBRUB
Internet: www.gordonsgrubrub.com

When Lance Gordon was dating his future wife in 1987, he invited her over for dinner. The two were chatting in the kitchen as Lance prepared chicken for the grill. He removed the skin, and as he was getting ready to add the dry seasoning, his date was concerned. "Where is the barbecue sauce?" she asked. She went on to explain that her dad made "the best barbecue sauce," and she wasn't accustomed to chicken being grilled without sauce.

Lance continued to make the chicken his way, using only the dry rub and no sauce. When it came off the grill, the couple sat down at the table, and by the third bite, his future wife suggested he sell the sensational concoction.

Lance named his creation Grub Rub®, a name which popped into his head one day as he was driving along Interstate 10. When he first began marketing his ingenious blend, he sold about seventy-five jars at a food show. Now he sells hundreds of jars at a time.

Lance comes from a family of cooks, including a grandmother who helped develop a cookbook. Lance's father originally created the Grub Rub formula. In fact, Lance still has the original recipe in his dad's handwriting. This MSG-free blend contains a unique combination of spices that creates a glaze. Simply rub the tasty concoction on meat or chicken, let it sit for ten minutes, and presto, you'll see the liquid glaze. From there, just toss the meat on the grill, and the rub seals in the flavor and juiciness. The final product is tasty and tender. The seasoning blend imparts a flavor that is not too sweet and not too spicy, but alive with a good balance of spices. If you have any leftovers (and that is a big if), cold chicken made with Grub Rub is sensational.

Grub Rub has won high acclaim. It is the secret ingredient for many successful cookoff teams, and the label clearly says, "Award winning." Lance is on the road quite a bit, demonstrating his product about thirty-five weekends a year. Some of Lance's favorite Grub Rub recipes include chicken, pork chops, shish kabob shrimp, brisket, and chuck roast. Hunters enjoy it on wild game and venison.

By the way, Lance's father-in-law (the one with the great barbecue sauce) is hooked on Grub Rub himself.

Where to Buy. Grub Rub has a very wide distribution to approximately 1,000 stores. Look for it in the spice aisle or meat counter of retailers such as Academy, Randalls, most HEB stores, Tom Thumb, Fiesta, Krogers, and Canton First Monday. You can order Grub Rub by mail, phone, or on the Internet.

Hummingbird Kitchens

P.O. Box 1286
Whitehouse, Texas 75791
Phone: (903) 839-6244
Toll-Free: (800) 921-9470
Internet: www.hummingbirdkitchens.com

In East Texas, about seven miles south of Tyler, is a town called Whitehouse, Texas. There, in the midst of the Piney Woods, is the home of a product worthy of presidential acclaim.

Bill Faulkner says his wife, Jan, has always been "a really good cook." When she started blending her own dry mixes for breads, dips, and soups, she gave them as Christmas gifts. Friends loved the fresh, spicy, fragrant packets and wanted to buy some. And Hummingbird Kitchens took flight.

It was 1993 when Bill and Jan sold their first soups, breads, and dips. Today they make fifty items, which are free of MSG and preservatives and as low salt as possible. Preparation is designed to be easy and, in most cases, quick.

One of their signature items is Texas Tortilla Soup, a quick version of this Lone Star favorite that can be made in less than half an hour. Add water, crushed tomatoes, and chicken if you like, and serve over crunchy tortilla chips.

The tortilla soup's success is based on a secret blend of nineteen different herbs and spices. And no, Bill and Jan aren't telling any more than that!

White Chili is another Hummingbird specialty. This low fat, low cholesterol bowl of red, or rather white, has no red chili powder but smells and tastes like the real thing. With only 1.6 grams of fat, including the chicken, it makes a hearty and healthy meal. Four types of white beans share the spotlight with a blend of "lots" of herbs and spices. Best of all, you can make the soup in the crock pot if you like. Your home will capture the aroma as this delightful blend simmers. There are many other soups to choose from including Texas Roasted Pepper and Garlic Soup Mix to name a few.

Soups are only the beginning. Hummingbird Kitchens is also well known for its delicious dips. Texas Fire and Smoke is a dip mix featuring classic Southwest flavors. With just the right amount of heat, customers say the dip "has an attitude." Simply mix in sour cream for an appealing appetizer.

Bill and Jan take a great deal of pride in their bread mixes, which are versatile enough for either a bread machine or the old-fashioned method. A popular choice is the Cheddar and Jalapeño bread mix. Cheese and dried jalapeño peppers team up in this easy-to-make bread that requires no kneading or rising. Many people buy chili and bread mixes for a special gift or a great meal to enjoy themselves.

Hummingbird Kitchen products are flying around the world. They have been shipped to Alaska (must have been the soup or chili) and have traveled as far away as Finland, Japan, Saudi Arabia, and Germany.

Where to Buy. Hummingbird Kitchens' soup, bread, and dip mixes are sold at a number of gift shops including The Market in Whitehouse, Village at Old Mill Market (Canton First Monday), Lindsay House in Gainesville, and other specialty shops. Orders are taken by mail, phone, fax, and the Internet.

Limestone Cottage

P.O. Box 26746
Austin, Texas 78755
Phone: (512) 345-9330
Toll-Free: (800) 597-8821
Fax: (512) 342-2495

Roger Serafine combines artistry and flavor in a line of soup, dip, and tea mixes. The blends are a rainbow of colors that taste as good as they look.

In 1998 Limestone Cottage mixes first appeared, offering three soups and five dips initially. Seven Bean Rice & Spice Soup mix was an instant hit and is still the company's top selling item. The beautiful blend features colorful layers of beans, rice, herbs, and spices. The layered packaging is a unique touch that adds charm and an artisan look.

Substantial Spud was another of Roger's inaugural soup mixes. The difference is that the soup is not creamy. It contains a flavorful blend of potato flakes, great northern beans, yellow split peas, brown rice, and spices. Preparation is a snap; simply add water. Or you can add chicken bouillon or pulled meat. The packet comes with recipe ideas.

The third original soup is Mama Mia Minestrone, a mixture of small white beans, red kidney beans, dehydrated veggies (green beans, carrots, celery), spices, herbs, and a separate packet of macaroni. The mix comes with complete directions for adding optional ingredients, such as beef or vegetable bouillon and a can of diced tomatoes for an authentic Italian soup.

The five original dip mixes are very versatile and come with recipe suggestions. They are: Down on the Border, Positively Tex Mex, Down on the Bayou, Creative Cajun, and Real Dill. The last mix is the real deal when mixed with butter and drizzled over fresh veggies. Using a phrase coined by my husband, it is "scrum-dilly-icious."

A newer dip, not part of the original five, is Eat Your Greens: The Ultimate Spinach Dip. Serve in a hollowed out loaf of bread for a gourmet spread.

Roger develops the mixes to taste good without using additives. He found culinary inspiration during family travels abroad where he tried new foods and acquired a taste for fresh herbs and spices. Limestone Cottage mixes are made in a commercial kitchen the old-fashioned way, by hand. Roger and two to four employees take care in every packet of mix. He has recently developed a line of fruit and herbal teas with no caffeine.

Limestone Cottage items are attractive enough to give as gifts. Unique gift sets, such as the Round o'Dip container, are available. The labels are tastefully decorated with an illustration of a charming limestone cottage.

Where to Buy. Look for the colorful Limestone Cottage products at Whole Foods, Sun Harvest, Wild Oats, and other natural food stores and upscale groceries, as well as tearooms and day spa gift shops. Orders are taken by mail, phone, and fax.

Obie-Cue's Texas Spice

P.O. Box 951
Lancaster, Texas 75146-7951
Phone: (972) 641-2660
Fax: (972) 227-0686
Internet: www.obiecue.com

Obie Obermark says, "Our job is to make you a barbecue legend in your neighborhood." Obie is a barbecue legend himself. Obie-Cue was the name for his barbecue team, which has won scores of awards, including three national championships. He is proud to be the only three-time winner of the American Royal, the world's largest barbecue cookoff, held in Kansas City. And he is a founding father and past executive director of the International Barbecue Cookers' Association, the sanctioning body in cookoffs.

As proud as Obie is of his awards and achievements, he really seems to enjoy talking about the attributes of his seasonings and rubs. His products are blended with top quality ingredients to impart award-winning flavors. Obie and his wife, Pat, are both fond of cooking, and they pride themselves on their ability to transfer that knowledge to their rubs. Obie has a natural knack for flavor, and most of his products are low sodium.

Obie explains that the value of a rub is that as meat is heated, the fibers open up and swallow the flavor from the seasoning. Juices come up, hit the spices, and dissolve them. Rubs keep the meat juicy and help the flavor penetrate, a tasty cycle that continues throughout cooking. Obie recommends adding the rub when you are ready to cook or just a bit in advance.

If you haven't tried Obie's products, he suggests starting with Steakmaker. This tangy blend of lemon, Worcestershire, garlic, and black pepper come together to perk up steaks, burgers, fish, shrimp, even veggies. There are many other products in the Obie-Cue line. Sweet Rub is another popular choice, and Obie recommends trying this "very low sodium" rub on grilled chicken. For some real heat try Yankeeblaster, a fiery blend of jalapeño and cayenne peppers. The website has a complete list of products and awards.

Gift sets are a way to combine Obie-Cue spices into a present for that special barbecue lover. The Backyard Hero Gift Set contains four rubs, and the Simple Pleasures Gift Set contains Gatorbreath (Cajun), Sweet 'N' Heat, Smooth Moove, and Moo-Cue for use indoors or out.

Where to Buy. Look for the line of Obie-Cue seasonings and rubs in Barbecue Galore stores and other specialty shops. Orders are taken by mail, phone, fax, or by sending in the form on his website.

Pecos Red Products, Inc.

13329 Veteran's Memorial Drive, #H
Houston, Texas 77014
Phone: (281) 440-8990
Fax: (281) 440-8990*11
Internet: www.pecosred.com

Jo Ann Oakman has successfully turned her chili cookoff hobby into a career. In 1989 the staff at The Chile Shop (one of my favorite places) in Santa Fe, New Mexico, asked her to come up with a packaged chili mix. She sent a sample, they loved it, and they have been selling it ever since.

The Pecos Red name was inspired by chili cookoffs, where the featured items are affectionately called "bowls of red." Jo Ann heads across the Pecos River for the Terlingua Chili Cookoff, so Pecos Red was a natural.

Jo Ann is a natural, too. The award-winning chili champ knows how to mix a fiery and flavorful blend. The single-use Pecos Red Chili mix is spicy enough for most people, but a packet of cayenne pepper is included for those who like it hotter. The chili mix contains four sealed cello bags: Chili Blend A, Chili Blend B, dry broth mix, and a packet of hot pepper (optional). The instructions are easy to follow. Just add ground beef or other meat, an eight-ounce can of tomato sauce, and three cups of water. While the meat is browning in a skillet, boil the water and dissolve the broth. Then add the browned meat, tomato sauce, Chili Blend A, and the hot pepper *if you want it hotter!* This aromatic blend cooks for thirty to forty-five minutes. Then Chili Blend B is added and simmered for fifteen minutes. From start to finish, you are only about an hour away from an award-winning bowl of red. Actually, you'll make more than a bowl; one mix yields one-and-a-half quarts of "homemade" chili.

The packets of Chili Blends A & B are separate because one is designed to release flavors over a longer time, while the other adds a burst of flavor just prior to eating. The final product is a smooth and spicy blend of meat and chili "gravy" sauce. It is truly a crowd-pleasing formula. Beans are disallowed in cookoffs, but Pecos Red instructions tell how to add them at home (for the toughest judges of all!).

Pecos Red Chili is complemented by several other products. Jo Ann wanted to create a ranch style bean mixture when she developed the Six-Shooter Bean Mix. Here, six bean varieties come together in a very flavorful blend. The beans are: Anasazi™, canary, great northern, pink, pinto, and small reds. Just soak the beans four hours or overnight, add the included spices, and in about two hours you will have a perfectly spiced pot of beans. The mix features Jo Ann's trademark of two separate sealed cello spice packets: one to add at the start and the second in the last thirty minutes of cooking.

A green chile connoisseur, Jo Ann wanted to develop a product using this popular pepper. Pecos Red Green Chile Chowder is a spicy blend of dehydrated carrots, potatoes, corn, red and green bell peppers, onion, cilantro, and chives. Add the liquid (and chicken if you like) and you'll have a savory soup to enjoy when those "blue northers" blow in off the plains.

To make the soup into a meal, Jo Ann created a Blue Cornbread mix featuring Indian Blue Corn. This quick bread is alive with sweetness and spice flavored by jalapeño peppers and lime. Bake in a muffin or square cake pan.

Chili—State Dish of Texas

On May 11, 1977, the Texas Legislature filed a proclamation with the state of Texas making chili the official state dish. Here is the final passage from the proclamation:

RESOLVED by the House of Representatives of the State of Texas, the Senate concurring, That the 65th Legislature, in recognition of the fact that the only real "bowl of red" is that prepared by Texans, hereby proclaims chili as the "State Dish of Texas."

(Special thanks to Jo Ann Oakman of Pecos Red for providing this information.)

Every food lover knows that taste is paramount. But we also know that appearance counts, too. Pecos Red products are tasteful inside and out. The package imparts a Western theme with its brown bag and colorful ribbon seal. The label, colored to match the ribbon, sports a Western-inspired design. The packages make an attractive gift presentation, and recipients will appreciate the professionally sealed cello bags containing the spice blends. Instructions are printed on heavy weight cards that have a rustic appearance and are easy to read. A variety of serving suggestions are included.

Where to Buy. Look for the perky Pecos Red labels at The Chile Shop in Santa Fe, New Mexico, and in upscale markets in Texas such as Rice Epicurean, Kroger signature stores, and other specialty shops. Orders are taken by mail, phone, or fax.

Red Eye Chili Company

1250 CR 249
Florence, Texas 76527
Phone: (254) 793-2799
Fax: (254) 793-3440
Internet: www.redeyechili.com

Red Eye Chili, an authentic chili blend that has spanned three generations of a Texas family, lives on because of the efforts of John and Mary Fenoglio. It was created by Mary's grandfather A.C. (Critt) Hill in the 1930s. The story is a fascinating one.

Critt Hill raised his three daughters in the small North Texas community of Vernon, where he ran Hill's Bakery during the latter part of the 1930s. His second daughter, Alma, married a local boy named James Rowlett, who ran a sales route for Hill's Bakery.

While the bakery was Critt's primary job, he was passionate about his hobby as an inventor. He was an avid cook and loved to tinker around with food-related gadgets. His hobby actually yielded a few patents, and one was for the Twin Cronies. (For the younger folk, "crony" means pal.)

Twin Cronies came in both floor and table models and were popular in their day. They tantalized many taste buds with their blend of hot dogs and chili on a bun with all the fixins'. Red Eye Chili was an integral part of this invention.

The Twin Cronies rotated hot dogs around a central vat containing hot chili mix. The contraption also had a bun warmer that heated an uncut hamburger-shaped bun wrapped in a wax paper bag. When the bun was warm, it was swiped with mustard and placed over a pair of hot wieners rotating on their spits. The machine operator lifted the bun and wieners, filling the space between the wieners with chili and topping it all off with onions, cheese, relish, or whatever condiments the customer ordered. The two wieners were the inspiration for the name "Twin Cronies" because they sat together like peas in a pod. Critt's invention allowed both the operator and customer to stay clean while handling this messy sandwich because the operator's hands barely touched the sandwich, and the wax paper bag caught any drips.

At first the buns were baked in Hill's Bakery in Vernon and delivered along specified routes. It wasn't long before Critt realized the future of the Twin Cronies was brighter than that of being the bun supplier. He sold the bakery and ran Hill's Café in the 1940s.

In the meantime Critt's son-in-law James built the Twin Cronies in his workshop. Each machine was sold under a lease/franchise agreement that required the lessee to buy Critt's chili mix. Critt supervised

Alley Oop Chili and BBQ Cookoff

Iraan, Texas, named for ranch owners Ira and Ann Yates, holds this annual cookoff in June. The event is named after the comic strip created by V.T. Hamlin, who was a reporter in Iraan when he developed it. Friday night's Beauty Pageant features the crowning of characters straight out of the comics, like Mr. Alley Oop Caveman. The Chili Cookoff is held on Saturday.

the blending of the chili mix at his café and shipped it to his customers. The recipe was never shared with any person outside the family. Hill's Café had become famous for its "bowl of red."

When Critt died, his daughter Alma and her husband James maintained the seasoning supply for a number of years, until health laws required that only stainless steel equipment be used for mixing foods. The Twin Cronies became obsolete because making them out of stainless steel was not feasible for James. (Today, there is one restaurant in Iowa using the chili mix.)

Eventually James and Alma gave the treasured chili blend recipe to their daughter Mary Elizabeth Fenoglio. She and her husband John felt that it was important to preserve this special family heirloom. They named the seasoning Red Eye Chili Blend and acquired a trademark. Today this delicious blend spices up bowls of red around the country as far away as Alaska.

The Red Eye Chili blend allows you to make a half-gallon of delicious, homemade tasting chili with ease. Start with two pounds of ground meat, and brown with onions and garlic. Add two cans of tomatoes with green chilies, water, and the seasoning blend. Cover and cook for at least an hour, and you will enjoy a bowl of red bursting with flavor. The hurried cook will appreciate directions for preparing the chili in less time. And if you'd like to use the crock pot, directions for that method of preparation are also included. If you prefer a spicier chili, the instructions include three options for adding heat.

In addition to the chili, Red Eye t-shirts and aprons are available to spice up your wardrobe. A gift that truly says "Texas" is a t-shirt and a few packs of chili. The chili blend box has a charming orange crate-inspired design created by Mary Fenoglio. Inside, the seasoning packet is professionally sealed in a bag tucked neatly into the box. The instruction sheet has an order form and company history.

Red Eye Chili is a family operation, and Mary, John, and their son are proud to carry on Critt Hill's delicious legacy.

Where to Buy. The legendary Red Eye Chili is available at a store in Florence, but the primary way to get your hands on a pack is by ordering direct. Orders are taken by mail, phone, fax, and the family is working on the Internet site (may be up by the time you read this). Each package comes with a handy order form.

Texas Gunpowder, Inc.

P.O. Box 852573
Mesquite, Texas 75185-2573
Toll-Free: (800) 637-9780

In the late 1970s Jan Pinnell's doctor told her to cut out the salt from her diet, leaving her taste buds craving some taste! Her husband, W.L. "Pappy" Pinnell, decided to take action. He was determined to perk up his wife's palate. What Pappy did next was the start of something hot.

The Pinnells' garden was a pepper haven, so Pappy picked some jalapeños, dried and ground them, then poured them into an empty saltshaker. He placed the shaker on the table without saying a word. Not only was his wife thrilled, the whole family became addicted to their new spice. Demand outgrew the Pinnells' garden. The family picked peppers from their daughter Dee's garden and friends' yards as well.

The Pinnell family eventually found a bigger source for the peppers and in 1980 started selling their fiery powdered seasoning. They incorporated in 1989, and the entire family became involved in the business.

Pappy died in 1999, and today the company continues to make Texas Gunpowder featuring ground jalapeño peppers. They have a Pappy Pinnell line of products with a sketch of Pappy on the label. Pappy Pinnell's Lemon Pepper is a salt-free seasoning, and Pappy Pinnell's Rojo Pepper is a tasty blend of red peppers. Mesquite Dust is another creation.

You can imagine the attention the company name draws. The name was inspired by a family friend who said, "Ya know, Pappy, I'd like some more of that gunpowder. You get too much of that pepper and it just blows your head off."

Where to Buy. Texas Gunpowder products are sold in a variety of gift shops throughout Texas, including Congress Avenue Gifts near the Capitol and the Oasis gift shop in Austin, and at the Alamo in San Antonio. It is also sold at a Tex-Mex store in Great Neck, New York, and through a popcorn company based in Illinois. Mail order catalogs, including Mo Hotta Mo Betta, feature the products. Texas Gunpowder accepts orders by mail and phone.

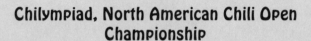

Chilympiad, North American Chili Open Championship

Up until 2001 this San Marcos event held in September was simply called Chilympiad. You will have a chance to sample a lot of chili and enjoy many other festivities.

Chapter 9

Tamales, Tortilla Chips, Fish Fry, and Hushpuppies

Tamales and tortilla chips are staple items in Texas. In the Lone Star State, many *bidness* deals have been made over a basket or two of chips. And throughout the year, but especially at Christmas, tamales take center stage. Start off the event with some chips and move on to the tamales. Does it get any better than that?

Tortillas have been around more than a while. Actually, their history spans thousands of years. Enter a Mexican restaurant and you're likely to be served a basket of warm crispy tortilla chips to dunk in the fiery salsa.

And tamales are a treat in a tube. A succulent filling nestled in stone-ground masa and wrapped in a genuine cornhusk just has to be sensational.

While pork is a tamale favorite, they are also available in beef, chicken, bean, veggie, or cheese. This section contains some tamale flavors you may have never dreamed you could find. Look in your grocer's freezer section, and you will have a pleasant surprise.

Eating a tamale is a fun and flavorful experience. First, there is the outer cornhusk layer. If you are new to Texas or to tamales, take the wrapper off! Once you have unwrapped your tamale, enjoy it plain or topped with salsa or anything else your heart desires. The stone-ground masa coating has a mild flavor and soft texture that always blends well with the meat, beans, or vegetables hidden inside. Whatever the filling, there is sure to be either a hint of spice or a great big kick, depending on if you're eating mild or spicy.

While the flavors of tamales are complex, heating them is simple. Steaming is the traditional cooking method, although some people simply pop them in the microwave. Manufacturers recommend steaming for the most authentic flavor and texture.

Fish fry batters and hushpuppies also fall into the category of corn-based cuisine. The batters coat everything from fish to pork chops to chicken. And since this is Texas, they are available in varying degrees of spiciness. Best of all, breaded foods can be baked for those who are fry shy. Hushpuppies are another Lone Star staple. Like a corn fritter, these cornbread balls complement a variety of main dishes. Batter up!

★ Adelante Tamales

P.O. Box 90112
San Antonio, Texas 78209
Phone: (210) 822-7681

Adelante means "forward thinking," and there is no doubt that restauranteur Dan Soder's tamale ideas are advanced. The theme of this unique restaurant owned by Dan and his wife says it all: "Where Heaven and Health Meet." Located in San Antonio's Alamo Heights district, the healthy theme spans from the food to the décor. Paper maché watermelons and car-

rots adorn the seating area. Traditional delights created with Dan's imaginative twists adorn the menu.

Now, back to the tamales. When the crowd has slimmed between lunch and dinner, the staff makes tamales for retail sale. They prepare a few hundred in an afternoon, freeze them immediately, and package them at night. The tamales are prepared by a machine that was tweaked to make each one heavy on the filling and lighter on the masa. By tamale standards, Adelante's are jumbo, about twice the size of your average tamale.

Now that we've covered how they are made and how big they are, let's get to the good part: the filling. This is where the "out of the husk" thinking comes into play. In stores, Adelante is available in Spinach, Black Bean, and Cheddar Cheese. The Spinach Tamales are embellished with jack and feta cheeses and red onion. Black Bean Tamales contain cilantro, jalapeño peppers, garlic, and black pepper. And the Cheddar variety is flavored with jalapeño peppers, tomatoes, and green onions. They use canola oil in their masa. The variety of fresh vegetables and spices add flavor without saltiness.

Additional tamale varieties are served at the restaurant. Choose from the flavors already mentioned or try Sweet Potato, Jack, Refried Bean, Vegetable, Pumpkin (sometimes), and Chicken made with all white meat.

Where to Buy. You can purchase Adelante tamales "to go" at the restaurant or at some Central Market stores.

A Tasty Visit

Adelante
21 Brees (in Alamo Heights)
San Antonio
Phone: (210) 822-7681

If Mother always told you to eat your vegetables, this is the place to go. In addition to tamales, the restaurant serves a variety of other Mexican foods with a healthy gourmet twist. The only meats used are chicken and turkey. Choose from veggie quesadillas and tacos, tofu enchiladas, and an array of other items. Spinach Quesadillas are a favorite, featuring homemade grilled corn tortillas filled with fresh spinach, mushrooms, red onions, and Jack cheese.

Royal Tortillas

Mayan legend says that tortillas were invented thousands of years ago by a peasant for his hungry king.
Source: Tortilla Industry Association

Alamo Tamales

3713 Jensen Drive
Houston, Texas 77026
Phone: (713) 228-6445
Toll-Free: (800) 252-0586
Fax: (800) 447-1980
Internet: www.alamotamale.com

ORDER FORM

Four Easy Ways to Order
Alamo Tamales

In 1960 Eduardo and Graciela Webster turned their authentic tamale recipe and a $5,000 investment into a family business. The Alamo Tamale factory got its start in a 2,000-square-foot building located in Houston.

Today Alamo's production takes place in a modern 25,000-square-foot facility under the leadership of the Websters' son, Louis. The company continues to use the family's traditional recipes made with top quality ingredients. Each tamale is wrapped by hand in a real cornhusk.

When it comes to selection, Alamo has something for everyone. Flavors include Pork (Hot or Mild), Beef, Chicken, Spinach & Cheese, and Bean Tamales. Not sure which one to try? Alamo suggests having a "tamalada," a Christmas party featuring a variety of tamales.

Speaking of entertaining, tamales are a perfect party food because they are so easy to prepare. Alamo Tamales can be placed in either the steamer or microwave. Unwrap them and top with chili and cheese or salsa, and serve with rice and beans for a hearty Mexican feast. Give your family and friends a real treat by serving a tamale dip. This recipe, and others that are just as tempting, can be found on the company's website. The tamale baked potatoes also sound intriguing.

If you leave your Alamo Tamales unopened in their original container, they can stay in the freezer for up to a year or in the refrigerator for ninety days. Can you resist them for that long?

Where to Buy. Purchase Alamo Tamales in Texas grocery stores, in most Sam's stores throughout the state, and Sam's in Oklahoma City. If you can't find them, Alamo ships overnight anywhere in the continental U.S. Order via fax, phone, or the Internet. The tamales are sent frozen, and the company says you can refreeze them if they have thawed a bit during shipping.

Cook's Choice

12021 Plano Road, Suite 170
Dallas, Texas 75243
Phone: (972) 644-5553
Fax: (972) 644-4201
Internet: www.cookschoice.com

Greg Broom loves to fish, but he wasn't always a fan of eating the fresh catch of the day. That changed in the mid-1980s when he had dinner at a friend's house. One bite of the breaded fish main course changed everything. Greg complimented his friend and said, "When you want to sell this batter, I'll do it for you."

It took Greg seven years to get the recipe, and when he finally did—in 1991—he founded Cook's Choice. A talented entrepreneur, Greg came up with the company name and began marketing his product. And that was just the beginning.

Today, Cook's Choice markets the batter under the Bass Pro Shops private label, "Uncle Buck's," and also under the Bill Dance name. And that's not all. There is a line of fifteen seasonings sold in four- to seven-ounce jars. Varieties include everything from Pork Rub to Rib Rub to wild game seasoning, fajita seasoning, and much more. Greg loves to test recipes, and twenty new products are being developed. They include pancake syrup and mixes for pancakes, cornbread, biscuits, cream and brown gravies, and cobbler, all under the Uncle Buck's name. (Bass Pro Shops owner, Johnny Morse, was introduced to the sport of fishing by his own Uncle Buck. The brand name carries on the legacy.)

The breading mixes come in an assortment of flavors: Seasoned, Original (a bit spicier than Seasoned), Hot-n-Spicy (spiciest), and Light 'n' Krispy, which is ideal for frying up Japanese tempura veggies. Although they are called "Fish Fry" mixes, Greg is quick to point out that the breading tastes great on chicken, pork, all meats, and vegetables as well. And don't let the word "Fry" scare you. Each package includes baking directions in addition to the frying instructions. A ten-ounce bag breads three to five pounds of product.

The Hot-n-Spicy flavor is a popular French fry batter. Simply cut up a fresh Idaho spud, batter it, fry, and savor the flavor. There is also a Hushpuppy mix, which fries up golden brown and light and fluffy.

Always the entrepreneur, Greg invented a kitchen tool called Better Breader™, for which he owns the patent. This unique product makes breading a breeze. It has only three dishwasher-safe parts: tub, sifter, and lid, and can bread several pieces of fish, chicken, meat, or vegetables at a time. Here is how it works: The breading goes in the bottom, then the sifter fits in, followed by the fish or meat on top. Cover the device with the lid, turn it upside down and shake three or four times. The breading falls through the sifter and coats the fish. Then turn it right side up and shake it three or four more times to allow the extra breading to fall back to the bottom. This remarkable device breads perfectly, which helps keep the frying oil clean.

Although Cook's Choice has grown phenomenally, quality remains a top priority for Greg, who is the president and CEO. Fresh corn is purchased directly from farmers, and the company makes over two million pounds of breading in a year in partnership with a milling company.

Where to Buy. Look for the breading products at Bass Pro Shops, over 10,000 grocery stores, Wal-Mart, by fax, and online. They are sold in Texas and throughout the nation. Stores to check include Albertson's, Kroger, Winn Dixie, Minyard's, Tom Thumb, Randalls, and HEB. The Better Breader is available at Wal-Mart, grocery stores,

Cowboy Chow

In the Old West, tortillas were a popular way to eat meat around a campfire without having to use a knife or fork.

Source: Tortilla Industry Association

tackle shops, and other locations. If you cannot find the products in a store near you, call Cook's Choice and they will direct you.

Doña Mariquita's TOTOPOS

2138 Welch
Houston, Texas 77019
Phone: (713) 522-2606
Fax: (713) 522-5702
Internet: www.totopos.com

Totopos, with the accent on the middle syllable, is a generic term for "chip" in Mexico. But Doña Mariquita's TOTOPOS are anything but generic. These specialty chips are sure to be the centerpiece of any gathering.

Mariquita Masterson grew up in Mexico City and stayed there until she was married. An avid entertainer, she hosted parties for the symphony and arts associations. Through these galas, Mariquita became known for her delicious and unique tortilla chips. The crispy texture and fresh flavor brought more than rave reviews. People began telling Mariquita to turn her chips into a business. Already a successful businesswoman, Mariquita decided to give it a try.

In 1994 she sold her Totopos at the Houston Nutcracker Market. Packaged in a plastic bag encased in a beautiful gold tin, Totopos chips were a big hit.

The best way to describe Totopos is to say it is a gourmet chip. Each pie-shaped crisp is crunchy and has enough body and substance to pick up virtually any dip without breaking. The lightly salted delicate flavor has a homemade, yet gourmet, appeal. They are the perfect size: big enough for a few bites, yet not so large that they fall apart.

The chips are available in the exquisite tin or in bags. If you buy the tin, serve them directly from it. The gold tin and purple label add elegance to any buffet table.

Where to Buy. You can find Totopos at Central Market or the Houston Nutcracker Market. Orders are taken by phone, fax, or mail, or check the Totopos website for a printable order form.

O'Shucks Tamales

618 E. 6th Street
Austin, Texas 78701
Phone: (512) 499-0766
Fax: (512) 499-0766 (call first and tell them to crank up the fax)
Internet: www.oshucks.com

Brian Rush's mom, Joy, started the tamale company in 1989, using a name inspired by the family's Irish heritage. Both mother and son were brought up in military settings, traveling quite a bit. The experience gave them the opportunities to explore other cultures and is now reflected in their cooking.

Brian and Joy are as conscious about health as they are about great taste. Their tamales feature canola oil, a lower fat alternative to lard. Each tamale contains the best ingredients they can find along with a flavorful blend of spices. The recipe took some time to develop, but as they say, "Practice makes perfect."

O'Shucks can make one hundred dozen in a day, a very full day! Flavors include Pork, Chicken, Veggie, and Black Bean.

Veggie leads the way in popularity and has been the company's signature since it was first rolled out. The Veggie tamales feature carrots and corn mixed with spices blended into a consistency similar to a moist cornbread. You can pack them in because one contains only about 137 calories (and 20 percent of the daily Vitamin A requirement to boot!).

The Pork tamales are made with fresh pork butt and a blend of spices to give them a kick. Chicken tamales are thighs seasoned with herbs and are milder than the pork. The most spiced-up variety is the Black Bean, with its smooth texture and rich flavor. Buy them frozen and steam for best results.

O'Shucks will also make venison tamales. Just call and arrange to bring in the meat.

Where to Buy. Purchase all varieties at the company's Austin store or some varieties at Whole Foods, Central Market, and Wheatsville Co-op. If you can't find O'Shucks in a store near you, order by phone, fax, or online.

A Tasty Visit 🍽️

O'Shucks/Tears of Joy
618 E. 6th Street
Austin, Texas 78701
Hours: Monday 10 a.m. - 4 p.m.
Tuesday - Friday 10 a.m. - 6 p.m.
Saturday Noon - 6 p.m.
Closed Sunday

Visit the O'Shucks/Tears of Joy store in Austin. The store is located two-and-one-half blocks west of Interstate 35 on 6th Street. In addition to tamales, browse through the books, gift baskets, and an assortment of fiery foods, such as salsas, marinades, barbecue sauces, and dressings. (O'Shucks also makes a hot sauce called Tears of Joy and described in Chapter 7.)

⭐ Pedro's Tamales, Inc.

"Sirloin in a Shuck"
P.O. Box 3571
Lubbock, Texas 79452
Phone: (806) 745-9531
Toll-Free: (800) 522-9531
Fax: (806) 745-5833
Internet: www.pedrostamales.com

Pedro (Pete Hale) learned to make tamales for one reason: He loved them! In 1977 he went to a Texas Tech dormitory equipment auction, purchased a hand-cranked tamale maker called "Old Number 1," and began making tamales in

the back of a warehouse. But Pedro didn't want to make just any tamale, he wanted to make "the best tamale ever."

He learned how to make masa using a 12,000-year-old technique that imparts a delicious flavor and texture. When it came to fillings, again Pedro was picky. A fan of sirloin, he decided to use this premium cut cooked by his wife, Sally. The fat was (and still is) picked out before the meat is shredded and mixed with the spices.

These days Pedro's sons Mike and Mark Hale are at the helm of Pedro's Tamales. They honor their dad's memory by insisting that the quality never change. The original tamale machine, "Old Number 1," has been archived and remains on the premises as a reminder of the company's roots. They now have about fifty employees who can crank out approximately six thousand dozen tamales in a day.

Flavors include Beef (Mild or Spicy), Shredded Pork, Premium Chicken, and Bean. The Beef tamale is the famous "Sirloin in a Shuck." This popular variety contains shredded sirloin, making it both tender and tasty. (The Mild has just the right amount of spice, and kids love it, too.) Try the Spicy Beef if you'd like just a bit more kick. They steam up beautifully, retaining their taste, texture, and shape. Premium Chicken contains all white meat and a delicious blend of spices. Bean is all bean (no fillers) and is reminiscent of another southern favorite, beans and cornbread. In all varieties, the corn flavor shines through in the delicious masa wrapped around the filling. If you eat one, you will have to have more!

The company's catalog features tamales and a host of other items, such as salsa, chili, and seasonings. A recipe section is delightful. The Mexican Lasagna, made with two packages of Pedros Tamales, sounds fabulous.

Taconite on Tuesday?

If you think "Taconite" is a special night of the week for eating crispy tortillas filled with seasoned meat and grated cheese, think again. It is actually the name of a type of iron ore that is pronounced tack-o-nite.

Where to Buy. In Texas, you can find Pedro's Tamales in the freezer section of most grocery stores including Albertson's, United, Lowe's, Tom Thumb, Randalls, and Winn Dixie. They also sell to restaurant chains. Pedros accepts orders by phone, fax, or the Internet. The tamales are shipped frozen and arrive in top condition sealed in a cooler.

A Tasty Visit 🍽️

Pedro's Tamales
8207 Highway 87
Lubbock, Texas
Company Store (drive-thru) Hours:
Monday - Wednesday 8 a.m. - 7 p.m.
Thursday - Saturday 8 a.m. - 8 p.m.

Mark and Mike Hale are happy to do guided factory tours by appointment. The drive-thru sells a variety of items, including fresh or frozen tamales, barbacoa, and carne guisada.

Rudy's Tortillas

535 Regal Row
Dallas, Texas 75247
Phone: (214) 634-7839
Toll-Free: (800) 878-2401
Fax: (214) 638-5317
Internet: www.rudystortillas.com

On March 15, 1945, Jose R. Guerra founded Rudy's, first calling it the Texas Tortillas Factory. In those days, tortillas were made by the "comal" method in which they were cooked on a hot griddle and turned by hand. The company now enjoys a history that spans over fifty years of family pride.

In 1949 the Texas Tortillas Factory moved to a different plant with their one tortilla machine and just three employees. With automation, they could make about six hundred tortillas in an hour.

In 1964 Mr. Guerra started the year by selling the Texas Tortillas Factory to his youngest son, Rudy Guerra Sr., and wife Carmen. In 1965, in response to the construction of the Dallas North Tollway, the company and its seven employees moved to a space boasting eight hundred square feet and two tortilla ovens. More growth was on the way as Mexican foods gained popularity. In 1971 the Texas Tortillas Factory tripled its leased space to 2,400 square feet. The company incorporated in 1975 and became Rudy's Tortillas. At that time, third generation family member Rudy Guerra Jr. joined the ranks. A few years later, in 1977, while enjoying continued growth, Rudy's purchased its first building, which had 9,000 square feet. The company's fifteen employees made more than 25,000 tortillas in just an hour.

Another family member, Louis Guerra, joined the company after finishing college and some time in the U.S. Army. Everything was coming up roses (or rather, tortillas) until tragedy struck on February 25, 1994, just one day after Rudy Sr.'s birthday. A fire totally destroyed the plant and every piece of equipment.

But Rudy's didn't give up. They had worked too long and too hard to build their business. With leased space and equipment, they were able to serve their customers within a week of the fire. Later that year Rudy Sr.'s youngest son, Joe (named for Jose, the company founder), took charge of rebuilding the kitchen and retail store areas. After completing this sizeable task, Joe went back to college and graduated in 1996 with a food service degree. He is now putting his degree to work with the business.

Today Rudy's Tortillas has over one hundred employees. They continue to use only choice ingredients—flour from Saginaw, Texas, and white corn from South Texas—to make their tortillas. And the staff at Rudy's grinds and cooks their own corn to make tortillas the authentic way. In other words, their products are made from scratch. The family-owned business is run by several generations, with the younger members feeling the pride and need to carry on what their parents and grandparents created.

The tortillas are made with yellow, white, and blue corn, designed for a variety of uses. The thicker tortillas stay soft, making them ideal for enchiladas or for serving at the table while the thinner varieties create crispy chips. Rudy's claim to fame is its Ultra-Thin white corn tortilla chip, perfect for dunking in a bowl of salsa. They also make dozens of other chip varieties and authentic tamales as well.

Where to Buy. Rudy's Tortillas are sold to many restaurants, so chances are you've tried them. They also take orders for tamales or tortilla chips (Party Paks) by phone or online. The Party Paks contain chips and salsa so you'll be equipped for your next fiesta!

Chapter 10

Food Organizations and a Dairy Good Museum

While food companies take center stage in the culinary arts arena, food organizations are behind the scenes offering a host of services.

The Texas Department of Agriculture, headquartered near the capitol building in Austin, is a major player in the world of Texas foods. Their GO TEXAN program does worlds of good for Texas food makers, and for those who chow down on Lone Star fare.

The Texas Beef Council works with cattle ranchers and consumers, offering helpful hints and delicious recipes. The Texas Pecan Growers Association is everything they are cracked up to be, and more. They have gobs of information, ranging from picking the perfect pecan to storage tips. The Texas Peanut Producers Board is the oldest commodity group in the state, offering support for the peanut farmers and the fans in the ballpark who want to make sure they are pitching the best possible peanut into their mouths. The Texas Food Processors Association is another group offering support to their industry.

The Tortilla Industry Association, a national organization, is headquartered in Dallas. They support the industry and offer a round of tasty tortilla information.

Disability Resources, Inc. is also mentioned in this section. This nonprofit group helps people with disabilities in countless ways. They offer employment opportunities, allowing these individuals to build their skills and make a huge contribution to Texas and the world.

And the Southwest Dairy Center and Museum in Sulphur Springs is a good way to enrich your next family vacation. A visit is sure to provide a great learning experience and a chance to eat at the state's oldest soda fountain.

Helpful people staff these organizations. Beyond their knowledge is a sense of enthusiasm and pride for the products they represent. I offer special thanks to these individuals, who so graciously helped shape this book: Disability Resources: Kris Anderson; Southwest Dairy Museum: Jodie Morris; Texas Beef Council: Anne Bried, Linda Bebee; Texas Department of Agriculture: Susan Combs, Susan Dunn, Chris Kadas; Texas Food Processors Association: Dr. Al Wagner; Texas Peanut Producers Board: Mary Webb; Texas Pecan Growers Association: Cindy Loggins Wise; and the Tortilla Industry Association: Irwin Steinberg.

Most of the organizations have websites filled with historical information, facts, and delicious recipes. Be sure to check them out.

Disability Resources, Inc.

3602 N. Clack
Abilene, Texas 79601
Phone: (915) 677-6815

In the West Texas town of Abilene lies a hidden jewel. Disability Resources is a nonprofit organization that brings **DisabilityResources.org** together the talents of disabled people with the needs of area businesses.

It all began back in 1987 when a local doctor needed help pickling the quail eggs laid on his farm. Disability Resources came to the rescue and got into the business of boiling, peeling, and pickling quail eggs.

Today a variety of award-winning products are made in this highly regarded organization. The group provides twenty-eight individuals with a home and transportation to and from work. When they arrive at the workplace, the individuals perform a variety of functions.

On an average day the group may be helping with the preparation of Billy Beans' famous salsa, West Texas Pepper Traders Bread and Butter Jalapeños, Carrie Belle's Sweet Hot Tomato Relish, or some other award-winning product. While this commercial kitchen is an ideal opportunity for the people who work there, it is a real plus for food company entrepreneurs.

Kris Anderson, business manager at Disability Resources, explains that the organization helps a variety of small businesses get their products made and packaged. And the folks who work there are paid for their time and find the job rewarding, making this a win-win situation. The group's goal is to raise funds so that more homes can be built.

Tony Dry from Billy Beans is a big supporter of the organization. He is proud that so many award-winning products are made under one roof, and he works tirelessly to promote the organization.

⭐ Southwest Dairy Center and Museum

1210 Houston Street
Sulphur Springs, Texas 75482
Phone: (903) 439-MILK (6455)
Internet: www.geocities.com/Heartland/Ranch/3541/museum.html

Step back in time and gaze at a butter-churning scene straight out of the 1930s. Watch cream being separated. See a skeleton riding a bicycle! And top it all off with a treat from an authentic old-time soda fountain. All of this and much more is available at the Southwest Dairy Center and Museum. The museum, funded by the Dairy Farmers of the Southwest, opened on June 8, 1991, and features visual and interactive exhibits as well as a creamery and gift shop.

Among the visual exhibits is the 1930s kitchen complete with an oil lamp, wood burning stove, and battery-powered radio. In the scene, a mother separates cream while a child churns butter. Nearby, the other children work on the historic farm, milking the cow and collecting eggs. As you progress through the exhibits, you'll see the dairy industry being transformed through the years.

Interactive exhibits are especially intriguing for school and other tour groups, encouraging participation in cream separating and butter making.

A highlight for many visitors is Cal C. Umm, the bicycle-riding robotic skeleton. Mr. Umm has a lot to say about osteoporosis, and guests enjoy learning from him. If all that talk about healthy bones stirs up your appetite, stop at the ice cream parlor, which features an authentic 1930s soda fountain moved to the museum from its original South Texas location. There, you can splurge on old-fashioned sundaes, sodas, banana splits, shakes, and even some lunch items. The malts are the real thing. Mr. Cal C. Umm would certainly approve!

A gift shop, appropriately called the Milk Cow Emporium, features something for everyone. Bring home a cap, shirt, toy farm set, or a package of note cards to help you remember this wonderful and educational place.

The Southwest Dairy Center and Museum is open 9 a.m. to 4 p.m. Monday through Saturday, and admission is free.

If you can't get to Sulphur Springs, the Mobile Dairy Classroom just might be able to make it to your hometown. A free service offered by the museum, the traveling classroom is available to schools throughout the Southwest. With lessons geared toward Grades K-6, the instructors teach modern milking techniques, the characteristics and anatomy of dairy cows, the importance of dairy foods, as well as proper food safety. There is a large demand for this service, so your school will need to call ahead to get on the schedule.

Texas Beef Council

8708 Ranch Road, 620 North
Austin, Texas 78726
Phone: (512) 335-2333
Fax: (512) 335-0582
Internet: www.txbeef.org

The Texas Beef Council was formed in 1987 to promote beef products, provide consumer education, and perform research.

Promotion is done through consumer marketing efforts. Education includes tips for teachers, consumer information about beef, cooking safety facts, and recipes.

The group has access to a variety of interesting beef news. What's the most popular steak in this country? Sirloin. What's the best way to make barbecue in Texas? No answer here, but the Council acknowledges that Texans have a whole slew of great ideas ranging from dry rubs to wet mops.

The organization's website is well done. It is colorful, friendly, and easy to use. A wide selection of mouth-watering recipes is offered.

The staff is friendly and willing to answer questions from consumers who want to know more about this popular Texas meat. Linda Bebee is the vice president of Domestic Marketing, and Anne Bried directs the Test Kitchen. Anne is the power behind the "Ask Anne" column featured on the website. This fact-filled column has the answers to questions you might have such as "Is there another name for a particular steak?"

If you enjoy Texas barbecue, backyard burgers, and sizzling steaks, you are sure to benefit from the services offered through this fine Texas organization.

Texas Department of Agriculture (GO TEXAN Program)

P.O. Box 12847
Austin, Texas 78711
Toll-Free: (877) 99GOTEX
Internet: www.agr.state.tx.us

If you want a sure-fire way to buy products made in the Lone Star State look for the GO TEXAN logo.

Back in 1999 Texas Department of Agriculture Commissioner Susan Combs consolidated the marketing programs for a variety of state-made products such as food, fiber, wine, forestry, horticulture, and livestock. She was looking for a way to let consumers

GO TEXAN.

know that a product was made or grown in the state. GO TEXAN is the outcome of her efforts, and the program's logo graces a variety of Lone Star products.

The old saying "A picture is worth a thousand words" holds true with the GO TEXAN logo. Cut out in the shape of Texas surrounded by a circle, the logo is designed to look like a cattle brand. Now that says "Texas!"

Texans love to buy food made in state. A customer survey by the Texas Department of Agriculture says it all. Here are some of the statistics revealed in the study. According to the Texans surveyed:

★ 89 percent make an effort to buy Texas products.

★ 89 percent would purchase more Texas products if they could identify them.

★ 87 percent determine their Texas purchases from Texas logos, ranking above all other mediums.

Many food companies mentioned in this book belong to the GO TEXAN program, and the logo proudly appears on their labels. As of this writing, there are over eight hundred food company members. To qualify as a GO TEXAN food member, a company must grow or process their products in Texas. Members are entitled to place the logo on their labels and to take advantage of a variety of marketing programs. Susan Dunn, Director for Food Marketing, and her staff promote Texas food companies at a wide variety of food shows and other events throughout the state. Their efforts cross the state boundaries as well. At events such as trade shows, they sell the rest of the world on the benefits of buying Texas products. And who wouldn't want to buy Texan products? After all, they are touted as "the grandest in taste, freshness, size, and appeal."

The Texas Department of Agriculture website is the icing on the cake for food companies as well as consumers. The site offers, among other things, a complete list of GO TEXAN food companies (look under TAME). There is a link to company information and in some cases hyperlinks to individual company websites. The list is extremely well organized and continuously updated.

Next time you head out to a Texas event, look for the GO TEXAN tent. In the stores, look for the label. And in the meantime, visit the website for a real treat, Texas style!

Texas Food Processors Association

HFSB 225
Texas A&M University
College Station, Texas 77843-2134
Phone: (979) 845-7023

This nonprofit trade organization represents companies that bring us many favorite foods such as salsas, sauces, jellies, cookies, pickles, and the list goes on. Our cupboards, refrigerators, and freezers are stocked with a variety of processed foods.

This group, founded in 1943 by five East Texas canners, was initially called the East Texas Canners' Association. Back then, canned items were the most common processed foods. Freezers as we now know them were a thing of the future. The name was later changed to Southwest Canners Association, Incorporated, and in 1970 it became the Texas Food Processors Association.

The organization has several functions. One is to raise funds for scholarships for Texas A&M and Texas Tech students studying Food Science. Another is to promote education in the food industry.

Today the group's membership represents a variety of food companies throughout the state.

Texas Peanut Producers Board

P.O. Box 398
Gorman, Texas 76454
Phone: (254) 734-2853
Toll-Free: (800) 734-0086
Fax: (254) 734-2017
Internet: www.texaspeanutboard.com

In 1969 the Texas Peanut Producers Board was formed and is the state's oldest commodity board. The group promotes all Texas peanut farmers with research and promotion. Mary Webb is the executive director.

In Texas, peanuts are grown around the state with the majority in the Southern High Plains of West Texas, south of Lubbock. They are also grown in East Texas, North Texas near the Red River, the southeast part of the Panhandle, and in South Texas. In other words, peanuts love Texas.

And Texans love peanuts! In fact, around 400,000 tons of peanuts are harvested in a year, although the drought of 2000 cut this number to about 347,000 tons.

Peanuts are harvested in the fall for about two months. They last longer in the shell than they do if shelled, and they are considered a perishable product. Processors keep the peanuts in cold storage so that they will be available year round. Usually one year's crop is used before a fresh crop is harvested.

To increase the shelf life, peanuts can be frozen indefinitely in or out of the shell. When you take them out of the freezer, use them fairly quickly.

The association's website has a great deal of educational information and taste-tempting recipes.

Texas Pecan Growers Association

P.O. Drawer CC
College Station, Texas 77841
Phone: (979) 846-3285
Internet: www.tpga.org

Autumn in Texas is delightful. The air is cool and breezy, football is in full swing, and pecans are at their peak. The Texas Pecan Growers Association, formed in 1921 and incorporated in 1967, began as a way for growers throughout the state to get together for fellowship and idea sharing.

It was actually Governor Hogg who inspired the need for such a group. Before his death on March 3, 1906, the governor requested that a pecan tree be planted at his grave in Austin. On the eve of his death, he said, "I want no monument of marble or stone, but plant at my head a pecan and at my feet an old-fashioned walnut, and when these trees shall bear let the nuts be given out among the plain people so that they may make Texas a land of trees." It was not known what type of pecan tree to plant—there are about one thousand varieties—and the growers initially got together to make that decision. (Two pecan trees, a Russell and a Stuart, were originally planted. In 1969 they were changed to Choctaw pecan trees.)

The Texas Pecan Growers Association is an informative, reliable resource. The group serves on behalf of the members as their spokesperson on pecan-related issues, and it promotes the industry as well. The association's website features educational information and a host of delicious pecan recipes. The staff, including executive vice president Cindy Loggins Wise, is exceptionally well versed on the subject of pecans.

Commercial pecan production is going on in over one hundred fifty counties throughout Texas. The trees are found in every part of the state, with the exception of the very tip of the Rio Grande Valley and some areas in the Panhandle. In the southern tip, there is not enough winter chilling. Two varieties common to West Texas are the Wichita and Western Schley. These particular species do not do well in humid areas, making the arid West Texas conditions ideal.

Pecan trees love water. In the summertime, the average pecan tree drinks about one hundred gallons of water a day. And you thought *you* were thirsty! Many growers rely on irrigation methods so their trees can thrive throughout the dry Texas summers. The most important time for rain is in August and September, when the nutmeat is growing and expanding in the shell.

When purchasing pecans, it is important to know what to look for. If you are buying unshelled pecans, look for a smooth shell with no cracks or holes. Most growers and stores will let you crack a few shells to inspect the nutmeat. Inside, the meat should not be a dark color and should be plump rather than shriveled. Check carefully for tiny black spots, indicative of an insect sting or bite.

If you are selecting shelled pecans, look for plump kernels ranging in color from light golden to golden brown. Avoid a dark brown color because it could indicate rancidity.

Pecans retain their freshness at room temperature for only a month or so. Refrigeration is recommended for both shelled and unshelled varieties. For a longer shelf life, they may be kept in the freezer up to two years.

Pecans are a highly seasonal nut and are most plentiful in the autumn months. For maximum freshness, it is recommended that you buy a year's supply and freeze them. When you need them for baking, simply pop them out of the freezer and use without thawing. However, you must thaw before chopping in a food processor to avoid a gummy texture. If you would like to purchase pecans throughout the year, make sure you are buying from a reputable grower who uses proper storage techniques.

New studies show the health benefits of pecans. Although they do contain oil, it is all unsaturated, making the pecan a healthy choice and a patriotic one since they come from the Texas State Tree!

Tortilla Industry Association

8300 Douglas Avenue, Suite 800
Dallas, Texas 75225
Phone: (214) 706-9193
Internet: www.tortilla-info.com

Texas is a tortilla-eating state, so it is not surprising that Dallas serves as the headquarters for the Tortilla Industry Association, a national organization. The group, which was formed in 1990, has several functions including the promotion of tortilla consumption and support for tortilla research. Irwin Steinberg is the executive director.

The group's website is flat-out great! It is filled with tortilla trivia, facts, history, and statistics. It has calorie values for the average corn and flour tortilla (sixty for corn and one hundred fifteen for flour, according to their figures from the USDA Handbook). Flour tortillas have about two to three grams of fat while corn tortillas have one gram of fat per serving. Both are considered low-fat foods.

Visit their website and learn more about this popular flat bread.

Chapter 11
Tasty Trips

A food company or farm tour offers a fun-filled trip for the whole family. The following food companies welcome visitors. Some offer tours, others give onlookers a chance to peer through glass windows as treats take shape, and still others have an on-site restaurant. Some require reservations, while others let you drop in on the spur of the moment. Many offer samples and a chance to buy their products.

The food companies are listed under the city where they are located, and cities are in alphabetical order. Get the full scoop by checking back to the company's listing in the appropriate chapter.

Happy trails!

Athens
New York, Texas, Cheesecake Co.® (Chapter 1)

Austin
Austinuts (Chapter 2)
Good Flow Honey & Juice Company (Chapter 2)
Hudson's on the Bend Restaurant (Chapter 7)
Lammes Candy Shops — Austin, Round Rock, San Antonio
(Chapter 2)
Stubb's Bar-B-Q Restaurant (Chapter 7)
Tears of Joy/O'Shucks (Chapters 7 & 9)
Tom's Tabooley (Chapter 6)

Brenham
Blue Bell Creamery (Chapter 3)

Buda
Jardine Foods (Chapter 7)

Lubbock
Goodart's Peanut Pattie (Chapter 2)
Pedro's Tamales (Chapter 9)

Lufkin
Atkinson Candy Company (Chapter 2)

Marshall
Bear Creek Smokehouse, Inc. (Chapter 5)

Midland
Susie's South Forty Confectioners (Chapter 2)

Mt. Pleasant
Main Street Bakery — inside Antiques & Uniques for
    Laura's Cheesecakes (Chapter 1)

New Braunfels
New Braunfels Smokehouse Restaurant (Chapter 5)

Plainview
Panhandle Popcorn (Chapter 2)

Pleasanton
Gifts Galore — Ashur Products' chocolate tamales (Chapter 2)

Richardson
La Chocolatiere (Chapter 2)

Richmond
Le Blanc Pecans (Chapter 2)

Rogers
Lone Star Honey Company (Chapter 2)

San Antonio
Adelante Restaurant (Chapter 9)
Creative Chocolates (Chapter 2)
Lammes Candies Since 1885 (Chapter 2)
The Guenther House® — Pioneer Brand (Chapter 1)

San Angelo
Talk O' Texas (Chapter 6)

San Saba
Sanderson Pecan Company (Chapter 2)

Chapter 12

Scrumptious Surfing

Here is a web guide to most of the products found in this book. (Some do not have websites and are not on this list.)

Chapter 1: Cakes, Cookies, and Baking Mixes

Austin Cheesecake Company
www.austincheesecakes.com
C.H. Guenther & Son (Pioneer Brand)
www.chguenther.com
Chocolate Chix
www.chocolatechix.com
Collin Street Bakery
www.collinstreetbakery.com
Country Fruitcakes
www.alpha1.net/~ashannon
Gladder's Gourmet
www.gladders.com
Lady Walton's Gourmet Cookies
www.ladywalton.com
Laura's Cheesecakes
www.laurascheesecakes.com
Marotti Biscotti
www.mbiscotti.com
Mary of Puddin Hill
www.puddinhill.com
Miss Sophia Fine Handicrafts (Old World Gingerbread)
www.misssophia.com

New York, Texas, Cheesecake® Co.
    www.nytxccc.com
The Original Texas Ya-Hoo! Baking Company
    www.yahoocake.com
Wunsche Bros. Chocolate Whiskey Cake
    www.whiskeycake.com

Chapter 2: Candy, Nuts, and Honey

All American Snacks (White Trash)
    www.allamericansnacks.com
Ashur Products (chocolate tamales)
    www.ashurproducts.com
Atkinson Candy Company
    www.atkinsoncandy.com
Aunt Aggie De's Pralines
    www.auntaggiede.com
Austinuts
    www.austinuts.com
Charlene's Sweets
    www.realfudgeandmore.com
Creative Chocolates
    www.creativechocolates.com
The Great Texas Pecan Candy Company
    www.texaspecancandy.com
La Chocolatiere
    www.trufflefactory.com
Lammes Candies Since 1885, Inc.
    www.lammes.com
Lone Star Honey & Walker Apiaries/Walker Honey
    www.walker-honey.com or www.lonestarhoney.com
LeBlanc Pecans
    www.leblancspecancompany.com
Panhandle Popcorn
    www.panhandlepopcorn.com
Quintessential Chocolates (liquor-filled chocolates)
    www.qechocolates.com
Southeast Texas Honey Company
    www.texasdrone.com

Susie's South Forty Confections
   www.susiessouthforty.com
Sweet Taste of Texas
   www.sweettasteoftexas.com
The Toffee Company
   www.toffeeco.com

Chapter 3: Cheese, Ice Cream, Milk, and More

Blue Bell Creameries, L.P.
   www.bluebell.com
Daisy Brand Sour Cream
   www.daisybrand.com
Mozzarella Company
   www.mozzco.com
Promised Land Dairy
   www.promisedlanddairy.com
Pure Luck Texas (goat cheeses)
   www.purelucktexas.com
Texas Jersey Specialty Cheese Company, Ltd.
   www.texasjersey.com
White Egret Farm (goat cheeses)
   www.whiteegretfarm.com
White Mountain Foods
   www.wmfoods.com

Chapter 4: Frozen Main Dishes

Michael Angelo's Gourmet Foods
   www.michaelangelos.com

Chapter 5: Jerky, Turkey, Sausage, and Ham

Bear Creek Smokehouse, Inc.
   www.bearcreeksmokehouse.com
Cain's East Texas Meats
   www.texascountrymall.com
Double B Foods, Inc.
   www.doubleb.com
Greenberg Smoked Turkeys
   www.gobblegobble.com

Meyer's Elgin Sausage
    www.elginsmokehouse.citysearch.com
New Braunfels Smokehouse
    www.nbsmokehouse.com
Opa's Smoked Meats
    www.opassmokedmeats.net
Pederson Natural Farms, Inc.
    www.healthypork.com
Smokey Denmark Sausage Company
    www.smokeydenmark.com
Texas Best Beef Jerky Company
    www.texasbestbeefjerky.com

Chapter 6: Pickles, Peppers, Relishes... and Tabooley to Boot!

Alberto's Food Products, Inc.
    www.albertosbrand.com
Carrie Belle Gourmet Foods, LLC
    www.carriebelle.com
Goldin Pickle Company, Inc.
    www.goldinpickle.com
Talk O' Texas
    www.talkotexas.com
West Texas Pepper Traders
    www.peppertraders.com

Chapter 7: Salsas, Sauces... and even some Jellies!

Austin Spice Company
    www.austinspice.com
Billy Beans
    www.billybeans.com
Brazos Country Foods
    www.brazoscf.com
Bronco Bob's Specialty Foods
    www.ladywalton.com
El Fenix Corporation
    www.elfenixtexmex.com

The El Paso Chile Company
    www.elpasochile.com
Fischer & Wieser Specialty Foods
    www.jelly.com
Hell on the Red
    http://home.texoma.net/~fcec0704
Hudson's on the Bend
    www.cookingfearlessly.com or www.hudsonsonthebend.com
Jardine Foods
    www.jardinefoods.com
Jimmy O's Texas Marinades
    www.jimmyos.com
Mother Teresa's Fine Foods
    www.italianfoodmot-teresas.com
New Canaan Farms, Inc.
    www.newcanaanfarms.com
The Original Habanero Company
    www.HabaneroCo.com
Renfro Foods, Inc.
    www.renfrofoods.com
Riba Foods, Inc.
    www.ribafoods.com
Sanderson Specialty Food Company
    www.texasfoodsdirect.com
Stubb's Legendary Kitchen, Inc.
    www.stubbsbbq.citysearch.com
Tears of Joy
    www.oshucks.com
Texas Firehouse Chili & Salsas
    www.texasfirehouse.com

Chapter 8: Soups, Spices, and Great Bowls of Red (Chili, that is)

Ant Hill Production
    www.pepperseasoning.com
Baldy's Seasoning
    www.baldysseasoning.com

Bolner's Fiesta Products, Inc.
www.fiestaspices.com
Carmie's Kitchen
www.peppersprings.com
Company's Comin'
www.companyscomin.com
EZ Fixins' Spice Company
www.ezfixins.com
Gordon Specialty Foods, Inc.
www.gordonsgrubrub.com
Hummingbird Kitchens
www.hummingbirdkitchens.com
Obie-Cue's Texas Spice
www.obiecue.com
Pecos Red
www.pecosred.com
Red Eye Chili Company
www.redeyechili.com

Chapter 9: Tamales, Tortilla Chips, Fish Fry, and Hushpuppies

Alamo Tamales
www.alamotamale.com
Cook's Choice
www.cookschoice.com
Doña Mariquita's TOTOPOS
www.totopos.com
O'Shucks Tamales
www.oshucks.com
Pedros Tamales, Inc.
www.pedrostamales.com
Rudy's Tortillas
www.rudystortillas.com

Chapter 10: Food Organizations and a Dairy Good Museum!

Southwest Dairy Center & Museum
    www.geocities.com/Heartland/3541/museum.html
Texas Beef Council
    www.txbeef.org
Texas Department of Agriculture (GO TEXAN program)
    www.agr.state.tx.us
Texas Peanut Producers Board
    www.texaspeanutboard.com
Texas Pecan Growers Association
    www.tpga.org
Tortilla Industry Association
    www.tortilla-info.com

Index

Looking for more?

Check out these and other great titles from Republic of Texas Press

Good Times in Texas: A Pretty Complete Guide to Where the Fun Is

Larry D. Hodge

1-55622-685-3 • $18.95
288 pages • 5½ x 8½ • paper

Tea for Texas: A Guide to Tearooms in the State

Lori Torrance

1-55622-828-7 • $18.95
288 pages • 5½ x 8½ • paper

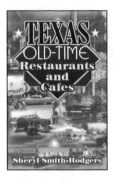

Texas Old-Time Restaurants and Cafes

Sheryl Smith-Rodgers

1-55622-733-7 • $18.95
288 pages • 7½ x 9¼ • paper

Barbecuing Around Texas

Richard K. Troxell

1-55622-697-7 • $18.95
312 pages • 5½ x 8½ • paper

Our Texas Heritage Ethnic Traditions and Recipes

Dorothy McConachie

1-55622-785-X • $19.95
232 pages • 7½ x 9¼ • paper

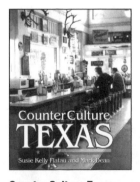

Counter Culture Texas

Mark Dean and Susie Kelly Flateau

1-55622-737-X • $24.95
272 pages • 7½ x 9¼ • paper